CU00666384

THE INSTITUTE OF INTERNATIO
ON STATE SUCCESSION AND S

Marcelo Kohen and Patrick Dumberry explore in an article-by-article commentary the Resolution adopted in 2015 by the Institute of International Law, on State succession in matters of State responsibility. They analyse the content and scope of application of each provision based on a comprehensive survey of existing State practice and judicial decisions (both domestic and international), as well as taking into account the works of scholars and that of the ILC Special Rapporteur in his proposed Draft Articles on the same topic. This book explains the rationale and the reasons behind why the Institute adopted specific solutions to address particular problems of succession to responsibility for each provision, including the need to achieve a fair outcome given the specific circumstances and relevant factors for each case.

MARCELO G. KOHEN is Professor of International Law at the Graduate Institute of International and Development Studies in Geneva, where he has been a member of the faculty since 1995. He is a Titular Member of the Institute of International Law, and has been its Secretary General since 2015. He has worked as legal counsel and advocate for a number of States before the International Court of Justice, the International Tribunal for the Law of the Sea and other tribunals. He also acts as an arbitrator. He has been visiting professor at several European universities, and the author of many publications in the field of International Law, in English, French and Spanish. He was the Rapporteur of the Institute of International Law on the question of State succession in matters of State responsibility and also co-rapporteur for the International Law Association and the Council of Europe on State succession and State immunity matters. He was awarded the Paul Guggenheim Prize in 1997 for his book *Possession contestée et souveraineté territoriale*.

PATRICK DUMBERRY is Professor of Law at the University of Ottawa (civil law section). He practised international arbitration for several years with Lalive in Geneva and Norton Rose in Montreal, as well as with Canada's Ministry of Foreign Affairs. He continues to work as counsel and expert in arbitration cases. He is the author of more than sixty publications in international investment law and international law, including five other books: *State Succession to International Responsibility* (2007); *The Fair and Equitable Treatment Standard: A Guide to NAFTA Case Law on Article 1105* (2013); *The Formation and Identification of Rules of Customary International Law in International Investment Law* (2016); *Fair and Equitable Treatment: Its Interaction with the Minimum Standard and its Customary Status* (2018); and *A Guide to State Succession in International Investment Law* (2018).

THE INSTITUTE OF INTERNATIONAL LAW'S RESOLUTION ON STATE SUCCESSION AND STATE RESPONSIBILITY

Introduction, Text and Commentaries

MARCELO G. KOHEN

Graduate Institute of International and
Development Studies, Geneva

PATRICK DUMBERRY

University of Ottawa

CAMBRIDGE
UNIVERSITY PRESS

CAMBRIDGE
UNIVERSITY PRESS

University Printing House, Cambridge CB2 8BS, United Kingdom

One Liberty Plaza, 20th Floor, New York, NY 10006, USA

477 Williamstown Road, Port Melbourne, VIC 3207, Australia

314–321, 3rd Floor, Plot 3, Splendor Forum, Jasola District Centre, New Delhi – 110025, India

79 Anson Road, #06-04/06, Singapore 079906

Cambridge University Press is part of the University of Cambridge.

It furthers the University's mission by disseminating knowledge in the pursuit of education, learning, and research at the highest international levels of excellence.

www.cambridge.org
Information on this title: www.cambridge.org/9781108496506
DOI: 10.1017/9781108677905

© Cambridge University Press 2019

First published 2019

Printed and bound in Great Britain by Clays Ltd, Elcograf S.p.A.

A catalogue record for this publication is available from the British Library.

Library of Congress Cataloging-in-Publication Data
Names: Kohen, Marcelo G., compiler. | Dumberry, Patrick, compiler.
Title: The Institute of International Law's resolution on state succession and state responsibility : introduction, text, and commentaries /
Marcelo G. Kohen, Patrick Dumberry.
Description: Cambridge [UK]; New York, NY:
Cambridge University Press, 2018.
Identifiers: LCCN 2018039210 | ISBN 9781108496506 (hardback) |
ISBN 9781108733892 (paperback)
Subjects: LCSH: State succession. | Government liability (International law) |
International law. | Institute of International Law.
Classification: LCC KZ4026.K64 2019 | DDC 341.26–dc23
LC record available at https://lccn.loc.gov/2018039210

ISBN 978-1-108-49650-6 Hardback
ISBN 978-1-108-73389-2 Paperback

CONTENTS

ABBREVIATIONS

AFDI	*Annuaire français de droit international*
AJIL	*American Journal of International Law*
ALJ	*Australian Law Journal*
Annual Digest	*Annual Digest of Public International Law Cases*
ASDI	*Annuaire suisse de droit international*
Badinter Commission	International Conference on the Former Yugoslavia, Arbitration Commission
BIT	bilateral investment treaty
British YIL	*British Yearbook of International Law*
Canadian YIL	*Canadian Yearbook of International Law*
CIS	Commonwealth of Independent States
Columbia LR	*Colombia Law Review*
Comp. & Int'l L.J. S. Afr.	*Comparative & International Law Journal of Southern Africa*
CUP	Cambridge University Press
EJIL	*European Journal of International Law*
Final Report	Institut de Droit international, 14th Commission, 'State Succession in Matters of State Responsibility/La succession d'Etats en matière de responsabilité internationale', Rapporteur Marcelo G. Kohen, 'Final Report', 28 June 2015, in: (2015) 76 *Annuaire de l'Institut de Droit international*, 511ff.
Finnish YIL	*Finnish Yearbook of International Law*
FLN	National Liberation Front (Algeria)
FRG	Federal Republic of Germany
FRY	Federal Republic of Yugoslavia
GDR	German Democratic Republic
George Washington ILR	*George Washington International Law Review*
German YIL	*German Yearbook of International Law*
GPO	Government Publication Office
ICJ	International Court of Justice
ICJ Rep.	International Court of Justice Reports of Judgments, Advisory Opinions and Orders
ICLQ	*International and Comparative Law Quarterly*

ICSID Rev.	*International Centre for Settlement of Investment Disputes Review – Foreign Investment Law Journal*
IDI	Institut de Droit international (Institute of International Law)
ILA	International Law Association
ILC	International Law Commission
ILC Articles on State Responsibility	Articles on Responsibility of States for Internationally Wrongful Acts Adopted by the Drafting Committee on Second Reading, 26 July 2001
ILC Special Rapporteur, First Report, 2017	ILC, First report on succession of States in respect of State responsibility, by Pavel Šturma, Special Rapporteur, 69th session, 2017, A/CN.4/708, 31 May 2017
ILC Special Rapporteur, Second Report, 2018	ILC, Second report on succession of States in respect of State responsibility, by Pavel Šturma, Special Rapporteur, 70th session, 2018, A/CN.4/719, 6 April 2018
ILC, Working-Group Recommendations	ILC, Report of the International Law Commission, Official Records of the General Assembly, Seventy-first session, Supplement No. 10 (A/71/10), recommendation of the Working-Group on the long-term programme of work, Annex B: 'Succession of States in respect of State responsibility', Syllabus by Pavel Šturma
ILM	International Legal Materials
ILR	International Legal Reports
Iran-U.S. C.T.R.	Iran-U.S. Claims Tribunal Reports
Jap. Ann. Int'l L.	*Japanese Annual of International Law*
JDI	*Journal du droit international*
JIDS	*Journal of International Dispute Settlement*
J. World Invest. & Trade	*Journal of World Investment & Trade*
La. L. Rev.	*Louisiana Law Review*
Lighthouse Arbitration case	*Sentence arbitrale en date des 24/27 juillet 1956 rendue par le Tribunal d'arbitrage constitué en vertu du Compromis signé à Paris le 15 juillet*

	1932 entre la France et la Grèce, Award of 24/27 July 1956, in: 12 UNRIAA 155; (1956) 23 ILR 91
Md. L.Rev.	*Maryland Law Review*
Michigan JIL	*Michigan Journal of International Law*
Nordic JIL	*Nordic Journal of International Law*
OUP	Oxford University Press
ÖZÖRV	*Austrian Journal of Public and International Law*
PCA	Permanent Court of Arbitration
PCIJ	Permanent Court of International Justice
Provisional Report	Institut de Droit international, 'Provisional Report' by Rapporteur Kohen, in: (2013) 75 *Annuaire de l'Institut de Droit international,* 127.
PUF	Presses universitaires de France
Rec. des cours	*Collected Courses of the Hague Academy of International Law*
Recueil des décisions des tribunaux arbitraux mixtes	*Recueil des décisions des tribunaux arbitraux mixtes institués par le Traité de Paix,* 10 vols., Paris, Librairie de la société du recueil Sirey, 1922-1930
RBDI	*Revue belge de droit international*
Rev. Égyptienne d.i.	*Rev. Égyptienne de droit international*
RGDIP	*Revue générale de droit international public*
RHDI	*Revue Hellénique de Droit International*
SFRY	Socialist Federal Republic of Yugoslavia
South African YIL	*South African Yearbook of International Law*
UN	United Nations
UNCC	United Nations Compensation Commission
UNCITRAL	United Nations Commission on International Trade Law
UNTS	United Nations Treaty Series
UNRIAA	United Nations Reports of International Arbitral Awards
UKTS	United Kingdom Treaty Series
USTS	United States Treaty Series
USSR	Union of Soviet Socialist Republics
US	United States
Yearbook ILC	*Yearbook of the International Law Commission*
ZaöRV	*Zeitschrift für ausländisches öffentliches Recht und Völkerrecht*

NOTE ON THE COVER IMAGE

The cover image is an official picture of the members of the Institute of International Law taken at the Session of Siena (Italy) in 1952 during which the Institute adopted a resolution on the 'Effects of Territorial Changes upon Patrimonial Rights' (Les effets des changements territoriaux sur les droits patrimoniaux).

Front row from left to right: Alejandro Alvarez, Jean Spiropoulos, Gustave Guerrero, Hans Wehberg, Albert de la Pradelle, Fernand De Visscher, Tomaso Perassi, Gilbert Gidel, Alexandre Makarov, Georges Sauser-Hall, Henri Rolin.

Then, following a vertical line from left to right: Frede Castberg, José-Maria Trias de Bes, Julio Lopez Oliván, Arthur Kuhn, Pierre Lalive (secretariat), Charles Rousseau, Paul de La Pradelle, Hans Lewald, J.H.W. Verzijl, and behind him Georges Ripert, Gerald Fitzmaurice, Abdel Hamid Badawi, Edvard Hambro, Humphrey Waldock, Hsu Mo, Maurice Bourquin, and at the top Jean-Flavien Lalive (secretariat) hiding partially Baron Frederik-Mari van Asbeck, Erik Castrén, Erik Brüel (sideways), Walter Schätzel, Wilhelm Wengler, Bohdan Winiarski (bottom), Petros Vallindas, Haroldo Valladão (sideways), Alf Ross, Hersch Lauterpacht (sideways), Jules Basdevant (bottom), Plinio Bolla, Max Gutzwiller, Geoffrey-Chevalier Cheshire (sideways), above Antonio Malintoppi (secretariat), next to him Jacques Dumas-Lairolle (secretariat), Gaetano Morelli, Max Huber (bottom), Charles-Robert Pusta, Antonio de Luna, Sir Arnold Duncan McNair, Alfred Verdross, Roberto Ago hiding Emil Sandström, below Karl-Gustaf Idman, Manlio Udina, Count Giorgio Balladore Pallieri, Claude Mercier (secretariat), at the bottom J.P.A. François.

I
INTRODUCTION

A   Past Codification Efforts Regarding the Question of State Succession in Matters of State Responsibility

1.   The Institute of International Law (known by its French name, *Institut de Droit international,* and hereinafter referred to as the 'Institute' or 'IDI') is the oldest institution in its field and was awarded the Nobel Peace Prize in 1904. The Institute adopted a Resolution on State succession and State responsibility (hereinafter the 'Resolution') at its 77th session held in Tallinn, Estonia, in August 2015. The Institute decided to work on this subject at its Bruges session of 2003 and appointed a Rapporteur, Marcelo G. Kohen, after its session held in Santiago (Chile) in 2007. The Resolution is the result of nearly eight years of work. The purpose of this book is to provide an article-by-article commentary to the Resolution and explain in detail the content and the scope of application of each provision. The text of the Resolution is provided in English and French, both texts being authoritative, in the Annex.

2.   This Commentary is based on the case law – both domestic and international – where courts and tribunals have applied the different solutions adopted for each provision. The content of each provision will be explained by referring to relevant past and recent examples of State practice. The scarce literature existing on the questions examined in the Resolution will also be assessed. The solutions adopted under the Resolution for each provision are therefore solidly grounded on precedents from judicial decisions and State practice. It should be added, however, that for a number of provisions, there is in fact only limited existing State practice and case law. Whenever this is the case, this Commentary explains the rationale and the motives for adopting any specific solution. As further examined in this Commentary, the different solutions adopted under the Resolution are not only based on solid legal precedents, but also on what would be the most reasonable, fair, just and logical outcome given the specific circumstances and relevant factors for each case.

3.   State succession has become a neglected topic of international law after the most important wave of decolonisation reached its peak towards the end of the 1970s. The subject of State succession again attracted the interest of scholars after the fall of the Berlin Wall with the emergence of new States, mainly as a result of the collapse of the so-called socialist federal States, such as the Soviet Union, Yugoslavia and Czechoslovakia, or the unification of other States, such as Germany and Yemen. The end of the overly lengthy processes of decolonisation in Namibia in 1991 and in Timor Leste in 2002 likewise contributed to renewed interest in the topic. The separation of Eritrea from Ethiopia (1993) led to the emergence of important disputes and to a bloody armed conflict. Unilateral declarations of independence were issued with respect to Kosovo in February 2008, and regarding Southern Ossetia and Abkhazia some months later. In January 2011, in a referendum held

in South Sudan on the basis of the Peace Agreement of 2005 between the Sudanese government and the Sudan People's Liberation Movement/Army, the overwhelming majority
of participants decided in favour of the creation of a new State,[1] which came into being
on 9 July 2011, and was the last member to be admitted to the United Nations.[2] Palestine,
whose statehood has been challenged (although the unanimous view is that it has the
right to be a State), requested its admission as a Member State to the United Nations on
20 September 2011. The Security Council failed to take any decision with regard to this
application, and on 29 November 2012, Palestine was granted non-member observer State
status by the General Assembly.[3] The exercise of the right to self-determination by the
people of Western Sahara, which includes the possibility of independent statehood, is still
on the international agenda. In the context of the Ukrainian crisis, Crimea and the City
of Sebastopol were incorporated into Russia, and self-proclaimed independent entities
appeared in the Eastern part of the country in 2014. Referenda on independence were
held in Quebec (1995) and Scotland (2014). At the time of writing this book, another referendum was scheduled to take place in New Caledonia at the end of 2018. Other controversial referenda were organised unilaterally in Iraqi Kurdistan and in Catalonia (Spain) in
2017. In sum, the question surrounding the creation of new States under international law
(and its consequences in terms of succession) remains of great importance today.

4.   The numerous examples of creation of new States, as well as the different attempts
at secession around the world, raise the question as to whether or not international law is
equipped to address the different aspects of State succession arising in general, and the
question of State responsibility in particular. The Institute's Resolution does not deal with
any of the particular situations referred to above. It does not take a stance regarding their
legal characterisation. This was not the task of the Rapporteur and the Commission that
led to the adoption of the Resolution at its Tallinn session in August 2015. The goal was to
set out general rules relating to situations of State succession in the field of international
responsibility. Specific situations (such as those mentioned in the previous paragraph) are
beyond the scope of the Resolution. Rather it concerns general international law, and in
particular the application of its fundamental principles.

5.   The Resolution deals with the consequences *after* the date of succession of an internationally wrongful act which took place *before* that date. Specifically, the Resolution
examines the consequences arising from an internationally wrongful act committed prior
to the date of the succession *by* the predecessor State against a third State (or another subject of international law). It also analyses the consequences arising from an internationally
wrongful act committed by a third State (or another subject of international law) *against*
the predecessor State before the date of succession. The scope of the Resolution is therefore different from the *Articles on Responsibility of States for Internationally Wrongful*

---

1   *The Comprehensive Peace Agreement between the Government of the Republic of the Sudan and the
     Sudan's People's Liberation Movement/Sudan People's Liberation Army* is available on the website of
     the United Nations Mission in Sudan at http://unmis.unmissions.org. The results of the referendum of
     9 January 2011 are discussed in the Report of the Secretary-General on the Sudan, 12 April 2011, UN
     doc. D/2011/239.
2   United Nations General Assembly Resolution 65/308 of 25 August 2011.
3   United Nations General Assembly Resolution 67/19 of 29 November 2012.

Acts of the International Law Commission ('ILC').[4] These articles, applied in situations of State succession, solely concern internationally wrongful acts committed *after* the date of the succession.

6.   The Resolution deals with the interaction between two important areas of international law: State succession and State responsibility. These two areas have been on the agenda of the ILC for decades. In the field of State responsibility for internationally wrongful acts, the ILC produced a set of articles that are largely regarded and employed in practice and case law as reflecting general international law.[5] The subject of succession of States has been analysed by the ILC and partially codified in two treaties: the Vienna Convention of 1978, dealing with State succession in respect of treaties,[6] and the Vienna Convention of 1983 concerning State property, archives and debts.[7] In 1993, soon after the end of the Cold War, the ILC undertook a study on the issue of State succession in matters of nationality of natural persons, adopting a set of articles in this respect.[8] It has been discussed at length whether these instruments, and particularly the two Vienna Conventions, reflect general international law and/or propose adequate solutions for the questions at issue.[9]

7.   The Institute has already devoted its attention to matters of State succession in the past. In 1952, it adopted a Resolution on '*Les effets des changements territoriaux sur les droits patrimoniaux*',[10] and in 2001 another on 'State Succession in Matters of Property and Debts'.[11]

8.   The question of the impact of matters of State responsibility on situations of State succession has remained neglected. Until very recently, no attempt at codifying this question was pursued by the work of the ILC in either the area of State responsibility

---

4   International Law Commission, 'Responsibility of States for Internationally Wrongful Acts', 2001, II(2) *Yearbook ILC*; annexed to United Nations General Assembly Resolution 56/83 of 12 December 2001, UN Doc. A/56/49(Vol. I)/Corr.4.

5   Ibid.

6   *Vienna Convention on Succession of States in Respect of Treaties*, 23 August 1978, entered into force on 6 November 1996, U.N. Doc. ST/LEG/SER.E/10, in: 1946 UNTS 3; (1978) 17 ILM.

7   *Vienna Convention on Succession of States in Respect of State Property, Archives and Debts*, 8 April 1983, not yet in force, Official Records of the United Nations Conference on Succession of States in Respect of State Property, Archives and Debts, vol. II (UN publication, Sales No. E.94.V.6), in: (1983) 22 ILM 306.

8   International Law Commission, 'Draft Articles on Nationality of Natural Persons in Relation to the Succession of States', adopted by the ILC on second reading in 1999, ILC Report, UN Doc. A/54/10, 1999, chp. IV, annexed to UN GA Resolution 55/153, 12 December 2000, (1999) II(2) *Yearbook ILC,* 13.

9   See International Law Association, 'Final Report on Aspects of the Law of State Succession', Co-rapporteurs Władysław Czapliński and Marcelo G. Kohen, Report of the Seventy-Third Conference, Rio de Janeiro, 2008, 250–363. See also: G. Distefano, G. Gaggioli & A. Hêche (eds.), *La Convention de Vienne de 1978 sur la succession d'État en matière de traités: Commentaire article par article et études thématiques* (Brussels: Bruylant, 2015).

10   Institut de Droit international, 'Les effets des changements territoriaux sur les droits patrimoniaux', in: (1952) 44-II *Annuaire de l'Institut de Droit international,* 471.

11   Institut de Droit international, 'State Succession in Matters of Property and Debts', in: (2000–2001) 69 *Annuaire de l'Institut de Droit international,* 712.

or that of State succession. At the beginning of the work of the ILC on the latter issue, it had been proposed to include the question of succession with respect to responsibility for torts,[12] but it was ultimately decided not to deal with this matter.[13] Furthermore, the 1978 Vienna Convention contains a clause that explicitly removed the question from the ambit of the treaty.[14] Similarly, the 1983 Vienna Convention includes a general article setting out the scope of its provisions, thereby also excluding matters of State responsibility.[15]

9.   Notwithstanding these two above-mentioned general provisions contained in the Vienna conventions on State succession, and the position taken by the ILC in its commentary to the Articles on State Responsibility, it remains that some situations in which internationally wrongful acts are committed before the date of succession have in fact already been addressed by these codification texts. These situations are the following: a) acts committed by an insurrectional movement leading to the subsequent creation of a new State; b) wrongful acts having a continuing character occurring both before and after the date of succession; and c) acts allowing for the exercise of diplomatic protection which were committed against the predecessor State before the date of succession. In situations a) and c), the ILC took a stance on matters related to State succession; in other cases it referred to them, but left the questions open. The Rapporteur and the Commission took into account the solutions adopted by the ILC on these matters when adopting the Resolution.

10.   For decades, the interaction between the fields of State succession and State responsibility aroused little interest in the literature. Thus, until the book published in 2007 by one of the authors of this Commentary,[16] only five articles had focussed on the issue.[17] Since

---

12   ILC, 'Proposal by the Chairman of the ILC Sub-committee on Succession of States and Governments, Manfred Lachs' (1963) II *Yearbook ILC*, 260.

13   Ibid., 299.

14   Article 39, *Vienna Convention on Succession of States in Respect of Treaties*: 'The provisions of the present Convention shall not prejudge any question that may arise in regard to the effects of a succession of States in respect of a treaty from the international responsibility of a State or from the outbreak of hostilities between States'.

15   Article 5, *Vienna Convention on Succession of States in Respect of State Property, Archives and Debts*: 'Nothing in the present Convention shall be considered as prejudging in any respect any question relating to the effects of a succession of States in respect of matters other than those provided for in the present Convention'.

16   P. Dumberry, *State Succession to International Responsibility* (Leiden: M. Nijhoff, 2007). Extracts of the book were later published by the writer in a number of articles: P. Dumberry, 'Obsolete and Unjust: The Rule of Continuous Nationality in the Context of State Succession' (2007) 76(2) *Nordic JIL* 153–183; P. Dumberry, 'The Use of the Concept of Unjust Enrichment to Resolve Issues of State Succession to International Responsibility' (2006) 39(2) *RBDI* 506–528; P. Dumberry, 'The Controversial Issue of State Succession to International Responsibility in Light of Recent State Practice' (2006) 49 *German YIL* 413–448; P. Dumberry, 'New State Responsibility for Internationally Wrongful Acts by an Insurrectional Movement' (2006) 17(3) *EJIL* 605–621; P. Dumberry, 'Is a New State Responsible for Obligations arising from Internationally Wrongful Acts Committed before its Independence in the Context of Secession?' (2005) 43 *Canadian YIL* 419–453.

17   C. Hurst, 'State Succession in Matters of Torts' (1924) 5 *British YIL* 163–178; J.-P. Monnier, 'La succession d'Etats en matière de responsabilité internationale' (1962) 8 *AFDI* 65–90; W. Czapliński, 'State Succession and State Responsibility' (1990) 28 *Canadian YIL* 339–359; M. Volkovitsch, 'Righting Wrongs: Toward a New Theory of State Succession to Responsibility of International Delicts' (1992) 92 *Columbia LR* 2162–2214; B. Stern, 'Responsabilité internationale et succession d'Etats', in: L. Boisson de Chazournes & V. Gowlland (eds.), *The International Legal System in Quest*

then a number of other articles have addressed this question.[18] The Arbitral Tribunal in the 1956 *Lighthouse Arbitration* case noted that 'the question of the transmission of responsibility in the event of a territorial change presents all the difficulties of a matter which has not yet sufficiently developed to permit solutions which are both certain and applicable equally in all possible cases.'[19] In the context of the elaboration of the final ILC Articles on State responsibility, the last Special Rapporteur, Professor James Crawford, highlighted the difficulties and uncertainties surrounding the question: '[i]t is unclear whether a new State succeeds to any State responsibility of the predecessor State with respect to its territory'.[20] Judge Xue in her Declaration in the *Croatia Genocide Convention* case also noted that 'little can be found about State succession to responsibility in the field of general international law',[21] adding that 'rules of State responsibility in the event of succession remain to be developed'.[22] The Badinter Commission, established within the framework of the Peace Conference for the former Yugoslavia, contributed to this perception by simply stating that '[t]he rules applicable to State succession and State responsibility fell within distinct areas of international law'.[23] The Badinter Commission made this remark in the context of a question relating to the incidence of damages of war in the distribution of debts, goods and archives among the successor States. Clearly, the question was not whether there was succession to war debts, but rather whether acts carried out by the successor States themselves would influence the distribution of debts and assets 'inherited' from the former Yugoslavia. In sum, there is uncertainty in doctrine and State practice regarding the question of State succession to responsibility.

11.   However complicated the issue may be, it clearly remains an important one under international law. The fundamental relevance of the question and the importance of the

---

of Equity and Universality, Liber Amicorum Georges Abi-Saab (Leiden: M. Nijhoff, 2001), 327–355. Two theses were also published on the topic: H.M. Atlam, *Succession d'Etats et continuité en matière de responsabilité internationale*, Thesis, Université de droit, d'économie et des sciences d'Aix-Marseille (France), 1986; M. Peterschmitt, *La succession d'États et la responsabilité internationale pour fait illicite*, Mémoire de DES, Université de Genève/Institut Universitaire de hautes études internationales (Switzerland), 2001.

18   V. Mikulka, 'State Succession and Responsibility', in: J. Crawford, A. Pellet & S. Olleson (eds.), *The Law of International Responsibility* (Oxford: OUP, 2010) 291–296; V. Mikulka, 'Succession of States in Respect of Rights of an Injured State', in: ibid., 965–967; M.G. Kohen, 'Succession of States in the Field of International Responsibility: The Case for Codification', in: M.G. Kohen, R. Kolb, & D. Tehindrazanarivelo (dir.), *Perspectives of International Law in the 21st Century. Liber amicorum Professor Christian Dominicé in Honour of his 80th Birthday* (Leiden: M. Nijhoff 2011), 161–174; Pavel Šturma, 'State Succession in Respect of International Responsibility' (2016) 48 *George Washington ILR* 653–678.

19   *Sentence arbitrale en date des 24/27 juillet 1956 rendue par le Tribunal d'arbitrage constitué en vertu du Compromis signé à Paris le 15 juillet 1932 entre la France et la Grèce* [hereinafter referred to as '*Lighthouse Arbitration* case'], Award of 24/27 July 1956, in: 12 UNRIAA 155; (1956) 23 ILR 91.

20   ILC, 'Commentaries to the Draft Articles on Responsibility of States for Internationally Wrongful Acts Adopted by the International Law Commission at its Fifty-Third Session (2001)', Report of the ILC on the Work of its Fifty-third Session. Official Records of the General Assembly, Fifty-sixth Session, Supplement No. 10 (A/56/10), 119, at para. 3, (2001) II(2) *Yearbook ILC*, 30.

21   *Application of the Convention on the Prevention and Punishment of the Crime of Genocide (Croatia v. Serbia)*, Judgment of 3 February 2015, ICJ Rep. 2015, Declaration of Judge Xue, para. 22.

22   Ibid., para. 23.

23   International Conference on the Former Yugoslavia, Arbitration Commission, Opinion No 13, 16 July 1993, in: 96 ILR 727.

work of the Institute is highlighted by the recent decision by the ILC to examine the question. At its sixty-ninth session, in May 2017, the Commission decided to place the topic of 'Succession of States in respect of State responsibility' on its current programme of work and appointed Professor Pavel Šturma as Special Rapporteur.[24] At the time of writing this Commentary, ILC Special Rapporteur Šturma had issued two Reports.[25] The Reports largely follow the solutions adopted by the Institute under its Resolution, as well as those found in the book *State Succession to International Responsibility* published in 2007 by one of the authors of this Commentary. When necessary, this Commentary will take into account the observations made by the ILC Special Rapporteur in his Reports regarding a number of questions addressed by the Resolution.

B   Summary of the Work of the Institute on the Issue

12.   The Institute's 14th Commission on 'State Succession in Matters of State Responsibility' was created at the Bruges Session in 2003 (hereinafter 'the Commission'). The Rapporteur was appointed following his election as an Associate Member of the Institute in 2007. At the Naples Session in 2009, the Commission discussed the general issues that should be covered by its work. The Rapporteur distributed a first version of his Preliminary Statement which was discussed by the Commission at the Rhodes Session in 2011. As a result of the discussion, a new version of the Preliminary Statement, including a questionnaire that took into consideration a variety of concerns raised by the Rapporteur as well as other members of the Commission, was issued on 31 August 2011. The Rapporteur submitted his Provisional Report including a draft Resolution on 9 August 2013.[26] The Commission met at the Tokyo Session. As a result of the Commission's discussion, the draft Resolution was adopted with some, although no substantial, changes and submitted to the plenary session. At the Tokyo Session, the second plenary session held a general discussion on the matter, and the fourth plenary session proceeded to an article-by-article discussion of the draft Resolution. Taking into account such discussions, the Rapporteur elaborated a first version of his final report and a new draft Resolution was sent to the members of the Commission on 7 March 2015. The Rapporteur's Final Report was issued on 28 June 2015 taking into account comments and proposals.[27] A draft Resolution was

---

24   See also: ILC, 'Report of the International Law Commission, Official Records of the General Assembly, Seventy-first session', Supplement No. 10 (A/71/10), recommendation of the Working-Group on the long-term programme of work, Annex B: 'Succession of States in respect of State responsibility', Syllabus by Pavel Šturma (hereinafter referred as 'ILC, Working-Group Recommendations').

25   ILC, First report on succession of States in respect of State responsibility, by Pavel Šturma, Special Rapporteur, 69th session, 2017, A/CN.4/708, 31 May 2017 (hereinafter referred as 'ILC Special Rapporteur, First Report, 2017'); Second report on succession of States in respect of State responsibility, by Pavel Šturma, Special Rapporteur, 70th session, 2018, A/CN.4/719, 6 April 2018 (hereinafter referred as 'ILC Special Rapporteur, Second Report, 2018').

26   Institut de Droit international, 'State Succession in Matters of State Responsibility', Provisional Report by Rapporteur Kohen, 9 August 2013, in: (2013) 75 *Annuaire de l'Institut de Droit international*, 123ff.

27   Institut de Droit international, 14th Commission, 'State Succession in Matters of State Responsibility/ La succession d'Etats en matière de responsabilité internationale', Rapporteur Marcelo G. Kohen, Final Report, 28 June 2015 (hereinafter referred to as 'Final Report'), in: (2015) 76 *Annuaire de l'Institut de Droit international*, 511ff.

attached to the Final Report. The Final Report was discussed by members of the Institute at the Plenary Session in Tallinn in August 2015. As a result of the discussion, a number of changes were made to the text of the Resolution. The final text of the Resolution was adopted at the Tallinn Session on 28 August 2015.

13.　　Although the Institute's Commission was conscious of the sensitive political aspects involved in some issues regarding the problem of State succession to international responsibility, it considered that an attempt at codifying the subject-matter was in order. The Commission considered that its task was not only to take into consideration the practice followed by States and international bodies, but also to propose solutions that are logically the most appropriate given the specific circumstances of each situation. This would be particularly important whenever State practice is scarce or non-existent. Indeed, the question of the impact of a situation of State succession in relation to a prior internationally wrongful act whose consequences remain open is more technical than a political one.

14.　　During the discussion on the adoption of the topic at the Bruges Session in 2003, some doubts were raised – including by some members of the Institute who later became members of the Commission – over the possibility of codifying this subject-matter and hence for the Institute to adopt a resolution.[28] The Provisional Report issued in 2013 explained that there was room for the codification and progressive development of the law in the form of a set of articles. The outcome achieved and the fact that the ILC has now decided to codify the matter further illustrates the importance of the question examined by the Resolution.

15.　　The Commission also discussed the scope and content of the future resolution. One question that arose was whether the Commission should confine itself to the analysis of responsibility for internationally wrongful acts or also cover issues relating to so-called 'responsabilité objective' or 'liability'. As further discussed below,[29] the Commission overwhelmingly supported the idea of focusing only on the question of State responsibility for internationally wrongful acts.

16.　　Finally, it should be added that while the original draft Resolution focused on situations in which the victim of the internationally wrongful act is a State, and extended them to situations in which the victim is a people entitled to the right to self-determination, the final text was drafted in a manner as to include other situations in which the victim is also an individual or another private subject, and human groups other than peoples. The main purpose of this change was to ensure that internationally wrongful acts concerning violations of human rights obligations would be covered by the Resolution.

28　Institut de Droit international, 'Provisional Report' by Rapporteur Kohen, para. 3, 127.
29　See analysis under Article 1 (the 'use of terms') examining the expressions 'internationally wrongful act' and 'international responsibility'.

ARTICLE-BY-ARTICLE COMMENTARY

A   The Preamble and the Rationale of the Resolution

The *Institute of International Law*,

Noting that the work of codification and progressive development carried out in the field of succession of States has not covered matters relating to international responsibility of States, and that work in the latter field has set aside matters relating to succession of States,

Convinced of the need for the codification and progressive development of the rules relating to succession of States in matters of international responsibility of States, as a means to ensure greater legal security in international relations,

Bearing in mind that cases of succession of States should not constitute a reason for not implementing the consequences arising from an internationally wrongful act,

Taking into account that different categories of succession of States and their particular circumstances may lead to different solutions,

Considering that law and equity require the identification of the States or other subjects of international law to which, after the date of succession of States, pertain the rights and obligations arising from internationally wrongful acts committed by the predecessor State or injuring it,

Noting that the principles of free consent, good faith, equity and *pacta sunt servanda* are universally recognized,

Recalling the principles of international law embodied in the Charter of the United Nations, such as the principles of the equal rights and self-determination of peoples, of the sovereign equality and independence of all States, of non-interference in the domestic affairs of States, of the prohibition of the threat or use of force, and of universal respect for, and observance of, human rights and fundamental freedoms for all,

Noting that respect for the territorial integrity and political independence of any State is required by the Charter of the United Nations,

Adopts the following Resolution:

Commentary

17.   The preamble follows the general considerations already mentioned in other instruments relating to State succession, such as the 1978 and 1983 Vienna Conventions, the ILC Articles on succession of States in matters of nationality and the Institute's Resolution on 'State Succession in Matters of Property and Debts'. In particular, references are made

to the fundamental principles and rules of international law that must be taken into consideration in the interpretation and application of the Resolution. Considerations regarding the need to formulate guidelines in situations of State succession in the field of international responsibility are also mentioned, particularly when taking into account that no attempt at codifying this area of international law has been carried out in the past.

18.   One important point to highlight at the outset is that the work of the IDI's Commission was not limited to the examination of the practice followed by States and international bodies. In fact, the Commission has proposed the solutions that logically seem to be most appropriate in a number of situations where State practice is scarce or when it is contradictory. This is why the preamble refers to the Resolution as being an effort at 'codification and progressive development of the rules relating to succession of States in matters of international responsibility of States'. The Resolution's emphasis on both elements has since then been endorsed by ILC Special Rapporteur Šturma,[1] who also took the position that the Draft Articles to be proposed 'should be both codification and progressive development of international law'.[2]

19.   In the following paragraphs, the two most fundamental goals of the Resolution are examined in more detail.

I   THE NEED TO PREVENT THE EXTINCTION OF RIGHTS AND OBLIGATIONS SOLELY BASED ON THE SUCCESSION OF STATES

20.   One approach to the problem of State succession to responsibility that writers have adopted in the past consisted in affirming that responsibility is an *intuitu personae* phenomenon, i.e. that it is intrinsically linked to the personality of the State concerned. For that reason, many writers have argued that there cannot be any succession to international responsibility. This is indeed the classical view that prevailed among scholars for many years.[3] In fact, this position was not adopted specifically in relation to the field of international responsibility. It was first advanced to deny the very existence of the phenomenon of State succession.[4] The position of writers accepting the possibility of succession in other fields, but rejecting it regarding international responsibility, is influenced by a criminal law perspective. Criminal law is based on the personal and non-transferable nature of responsibility and punishment. However, State responsibility in international law does not take the form of 'criminal' responsibility, and the analogy is consequently misleading.[5]

---

1   ILC Special Rapporteur, First Report, 2017, para. 16.
2   Ibid., para. 27.
3   For a list of authors supporting that position, as well as the different arguments in support thereof, see: Dumberry, *State Succession to International Responsibility*, 35-35; Stern, 'Responsabilité internationale et succession d'États', 327–330; J. Crawford, *State Responsibility: The General Part* (Cambridge: CUP, 2013), 437ff; Šturma, 'State Succession in Respect of International Responsibility', 656ff; ILC Special Rapporteur, First Report, 2017, para. 33.
4   Notably those adhering to the school of voluntarist positivism. See the analysis by S. Torres Bernárdez, 'Succession of States', in: M. Bedjaoui (ed.), *International Law: Achievements and Prospects* (Dordrecht: M. Nijhoff/Unesco, 1995), 384.
5   See G. Abi-Saab, 'The Uses of Article 19' (1999) 10 *EJIL* 339–351; G. Abi-Saab, 'Que reste-t-il du «crime international»', in: *Droit du pouvoir, pouvoir du droit: mélanges offerts à Jean Salmon*

A number of scholars have in recent years refuted the arguments put forward by those rejecting any possibility of succession to the consequences of the commission of wrongful acts.[6] The Resolution clearly distinguishes[7], on the one hand, the question of which State bears responsibility for the commission of an internationally wrongful act, and, on the other hand, the issue of which State (or other legal subject) is successor to the rights or obligations arising from an internationally wrongful act.

21.   Furthermore, that perception, analogous to a kind of generalised non-succession rule, does not take into consideration the crucial importance of responsibility in international law. Without international responsibility, international law would not be a legal system – hence the need for rules establishing consequences for the commission of an internationally wrongful act. The sort of 'clean slate' rule applicable to all cases of State succession in the field of international responsibility, which is supported by some writers, would result in numerous situations where the consequences of illegality would simply be erased and unaccounted for. Such an outcome flies in the face of the requirement for stability in international relations as well as the very idea of equity and justice. Such an outcome would also be contrary to the interests of all States affected by an event of State succession, i.e. both the successor and predecessor States as well as third States. It would crucially affect the interest of the holder of a right to reparation following the commission of the wrongful act. In sum, the application of a strict non-succession rule would result in the victim no longer having any possibility of obtaining reparation if the wrongdoer State ceased to exist. Not only would such an outcome constitute a rather unusual way to end a relationship of responsibility, it would also be, most importantly, fundamentally contrary to the principles of justice and equity governing international relations.

22.   The approach adopted under the Resolution is by no mean a novel one. Judge van Eysinga, in his dissenting opinion in the *Panevezys-Saldutiskis Railway Case*, when commenting on the effects of the application of the rule of continuous nationality (further discussed below[8]) to situations of State succession (which was espoused by Lithuania and applied by the Court), asserted:

> The question arises whether it is reasonable to describe as an unwritten rule
> of international law a rule which would entail that, when a change of sover-
> eignty takes place, the new State or the State which has increased its territory
> would not be able to espouse any claim of any of its new nationals in regard
> to injury suffered before the change of nationality. It may also be questioned
> whether indeed it is any part of the Court's task to contribute towards the

---

(Brussels: Bruylant, 2007), 69–91; A. Pellet, 'Le crime international de l'Etat: un phœnix juridique', in: Kalliopi Koufa (ed.), *The New International Criminal Law: 2001 International Law Session* (Thessalonika: Sakkoulas, 2003), 281–351.

6   See, inter alia: Volkovitsch, 'Righting Wrongs: Toward a New Theory of State Succession to Responsibility of International Delicts'; Stern, 'Responsabilité internationale et succession d'Etats'; Dumberry, *State Succession to International Responsibility*, 35ff; Crawford, *State Responsibility: The General Part*, 438–442. See also, more recently, Šturma, 'State Succession in Respect of International Responsibility', 655, 677.

7   The distinction is examined when analysing Article 2, below.

8   See analysis of Article 10 of the Resolution.

crystallization of unwritten rules of law which would lead to such inequit-able results.[9]

23.   The general policy followed by the Resolution is to favour finding solutions where a State is required to assume the obligations stemming from the commission of an inter-nationally wrongful act. In other words, one of the most fundamental goals guiding the Resolution, as mentioned in the Final Report, is to 'prevent situations of State succession from leading to an avoidance of the consequences of internationally wrongful acts, particu-larly in the form of the extinction or disappearance of the obligation to repair, by virtue of the mere fact of the State succession.'[10] One of the Resolution's central themes is there-fore to discard the application of a general strict non-succession 'clean slate' solution for matters involving State succession to the consequences of international responsibility.

24.   Interestingly, this is the position which was adopted by one State in a recent case before the International Court of Justice (ICJ or the Court). In its pleading in the *Croatia Genocide Convention* case, Croatia argued that Serbia should be held responsible for acts committed by the Socialist Federal Republic of Yugoslavia (SFRY) based on the principle of succession to international responsibility (its position is further examined below[11]). In its pleadings, Croatia thus mentioned, 'we say the rule of succession can occur in particular circumstances if it is justified', adding that there is 'no general rule of succession to responsibility but there is no general rule against it either.'[12] Serbia rejected this position arguing that there was no principle of succession to responsibility in general international law.[13] It also argued that all matters of succession to responsibility were in fact governed by the 2001 Agreement on Succession Issues entered into by the successor States[14] (a point further discussed below[15]).

25.   While the Court in the *Croatia Genocide Convention* case did not formally take pos-ition on the issue, what is clear is that it did not reject the possibility for a new successor State to be held responsible for obligations arising from the commission of wrongful acts by the predecessor State before the date of succession. The ILC Special Rapporteur also follows this interpretation.[16] In fact, a number of judges (in their individual opinions) have considered the reasoning of the Court on this issue to be based upon a *presumption* in favour of succession to international responsibility.[17] It should be added, however, that at

---

9   *Panevezys-Saldutiskis Railway Case*, PCIJ, Series A/B No. 76, 35.
10   Final Report, para. 53, in: (2015) 76 *Annuaire de l'Institut de Droit international*, 534.
11   See analysis of Article 15 of the Resolution.
12   *Application of the Convention on the Prevention and Punishment of the Crime of Genocide (Croatia v. Serbia)*, Verbatim Record, 21 March 2014, CR 2014/21, 21, para. 42 (Crawford).
13   Ibid., Judgment of 3 February 2015, para. 108.
14   Ibid., Verbatim Record, CR 2014/22, Mar. 27, 2014, 27, paras. 52–53 (Zimmermann).
15   See analysis of Article 15 of the Resolution.
16   ILC Special Rapporteur, First Report, 2017, para. 54: 'the judgment seems to be the most recent pro-nouncement in favour of the argument that the responsibility of a State might be engaged by way of succession'. See also at para. 58 ('It is worth mentioning that the Court did not refuse and thus accepted the alternative argument of Croatia as to its jurisdiction over acts prior to 27 April 1992'). See also: ILC Special Rapporteur, Second Report, 2018, para. 179.
17   *Application of the Convention on the Prevention and Punishment of the Crime of Genocide (Croatia v. Serbia)*, Judgment of 3 February 2015, ICJ Rep. 2015, Declaration of Judge Xue, para. 22; Separate Opinion of Judge Skotnikov, para. 5; Separate Opinion of Judge Kreca, paras. 60–61.

the plenary session in Tallinn for the adoption of the final text of the Resolution, Judge Tomka (an Associate Member of the Institute and former President of the ICJ) emphasised that the 2015 decision 'should not be perceived as an authoritative statement on state succession in matters of State responsibility' since the Court 'found that no breach of the Genocide Convention had been established' and therefore 'did not have to address the issue of succession to responsibility'.[18]

26.   In any event, a number of judges have specifically addressed the issue in their individual opinions in the *Croatia Genocide Convention* case. Thus, Judge Xue in her declaration mentioned that 'when a State ceases to exist, it does not necessarily mean that all its rights and obligations simultaneously cease to exist.'[19] A different position, however, was adopted by Judge Skotnikov, indicating that it would have been an 'impossible task' for the Court 'to establish that the doctrine of succession to responsibility was part of general international law at the time of Serbia's succession to the Genocide Convention on 27 April 1992' for the simple reason that there is 'no jurisprudence or State practice to support this hypothesis'.[20] Judge Skotnikov clearly rejected the possibility of any such succession to responsibility:

> Moreover, the Court clearly pointed towards rejection of the notion of succession to responsibility when it decided, both in its 2007 *Bosnia* Judgment and in its 2008 Judgment on Preliminary Objections in this case, that Montenegro, a successor State to Serbia and Montenegro (formerly the FRY), had not consented to the jurisdiction of the Court and could not be a Respondent in the respective cases (*Application of the Convention on the Prevention and Punishment of the Crime of Genocide (Bosnia and Herzegovina* v. *Serbia and Montenegro), Judgment, I.C.J. Reports 2007 (I)*, pp. 75–76, paras. 75–77; *Application of the Convention on the Prevention and Punishment of the Crime of Genocide (Croatia* v. *Serbia), Preliminary Objections, Judgment, I.C.J. Reports 2008*, p. 423, paras. 32–33). Likewise, the FRY (now Serbia) is a successor State to the SFRY. Like Montenegro, in respect of the State Union of Serbia and Montenegro, Serbia did not inherit the right to the international legal personality of the SFRY. Like Montenegro, Serbia did not accept responsibility in the present case for the conduct of its predecessor State, and thus did not consent to the Court's jurisdiction in respect of that State.[21]

27.   The same position, which reflects the traditional view followed in the past by many scholars, was taken by Judge *ad hoc* Kreca in his separate opinion. He started his analysis by noting that 'the impression is that the Court qualified succession to responsibility as a rule of general international law with amazing ease,'[22] adding that the Court 'gives no

18   Institut de Droit international, Session de Tallinn – 2015, PVPL plénière n° 1, 1ère séance plénière, 14ème Commission, in: (2015) 76 *Annuaire de l'Institut de Droit international*, at 626.

19   *Application of the Convention on the Prevention and Punishment of the Crime of Genocide (Croatia v. Serbia)*, Judgment of 3 February 2015, ICJ Rep. 2015, Declaration of Judge Xue, para. 25.

20   Ibid., Separate Opinion of Judge Skotnikov, para. 4.

21   Ibid., para. 5.

22   Ibid., Separate Opinion of Kreca, para. 60.

indication of any source of international law that would vindicate the qualification that the rules of succession of States to responsibility pertain to the *corpus* of rules of general international law.'[23] For him, there are only 'a few isolated decisions' on the issue which 'seemingly (…) stand on diametrically opposed positions'.[24] Judge *ad hoc* Kreca is of the view that 'the opinions expressed in that regard are a doctrinal plea for the formulation of a comprehensive doctrine of succession to responsibility rather than an all-embracing and comprehensive doctrine *per se.*'[25] He thus observed that 'the focus of the theory of succession to responsibility is on the responsibility for delictual debts, as a rule in the relations between the State and physical or legal personalities which possess specific characteristics'.[26] He referred specifically to the doctrine of acquired rights and the principles of international servitudes and unjust enrichment.[27] For him, these 'principles are, by their nature, unsuitable to uphold the idea of responsibility *in personam,* such as responsibility for violation of the Genocide Convention, although they carry certain weight as regards responsibility *in rem.*'[28] Judge Kreca therefore concluded that 'it seems clear that, in the present phase of development, succession to responsibility *in personam* is not a part of the *corpus* of general international law'.[29] Later in his opinion, he added that 'the only possible form of succession to responsibility in the circumstances surrounding the case could be succession to the responsibility of SFRY *ex consenso'*[30] (referring to the *Agreement on Succession Issues* entered into between the successor States to the SFRY[31]).

28.   The different positions adopted by ICJ judges in the *Croatia Genocide Convention* case illustrate the fact that the question of succession in matters of State responsibility still needs scrutiny. It also shows that the general traditional doctrinal position of non-succession is still supported by many. The Resolution firmly takes the position that such an all-encompassing non-succession solution should not be the guiding principle governing the matter. At the same time, as noted by the Final Report, 'the purpose of ensuring that obligations stemming from the commission of internationally wrongful acts must be carried out even in cases of State succession must not lead to the adoption of an opposite, general

---

23   Ibid., para. 61.
24   Ibid., para. 62, referring to the *Lighthouse Arbitration* case as the 'paradigm of succession to responsibility' and the *Brown* case as the 'paradigm of non-succession to responsibility'. He is specifically critical of the Court's reliance only on the *Lighthouse Arbitration* case (para. 61), adding that the 'qualification of the decision as the expression of the acceptance of succession to responsibility is exaggerated' (para. 64).
25   Ibid., para. 65.1.
26   Ibid.
27   Ibid. He further states that: Responsibility *in personam* is too much linked with the legal identity and continuity of the State which makes it difficult to ascertain it in terms of *ipso iure* succession to responsibility without prejudice to the fundamental principles of equality and independence of States. The legal identity and continuity of a State appears to be the powerful argument in favour of the general principle of *action personalis moritur cum persona*' (para. 65.2).
28   Ibid., para. 65.2.
29   Ibid., para. 65.4.
30   *Application of the Convention on the Prevention and Punishment of the Crime of Genocide (Croatia v. Serbia)*, Judgment of 3 February 2015, ICJ Rep. 2015, Separate Opinion of Kreca, para. 79.
31   *Agreement on Succession Issues* of 29 June 2001, 2262 UNTS 251; (2002) 41 ILM 1–39. The Agreement is further examined below when analysing Article 15.

rule of succession to these obligations in all cases'.[32] The same conclusion is adopted by the ILC Special Rapporteur in his First Report.[33]

29.   Whether or not there should be any succession to the rights and obligations arising from the commission of a wrongful act simply cannot be decided in the abstract without taking into account several circumstances. This important point is examined in the next section.

2   SUCCESSION TO THE CONSEQUENCES OF RESPONSIBILITY DEPENDS ON THE TYPE OF SUCCESSION INVOLVED AND ON A NUMBER OF FACTORS AND CIRCUMSTANCES

30.   The second most important goal of the Resolution is to emphasise that different solutions regarding the question of State succession in matters of State responsibility should be adopted depending on the situations prevailing in each case. Thus, neither the extreme solution of clean slate nor any general rule of succession is fit to accommodate the varieties of situations arising in the context of succession to responsibility. In other words, neither the position in favour of or against the *automatic* transfer of responsibility is satisfactory. This is the position which has been adopted by a number of scholars,[34] and is also followed by the ILC Special Rapporteur.[35] As noted by the Arbitral Tribunal in the *Lighthouse Arbitration* case, 'It is no less unjustifiable to admit the principle of transmission as a general rule than to deny it. It is rather and essentially a question of a kind the answer to which depends on a multitude of concrete factors'.[36] This is also the position which was adopted by the Applicant in the *Croatia Genocide Convention* case. It referred to the *Lighthouse Arbitration* case indicating that 'whether there would be a succession to responsibility would depend on the particular facts of each case'.[37] In fact, for Croatia,

---

32   Final Report, 24, in: (2015) 76 *Annuaire de l'Institut de Droit international*, at 534.
33   ILC Special Rapporteur, First Report, 2017, para. 83; ILC Special Rapporteur, Second Report, 2018, para. 16.
34   Dumberry, *State Succession to International Responsibility,* 7–8; D.P. O'Connell, *State Succession in Municipal Law and International Law*, vol. I (Cambridge: CUP, 1967), 482–493; Volkovitsch, 'Righting Wrongs: Toward a New Theory of State Succession to Responsibility of International Delicts', 2198–2199.
35   ILC Special Rapporteur, First Report, 2017, para. 83; ILC Special Rapporteur, Second Report, 2018, para. 16, see also, at para. 167 (rejecting the strict and automatic application of the principle of non-succession in the context of dissolution, but adding that 'This does not mean, however, the endorsement of the opposite solution of the automatic transfer of all obligations arising from the responsibility of the predecessor State to all new successor States. Whether the obligations arising from internationally wrongful acts (and what obligations) may be transferred to the successor States depends on the particular circumstances of each case'). It should be noted that at para. 148, he refers to the existence of a 'presumption' in favour of succession: 'the general rule of non-succession should be replaced rather by a presumption of succession in respect of obligations arising from State responsibility. Of course, this is not an unqualified or absolute succession, because the presumption of such transfer of obligations may be confirmed, rebutted or modified by agreements, including agreements on distribution (sharing) of such obligations, where appropriate'.
36   *Lighthouse Arbitration* case, at 91.
37   *Application of the Convention on the Prevention and Punishment of the Crime of Genocide (Croatia v. Serbia)*, Judgment of 3 February 2015, ICJ Rep. 2015, para. 107.

'the responsibility of a State might be transferred to a successor if the facts were such as to make it appropriate to hold the latter responsible for the former's wrongdoing'.[38] However, as explained above and developed below,[39] the question at the heart of the Resolution is not that of a transfer or succession to responsibility, but one of succession to the obligations arising from wrongdoing which occurred before the date of succession.

31.   The Resolution's basic position is that different categories of succession may be subject to specific solutions.[40] Clearly, the solution adopted for one specific type of succession may very well not be appropriate for other instances of succession. As noted by the Arbitral Tribunal in the *Lighthouse Arbitration* case: 'It is impossible to formulate a general, identical solution for every imaginable hypothesis of territorial succession, and any attempt to formulate such a solution must necessarily fail in view of the extreme diversity of cases of this kind.'[41] Thus, for the Tribunal, whether or not a situation involves one type of succession or another 'cannot but exercise a decisive influence on the solution of the problem of State succession even in cases of delictual obligation'.[42] For instance, the fact that the predecessor State continues to exist after the date of succession in some instances of State succession has important consequences with respect to the determination of whether there is any succession to rights and obligations arising from international responsibility.

32.   In addition, a number of different factors and circumstances (other than the types of succession involved) must be taken into account in order to determine whether there should be succession to the obligation to repair and to the right to reparation from the predecessor State(s) to the successor State(s). Some of the relevant factors and circumstances include the existence of a continuous internationally wrongful act, whether or not there exists a 'direct link' between the consequences of a wrongful act and the territory or the population of the successor State(s) and, finally, whether the author of the act was an organ of a territorial unit of the predecessor State that has later become an organ of the successor State. These different factors and circumstances, as well as others, are examined in detail below.

33.   The approach adopted by the Resolution also corresponds to the position taken by the Arbitral Tribunal in the *Lighthouse Arbitration* case noting that 'it is no less unjustifiable to admit the principle of transmission as a general rule than to deny it' and that 'it is rather and essentially a question of a kind the answer to which depends on a multitude of concrete factors'.[43] O'Connell was the first scholar to recognise this important fact.[44] When addressing the issue of succession to international responsibility, he elaborated on the importance of taking into account different factors and circumstances:

---

38   Ibid.
39   See discussion below and the analysis of Article 2.
40   The same position is adopted by ILC Special Rapporteur, First Report, 2017, para. 84.
41   *Lighthouse Arbitration* case, at 91.
42   Ibid., 91–92.
43   *Lighthouse Arbitration* case, at 91.
44   O'Connell, *State Succession in Municipal Law*, 301.

It is exasperating not to be able to propose a synthetic structure of State succession doctrine which can accommodate the problem of torts, but the truth is that the matter cannot be brought to any finer focus than in Verzijl's conclusion in the *Lighthouse* case that many concrete factors, including the continuing nature of the wrong, and its liquidated or unliquidated character, are to be taken into account, and the factors may require different evaluation in different types of successions of States.[45]

34.   The approach refuting the traditional doctrine of non-succession and adopting the above-mentioned criteria was subsequently developed by one of the authors of this Commentary in his 2007 book. It has since then been endorsed by several scholars,[46] including by Professor Crawford (former ILC Special Rapporteur and now a judge at the ICJ).[47] The ILC Special Rapporteur has recently highlighted the evolution of the point of view of Crawford on the matter.[48]

35.   In sum, the approach adopted by the Resolution is, on the one hand, to reject, as a matter of principle, the strict and automatic principle of non-succession to responsibility and, on the other hand, to codify the different solutions regarding succession to the rights and obligations arising from international responsibility which should prevail depending on the different types of succession involved as well as the existing factors and circumstances in each situations. This approach has been endorsed by the ILC Special Rapporteur in his First Report.[49]

B   Chapter I: General Provisions

36.   The first chapter of the Resolution contains general provisions regarding the use of terms (Article 1) and the scope of the Resolution (Article 2).

---

45   D.P. O'Connell, 'Recent Problems of State Succession in Relation to New States' (1970) 130 *Rec. des Cours* 120–121.

46   See, for instance, A. Jakubowski, *State Succession in Cultural Property* (Oxford: OUP, 2015), 190, 265–266, but see critics at 270–271.

47   Crawford, *State Responsibility: The General Part*, 447ff.

48   ILC Special Rapporteur, First Report, 2017, para. 10: 'While in the 1998 report the Special Rapporteur, Mr. James Crawford, wrote that there was a widely held view that a new State does not, in general, succeed to any State responsibility of the predecessor State [referring to (1998) II(1) *Yearbook ILC*, A/CN.4/490 and Add.1–7, para. 279], the Commission's commentary to the 2001 draft articles on responsibility of States for internationally wrongful acts reads differently, saying: "In the context of State succession, it is unclear whether a new State succeeds to any State responsibility of the predecessor State with respect to its territory"' [para. (3) of the commentary to article 11 of the draft articles on responsibility of States for internationally wrongful acts, (2001) II(2) *Yearbook ILC* and corrigendum, para. 77]. See also, at para. 35 ('from a refusal in 1998 to a partial acceptance in 2001').

49   ILC Special Rapporteur, First Report, 2017, para. 36: 'One idea, which could provide useful guidance for possible codification by the International Law Commission, calls for flexibility to allow for the tailoring of different solutions to different situations'. See also: ILC Special Rapporteur, Second Report, 2018, para. 16: '[The Special Rapporteur] does not suggest replacing one highly general theory of non-succession by another similar theory in favour of succession. Instead, a more flexible and realistic approach is needed. The outcome might well be a confirmation of non-succession in certain legal relations arising from State responsibility and a formulation of special rules (or possible exceptions) on succession in others.'

ARTICLE 1:

Use of terms

For the purposes of this Resolution:

a)   "Succession of States" means the replacement of one State by another in the responsibility for the international relations of territory.

b)   "Predecessor State" means the State which has been replaced by another State on the occurrence of a succession of States.

c)   "Successor State" means the State which has replaced another State on the occurrence of a succession of States.

d)   "Date of the succession of States" means the date upon which the successor State replaced the predecessor State in the responsibility for the international relations of the territory to which the succession of States relates.

e)   "Newly independent State" means a successor State the territory of which immediately before the date of the succession of States was a dependent territory for the international relations of which the predecessor State was responsible.

f)   "Devolution agreement" means an agreement, concluded by the predecessor State and the successor State or a national liberation, insurrectional or other movement, or an entity or organ that later becomes the organ of the successor State, providing that rights and/or obligations of the predecessor State shall devolve upon the successor State.

g)   "Internationally wrongful act" means conduct consisting of an action or omission which: (i) is attributable to the State or another subject under international law; and (ii) constitutes a breach of an international obligation of the State or the other subject. The characterization of an act as internationally wrongful is governed by international law.

h)   "international responsibility" refers to the legal consequences of an internationally wrongful act.

Commentary

37.   There is a general consensus regarding the definition of 'Succession of States' which has been adopted in the past by the different instruments dealing with the issue of State succession,[50] including the Resolution adopted by the Institute in 2001.[51] For this

---

50   Article 2 (1)b), *Vienna Convention on Succession of States in Respect of Treaties*; Article 2 (1)a), *Vienna Convention on Succession of States in Respect of State Properties, Archives and Debts.* The same definition can also be found at Article 2 of the ILC's 'Draft Articles on Nationality of Natural Persons in Relation to the Succession of States'.
51   Institut de Droit international, 'State Succession in Matters of Property and Debts'.

reason, the Resolution has simply adopted the definition found in these instruments. The ILC Special Rapporteur also follows the same approach.[52]

38.   The Final Report explains that while it is true that the reference to succession as 'the replacement of one State by another in the responsibility for the international relations of territory' generally involves a change of sovereignty, it remains that this is not always the case.[53] Thus, such a 'replacement' can also occur in cases of succession not involving any *change* in sovereignty.[54] This has particularly been the case at the end of the different forms of protectorate. Thus, the protected State was the sovereign of the territory although some important State functions, including 'the responsibility for the international relations of the territory', were delegated to the protector State. States administering territories under international regimes, such as Mandates, Trusteeship and Non-Self-Governing Territories, are other examples.

39.   The Resolution also follows the definitions adopted in the instruments mentioned above regarding other terms such as 'predecessor' and 'successor' States, 'date of State succession' (hereinafter simply referred to as the 'date of succession') and 'newly independent States'.[55] For reasons further explained below, the Resolution has retained the category of 'newly independent States' as a specific type of the phenomenon of State succession.[56]

40.   The terms 'internationally wrongful act' and 'international responsibility' have been defined based on the work of the ILC on State responsibility and are consequently adopted by the Resolution. Again, the same approach was recently adopted by the ILC Special Rapporteur.[57]

41.   The IDI Commission discussed whether it should confine itself to the analysis of responsibility for 'internationally wrongful acts' or, on the contrary, whether its work should also cover issues relating to so-called '*responsabilité objective*' or 'liability'. The first option was privileged.[58] The ILC Special Rapporteur followed the same line.[59] One reason why the IDI Commission adopted such a position is because the rules relating to responsibility for internationally wrongful acts are of 'secondary' character (in the sense employed by Roberto Ago when he acted as ILC Special Rapporteur on matters of State responsibility[60]). As such, these rules are applicable no matter the content of the obligation breached. On the contrary, the rules relating to liability for injurious consequences

---

52   ILC Special Rapporteur, First Report, 2017, paras. 65ff.
53   Final Report, para. 37, in: (2015) 76 *Annuaire de l'Institut de Droit international*, at 528.
54   The other more theoretical question as to whether or not 'succession' to sovereignty is at all possible is briefly mentioned in the Final Report, ibid.
55   For an analysis of these terms, see: L. Gradoni, 'Article 2', in: G. Distefano, G. Gaggioli & A. Hêche (eds.), *La Convention de Vienne de 1978 sur la succession d'États en matière de traités: Commentaire article par article et études thématiques* (Brussels: Bruylant, 2015), 87ff.
56   See discussion regarding Article 16 below.
57   ILC Special Rapporteur, First Report, 2017, para. 74.
58   Final Report, paras. 13–15, in: (2015) 76 *Annuaire de l'Institut de Droit international*, 518–519.
59   ILC Special Rapporteur, First Report, 2017, para. 21.
60   See (1970) II(2) *Yearbook ILC*, 306, para. 66(c).

arising out of acts not prohibited by international law are considered as 'primary' rules. Some members also mentioned the fact that the rules relating to liability are controversial with regard to their content and in some cases their very existence in positive international law is a matter surrounded by uncertainty.[61] Another member of the Commission also mentioned the fact that the Institute already had distinguished the specificity of both kinds of responsibility in its Resolution on 'Responsibility and Liability under International Law for Environmental Damage' adopted in Strasbourg in 1997.[62] However, the same member noticed that in both cases the injured State has a right to be repaired, and this would constitute a point of junction between the two kinds of responsibility.

42.   As further discussed below,[63] the Institute decided that the matter under study should be addressed with regard to the succession (or not) to the rights and obligations stemming from an internationally wrongful act, and would therefore not be envisaged as one of succession to the international responsibility of a State. The conclusion reached with regard to such rights and obligations could have also been considered as transposable to those stemming from the liability for injurious consequences arising out of acts not prohibited by international law. The IDI Rapporteur was sympathetic with this opinion. However, given the sound preference expounded by the other members of the Commission and possible difficulties which could result from such an extension of scope, it was decided to explicitly limit the matter under investigation within the realm of responsibility for internationally wrongful acts. It was decided to leave open the question as to whether or not the rules contained in the Resolution could also be applicable to acts not prohibited by international law.

43.   As explained in the Final Report, one question which arose during the debates among members of the Commission was whether a specific solution should be envisaged for violation of obligations having an *erga omnes* character.[64] The Rapporteur considered that the consequence of the distinction between *erga omnes* obligations and other kinds of obligations was a matter regarding the law of State responsibility which had no bearing in the field of State succession. In other words, the successor State inherits, or not, the rights or obligations stemming from the commission of an internationally wrongful act, no matter the *nature* of the obligation breached. The same conclusion has also been reached by the other author of this Commentary regarding the so-called 'odious debts' and the breach of *jus cogens* norms.[65] Thus, while it has been suggested by some scholars that when the predecessor State breaches a peremptory (*jus cogens*) norm of international law, the successor State(s) should automatically be held responsible for the consequences of such grave acts,[66]

61   Final Report, para. 13, in: (2015) 76 *Annuaire de l'Institut de Droit international*, at 519.
62   Ibid., para. 14, at 519. See: Institut de Droit international, 'Responsibility and Liability under International Law for Environmental Damage', Session of Strasbourg, 4 September 1997, in: (1997) 67-II *Annuaire de l'Institut de Droit international*, 486–513.
63   See discussion regarding Article 2 below.
64   Final Report, para. 25, in: (2015) 76 *Annuaire de l'Institut de Droit international*, at 523.
65   Dumberry, *State Succession to International Responsibility*, 294–298.
66   See, for instance, Volkovitsch, 'Righting Wrongs: Toward a New Theory of State Succession to Responsibility of International Delicts', 2200; Jakubowski, *State Succession in Cultural Property*, 270–271.

there is, in fact, no logical necessity for establishing such as rule. No State practice supports this position either.[67]

44.   The Resolution also does not distinguish between the different *origins* of internationally wrongful acts breached by the predecessor State (i.e. conventional violations, violations of customary international law). It does not address the position adopted by some writers for whom whenever a successor State becomes party to a treaty by way of succession, there should, consequently, be an automatic transmission of obligations arising from prior treaty violations committed by the predecessor State before the date of succession.[68] The ILC Special Rapporteur has adopted the same position in his First Report.[69] Interestingly, one of the arguments put forward by Croatia in the *Croatia Genocide Convention* case before the ICJ was based on this proposition: 'Croatia argues that the FRY, by the declaration of 27 April 1992 already discussed, indicated not only that it was succeeding to the treaty obligations of the SFRY, but also that it succeeded to the responsibility incurred by the SFRY for the violation of those treaty obligations'.[70]

45.   Finally, the Resolution includes a definition of the term 'devolution agreement' which is fundamental to the interpretation and application of Article 6 specifically dealing with the consequences of the conclusion of such an agreement between the predecessor State and the successor State, in terms of succession to the consequences of international responsibility.[71]

ARTICLE 2:

Scope of the present Resolution

1.   The present Resolution applies to the effects of a succession of States in respect of the rights and obligations arising out of an internationally wrongful act that the predecessor State committed against another State or another subject of international law prior to the date

---

67   Stern, 'Responsabilité internationale et succession d'Etats', 349; Dumberry, *State Succession to International Responsibility*, 297–298.

68   See: Stern, 'Responsabilité internationale et succession d'Etats', 344–348. This question is examined in: Dumberry, *State Succession to International Responsibility*, 290; P. Dumberry, 'La succession d'Etats en matière de responsabilité internationale et ses liens avec la responsabilité des Etats en matière de traités', in: G. Distefano, G. Gaggioli & A. Hêche (eds.), *La Convention de Vienne de 1978 sur la succession d'État en matière de traités: Commentaire article par article et études thématiques* (Brussels: Bruylant, 2015), 1581–1608.

69   ILC Special Rapporteur, First Report, 2017, para. 73: 'the application of rules governing succession of States in one area does not prejudge or condition the applicability of rules governing succession of States in respect of another category of relations. In other words, while it may be a presumption that a successor State that succeeded to a treaty of the predecessor State could also succeed to obligations arising from the violation of the treaty, it should not be taken as granted. The two areas of succession of States are independent and governed by special rules. The question whether or not the successor State has certain obligations or rights arising from the responsibility of the predecessor State is a separate question from the succession in respect of primary obligations (under the given treaty)'.

70   *Application of the Convention on the Prevention and Punishment of the Crime of Genocide (Croatia v. Serbia)*, Judgment of 3 February 2015, ICJ Rep. 2015, para. 107.

71   The concept of 'devolution agreement' is examined in detail below; see analysis of Article 6.

of succession, or that a State or another subject of international law committed against the predecessor State prior to the date of succession.

2.   The present Resolution applies only to the effects of a succession of States occurring in conformity with international law and, in particular, the principles of international law embodied in the Charter of the United Nations.

3.   The present Articles do not govern the situations resulting from political changes within a State, including changes in the regime or name of the State.

Commentary

46.   Article 2 deals with the preliminary and fundamental question of the scope of the Resolution. The three different paragraphs focus on the following five questions, which will be examined in the next sections:

- The Resolution deals with the question of succession to the rights and obligations arising from an internationally wrongful act and *not* with the issue of succession to responsibility per se (Section 1);

- The Resolution also covers wrongful acts committed against or by non-State actors which are considered as subjects of international law (Section 2);

- The Resolution does not deal with either municipal torts or breaches of rules of State succession (Section 3);

- The Resolution applies only to situations of State succession which are 'in conformity' with international law (Section 4);

- The Resolution applies only to situations of State succession, and not to changes of *governments* (Section 5).

1   The Resolution Does Not Deal with the Question of State Succession to Responsibility per se

47.   The first paragraph of Article 2 indicates that the Resolution deals with two related issues:

- The consequences arising from an internationally wrongful act committed prior to the date of the succession *by* the predecessor State against another State (or another subject of international law); and

- The consequences arising from an internationally wrongful act committed by another State (or another subject of international law) *against* the predecessor State before the date of succession.

48.   Article 2(1) makes it clear that the Resolution concerns the question of succession to the *rights and obligations* arising from the commission of an internationally wrongful act. This important aspect had been highlighted by the Rapporteur from the very beginning of the work of the Institute on this subject. Following remarks made by some members of the Commission and others at the Tokyo and Tallin sessions, it was decided to add this general provision in order to clarify this important point.[72] For that purpose, the expression '*rights and obligations arising out of an internationally wrongful act*' is used at Article 2 instead of the phrase '*responsibility* arising out of an internationally wrongful act'.

49.   The question addressed by the Resolution is therefore not whether there is any succession to *responsibility per se*.[73] In other words, it is *not* whether the successor State(s) should be '*responsible*' for internationally wrongful acts committed by the predecessor State(s) before the date of succession. As a matter of principle, the successor State(s) cannot be *liable for* internationally wrongful acts committed by *another State* (the predecessor State).[74] The right question to be asked is instead whether there is any succession to the rights and obligations *arising from* internationally wrongful acts committed or suffered by the predecessor State. In other words, the issue is not one of transfer of *responsibility* for internationally wrongful acts, but rather that of the succession to the *consequences* of international responsibility *arising from* the commission of such acts.[75] These are two fundamentally different questions which, however, have often not been treated as such in doctrine.[76] Thus, Stern rightly speaks of the 'transmission des conséquences de la responsabilité, plus que de transmission de la responsabilité elle-même'.[77] Judge Kreca, in his separate opinion in the *Croatia Genocide Convention* case, reached the same conclusion.[78] The same approach was recently adopted by the ILC Special Rapporteur.[79] However, the text of his proposed draft Article 1 ('Scope') does not make this

72   Session de Tallinn – 2015, PVPL plénière n° 1, 1ère séance plénière, 14ème Commission, 16, 20, 22–23, in: (2015) 76 *Annuaire de l'Institut de Droit international*, at 630ff.
73   Final Report, para. 31, in: (2015) 76 *Annuaire de l'Institut de Droit international*, at 526.
74   Crawford, *State Responsibility: The General Part*, 439.
75   Ibid.
76   See the analysis in: Dumberry, *State Succession to International Responsibility*, 4–6, 443–446.
77   Stern, 'Responsabilité internationale et succession d'Etats', 338.
78   *Application of the Convention on the Prevention and Punishment of the Crime of Genocide (Croatia v. Serbia)*, Judgment of 3 February 2015, ICJ Rep. 2015, separate opinion of Judge Kreca, para. 65.4: 'Succession to responsibility *in personam* is not *strict sensu* legally possible... Even if responsibility of a State for acts or omissions of another State is established on the basis of consented succession to responsibility, it is not *strict sensu* a matter of succession to responsibility as subjective, of the *intuit personae* category, but of assuming the *consequences* of responsibility in a proper form' (emphasis in the original).
79   ILC Special Rapporteur, First Report, 2017, para. 75 ('the report does not envisage the succession of States in respect of State responsibility as a transfer of the responsibility as such but as a transfer of rights and obligations arising from international responsibility of a (predecessor) State'). See also ILC Special Rapporteur, Second Report, 2018, para. 148: 'This is why the distinction drawn in the present report in relation to draft article 6 seems to be of great importance. On the one hand, even in these cases, succession of States has no impact on the attribution of the internationally wrongful act committed before the date of succession of States. In other words, the internationally wrongful act was and remains attributed to the predecessor State only. On the other hand, however, the legal consequences of the act (namely the obligation of reparation) do not disappear. To this end, the general rule of non-succession should be replaced rather by a presumption of succession in respect of obligations arising from State responsibility'.

distinction clear, since it simply refers to 'the effect of a succession of States in respect of responsibility of States for internationally wrongful acts.'[80]

2   The Resolution Covers Wrongful Acts Committed against or by Non-State Actors which Are Subjects of International Law

50.   The text of the first paragraph of Article 2 not only refers to the acts committed by or against a State, but also to those committed against or by 'another subject of international law'. A similar reference is found in other provisions of the Resolution.[81] In response to questions from some members of the Institute at the Tallinn Session, the Rapporteur explained that the expression 'another subject' of international law 'was open and included any non-state actor recognized by international law, including but not limited to individuals'.[82] He further explained that:

> The *Rapporteur* confirmed that the idea discussed in Tokyo was to define the scope of the draft Resolution broadly. The term 'another subject' of international law referred not only to individuals. The two types of situation foreseen were, firstly where an individual was the victim of an internationally wrongful act such as breach of a human rights obligation, and secondly where the predecessor State was the victim of an internationally wrongful act and the author was a non-State actor such as a national liberation movement.[83]

51.   One example of a subject of international law relevant for the application of the Resolution are 'national liberation movements' representing a people entitled to self-determination in the context of newly independent States.[84] One concrete illustration of an internationally wrongful act committed prior to the date of succession *by* a non-State actor (a subject of international law) against another State is found at Article 16(3) of the Resolution. Under this provision,[85] the conduct of a 'national liberation movement' before the date of succession which 'succeeds in establishing a newly independent State shall be considered the act of the new State under international law'. In other words, the new State takes over the consequences of a wrongful act initially committed by a 'national liberation movement'.

52.   Another subject of international law envisaged by the Resolution is a 'people entitled to self-determination', also in the context of newly independent States.[86] One illustration of an internationally wrongful act committed prior to the date of succession

---

80   ILC Special Rapporteur, First Report, 2017, para. 29.
81   See, for instance, Articles 3, 4, 5, 6 and 7.
82   Session de Tallinn – 2015, PVPL plénière n° 1, 1ère séance plénière, 14ème Commission, 23, in: (2015) 76 *Annuaire de l'Institut de Droit international*, at 633
83   Ibid.
84   Final Report, para. 103, in: (2015) 76 *Annuaire de l'Institut de Droit international*, 548.
85   See analysis below examining Article 16(3).
86   Final Report, para. 102, in: (2015) 76 *Annuaire de l'Institut de Droit international*, 548.

by the predecessor State *against* this non-State actor is found at Article 16(4) of the
Resolution. Under this provision, the rights arising from such an act committed against a
'people entitled to self-determination' will pass to the 'newly independent State created
by that people'.[87]

53.   Importantly, the expression 'another subject of international law' used at Article 2
also has broader significance outside the specific situation of newly independent States. As
explained in the Final Report, it also covers an 'individual or a human group':

> The new draft Resolution consequently takes into account the fact that the
> subject victim of a breach can be an individual or a human group and not only
> a State. In case of a breach of human rights obligations committed by the pre-
> decessor State before the date of State succession, the victim individuals or
> groups enjoy all the benefits that the prior draft Resolution only recognized
> to the injured *State*. Since the main policy of the draft Resolution has been
> that no internationally wrongful act must remain unpunished as a result of the
> emergence of a case of State succession, the individuals or groups victims of
> human rights obligations will always find a State that will be obliged to repair
> that breach.[88]

54.   Examples of such subjects of international law include human communities that,
although not recognised as 'peoples' under international law in the sense of being holders
of the right to self-determination, nevertheless possess other collective rights, such as
national, religious or linguistic minorities. Indigenous peoples also constitute another
example of a non-State subject of international law that can be the victim of an internationally wrongful act committed by the predecessor State.

55.   The Final Report refers to situations where there is 'a direct link between the
consequences of the internationally wrongful act and the territory or the population that
becomes part of the territory or the population of the successor State.'[89] The existence of
such a 'direct link' is considered as one *exception* to the 'general non-succession rule in
cases in which the predecessor State continues to exist after the date of State succession.'[90]
The expression 'direct link' is used at Article 11(2) (transfer of territory), Article 12(2)
(separation), and Article 16(2) (newly independent States). Under these provisions, the
rights arising from an internationally wrongful act committed *against* the predecessor State
pass to the successor State whenever there exists a 'direct link' between the consequences
of this act and the population of the successor State. In the context of dissolution (Article
15(2)), the existence of such a 'direct link' is also a 'relevant factor' to determine which
of the different successor States becomes bearer of such rights after the date of succession.
These provisions are specific illustrations of the basic principle set out at Article 5(2)
whereby when the injury caused by an internationally wrongful act committed against a

---

87   The question is further examined in the section dealing specifically with newly independent States
       (Article 16).
88   Final Report, para. 26, in: (2015) 76 *Annuaire de l'Institut de Droit international*, 524.
89   Ibid., 536.
90   Ibid., 535.

predecessor State affects 'persons' which, after the date of succession, 'are under the jurisdiction of a successor State', that State can request reparation for the injury caused by such act.[91]

3   The Resolution does not Deal with either Municipal Torts or Breaches of Rules of State Succession

56.   The Resolution deals with internationally wrongful acts committed by the predecessor State against *another State* (or another subject of international law) or acts committed against the predecessor State by *another State*. In other words, it does not cover the different situation of what happens after the date of succession to acts committed by the predecessor State against *its own* nationals and corporations that are considered as breach of domestic law only. The Resolution does not address the question of whether or not the successor State is bound to provide reparation for the consequences of such acts committed against individuals (and corporations) who are now its nationals. This is because these acts are not internationally wrongful acts per se, but rather municipal law *torts*.[92] Yet, some of the examples of State practice and municipal court decisions examined below involve the commission of such domestic torts. While they are conceptually of a different nature, these examples are nevertheless relevant for the analysis of State succession. For this reason, the specific nature of these examples will be highlighted whenever they are referred to below.

57.   Finally, a member of the Commission raised the different issue of wrongful acts committed as a result of State succession per se or in cases of a disregard for the rules governing State succession themselves. The Final Report makes it clear that any such questions can only arise *after* the date of succession.[93] As such, they are not regulated by the rules of State succession.[94] This is therefore an issue that falls outside the scope of the Resolution.

4   The Resolution Only Covers Situations of State Succession in Conformity with International Law

58.   The second paragraph of Article 2 explains that the Resolution only covers situations of succession which are considered *legal* under international law. The text of the provision refers to those succession cases 'occurring in conformity with international law and, in particular, the principles of international law embodied in the Charter of the United Nations'. The source of inspiration for adding such a reference is the presence of similar language found in other instruments dealing with State succession issues. Thus,

---

91   Article 5(2) is further examined below.
92   Dumberry, *State Succession to International Responsibility*, 29–30; Crawford, *State Responsibility: The General Part*, 436.
93   Final Report, para. 23, in: (2015) 76 *Annuaire de l'Institut de Droit international*, 522.
94   Dumberry, *State Succession to International Responsibility*, 27.

both the 1978 and the 1983 Vienna Conventions as well as the ILC Articles on succession to nationality contain an identical provision to that effect.[95] Yet, as noted by one member at the Tallinn session,[96] the 2001 Institute's Resolution on 'State Succession in Matters of Property and Debts'[97] does not contain such a clause, but only a reference to this legality requirement in its preamble.

59.   Twelve members of the Institute issued the following statement with regard to this provision:

> We would like to express our reservation on Article 2(2). The draft Article in its present form limits the application of the principles adopted *only* to situations of State Succession achieved in accordance with international law and the principles embodied in the Charter of the United Nations.
>
> We believe that the question of lawfulness of State Succession may be applicable or relevant only in respect of rights to be enjoyed or succeeded to by State(s) claiming succession. However, in respect of obligations arising out of succession, the State or States claiming succession and exercising effective control over the territory, people and its resources is or are deemed to be accountable for them. Any other view is likely to deny the victims or injured State of seeking remedies necessary for consequences arising from the internationally wrongful act.[98]

60.   The Final Report explains that an entity which has employed illegal means under international law in order to claim statehood should be excluded from the scope of this Resolution simply because such an entity cannot claim to be a State.[99] One illustration would be the declaration of independence of Southern Rhodesia in 1965 which was considered contrary to the principle of self-determination and, consequently, resulted in an obligation of non-recognition for all States. In such a situation, there is simply no State succession.[100] The question of the pertinence of including any reference to the legality requirement in the final resolution (and, specifically, the use of the word 'only' in Article 2(2)) was debated by members of the Commission at the Tokyo session[101] and

---

95   Article 6, *Vienna Convention on Succession of States in Respect of Treaties*; Article 3, *Vienna Convention on Succession of States in Respect of State Property, Archives and Debts*; Article 2(2), ILC draft Articles on Nationality of Natural Persons in Relation to the Succession of States'.
96   Session de Tallinn – 2015, PVPL plénière n° 1, 1ère séance plénière, 14ème Commission, 26, in: (2015) 76 *Annuaire de l'Institut de Droit international*, at 635–636.
97   Institut de Droit international, 'State Succession in Matters of Property and Debts', 713ff.
98   See statement (emphasis in the original) in: (2015) 76 *Annuaire de l'Institut de Droit international*, 683–684.
99   Final Report, para. 24, in: (2015) 76 *Annuaire de l'Institut de Droit international*, 522. See also: ILC Special Rapporteur, Second Report, 2018, para. 39: 'However, it is far from settled and one may even say it is rather doubtful that, in the situations occurring not in conformity with international law, it is possible to speak about the presence of the successor State at all. Indeed, as shown in the overview of the selected practice, the entities created in violation of international law were, on numerous occasions, declared illegal and null and void, took the same position on the matter'.
100   ILC Special Rapporteur, Second Report, 2018, para. 36, took the same position on the matter.
101   The debate is summarised in the Final Report, para. 24, in: (2015) 76 *Annuaire de l'Institut de Droit international*, 522.

the Tallinn plenary session.[102] Some members had in mind specific situations which had recently occurred and were worried about their exclusion from the scope of application of the Resolution. The Rapporteur insisted, however, that the task of the Institute was not to decide whether any specific event was in accordance with international law or not, but rather to provide general guidance. At the end of the day, if one considers that a specific situation is illegal under international law, this qualification results in the rules contained in the Resolution not finding application. On the contrary, the Resolution applies if the event is considered to be in conformity with international law.

61.   While recognising that the wording of Article 2(2) is not entirely appropriate, the Rapporteur nevertheless considered that it enjoyed the benefits of having been consistently adopted by other instruments dealing with State succession. He insisted that the Resolution 'ought only to be applicable if the succession was in accordance with international law'[103] and that 'such a limitation was necessary in order to promote respect for international law'.[104] He also agreed with the observation made by one member noting that 'adverse inferences would be drawn from an omission' and that 'the Institute would hence convey a strong message either way, by deciding to include a condition of lawfulness or by deciding not to do so'.[105] This is precisely the reason why the provision was kept in the final version of the Resolution. The ILC Special Rapporteur adopted the same position and in his Second Report proposed the inclusion of a similar article.[106]

62.   It should be added that although the IDI Rapporteur was not willing, in the context of the Resolution, to improve the language of the provision which has been adopted by precedent instruments dealing with State succession, it would be advisable for the ILC to review the wording of such similar clause in its future work. For example, the provision could read as follows:

These Articles apply only to the effects of situations of succession of States. Situations of claims of the replacement of one State by another in the responsibility for the international relations of territory not occurring in conformity with international law and, in particular, the principles of international law embodied in the Charter of the United Nations, are not covered by these Articles.

63.   A number of members of the Institute declared that even in illegal situations, the wrongdoer should be held responsible for its actions. They referred specifically to what

---

102 Session de Tallinn – 2015, PVPL plénière n° 1, 1ère séance plénière, 14ème Commission, 16–17, 25–27, in: (2015) 76 *Annuaire de l'Institut de Droit international*, at 634ff. See also: Institut de Droit international, Session de Tallinn – 2015, PVPL plénière n° 7, 6ème séance plénière, 14ème Commission, 20ff, in: (2015) 76 *Annuaire de l'Institut de Droit international*, at 675ff.
103 Session de Tallinn, – 2015, PVPL plénière n° 1, 1ère séance plénière, 14ème Commission, in: ibid., at 636.
104 Ibid., at 627.
105 Ibid., at 636.
106 See Draft Article 5 and its analysis in: ILC Special Rapporteur, Second Report, 2018, paras. 22–41. Draft Article 5: 'The present draft articles apply only to the effects of a succession of States occurring in conformity with international law and, in particular, the principles of international law embodied in the Charter of the United Nations'.

the Court mentioned with regard to the situation of the illegal occupation of Namibia by South Africa.[107] The Rapporteur considered that this example is indeed one clear illustration where a State is responsible for the commission of a wrongful act. Yet, this is a situation falling outside the scope of the Resolution since this responsibility arises from the illegal territorial control and conduct by the wrongdoer.

64.   Finally, reference should be made to a number of pending investment arbitration proceedings in which the matter of the status of Crimea is discussed. Thus, eight arbitration claims were recently filed by Ukrainian investors against Russia under the Ukraine–Russia bilateral investment treaty (BIT) alleging violations committed in Crimea after the integration of that territory in Russia in 2014. The questions at issue, however, do not concern a situation of alleged international illegal conduct by the alleged predecessor State for which the alleged successor State would have to bear the obligations arising as a result of such conduct. The main controversial legal issue is whether the conduct of Russia after having taken control of Crimea falls within the realm of the Ukraine–Russia BIT. Consequently, these cases do not fall within the scope of the Resolution.

5   The Resolution does not Deal with Changes of Government

65.   The third paragraph of Article 2 explains that the Resolution only concerns the effect of State succession and does not cover 'situations resulting from political changes within a State, including changes in the regime or name of the State.' In other words, the Resolution deals with *State* succession, not change of *government*. The basic distinction between these two concepts is well established. Changes in relations to the type or nature of a government or even regarding the name of a State do not affect its international personality. The same is true even in situations when the change of government is radical, such as, for instance, in the context of the transition from a dictatorship to a new democratic government.[108] In other words, these events do not affect the *identity* of that State. That State is (legally speaking) 'identical' before and after the events; it has the same international legal personality. No issue of State succession arises in such a situation. The concept of State 'continuity' is further examined below when analysing Article 4.

C   Chapter II: Common Rules

INTRODUCTION

66.   The second part of the Resolution contains common rules applicable irrespective of the categories of State succession involved. Article 3 highlights the subsidiary character of the guidelines contained in the Resolution. Two other clauses (Articles 4 and 5) examine the situation where the predecessor State is the perpetrator or the victim of a wrongful

---

107   Ibid., 637.
108   The matter is briefly discussed in: Final Report, para. 22, in: (2015) 76 *Annuaire de l'Institut de Droit international*, 522.

act committed before the date of succession and continues to exist after that date. Article 6 deals with the nature and the effect of the existence of devolution agreements between the parties concerned on matters of succession to the consequences of the commission of a wrongful act. Article 7 addresses problems arising when there is a plurality of successor States. Article 9 contains guidelines relating to cases of wrongful acts having a continuing or composite character. Finally, Article 10 concerns the exercise of diplomatic protection in the context of succession of States.

ARTICLE 3:

Subsidiary character of the guiding principles

The guiding principles mentioned below apply in the absence of any different solution agreed upon by the parties concerned by a situation of succession of States, including the State or other subject of international law injured by the internationally wrongful act.

Commentary

67.   This provision highlights the subsidiary character of the solutions proposed in the Resolution and the prevalence of agreements concluded by the parties to govern the matter. Clearly, rules relating to State succession do not possess a peremptory (*jus cogens*) character. Consequently, they may be substituted by other rules if so agreed by the interested parties.[109] The subsidiary character of any codification effort in the context of State succession to responsibility is also followed by the ILC Special Rapporteur in his First Report:

> like in the two Vienna Conventions and articles on nationality of natural persons in relation to the succession of States, the rules to be codified should be of a subsidiary nature. As such, they may serve two purposes. First, they can present a useful model that may be used and also modified by the States concerned. Second, in cases of lack of agreement, they can present a default rule to be applied in case of dispute.[110]

68.   Like any other agreement, those regulating situations related to the consequences of internationally wrongful acts in cases of State succession must not conflict with a peremptory norm of general international law. *Jus cogens* norms are, of course, quite limited in number.[111] Grave violations of fundamental norms of human rights or permanent sovereignty over natural resources, for example, may be at stake in these situations. Consequently,

---

109   Final Report, paras. 44ff, in: (2015) 76 *Annuaire de l'Institut de Droit international*, 530.
110   ILC Special Rapporteur, First Report, 2017, para. 86.
111   According to the ILC work on State responsibility ('The Report of the International Law Commission on the work of its Fifty-third session', Official Records of the General Assembly, Fifty-sixth session, Supplement No. 10 (A/56/10), chp. IV.E.2, 208, (2001) I *Yearbook ILC*, p. 202), peremptory norms include the prohibitions of aggression, genocide, slavery, racial discrimination, crimes against humanity and torture, and the right to self-determination.

it was important to explicitly include this caveat in the Resolution, following the examples of the 1978 and 1983 Vienna Conventions but improving their content.[112]

69.   Article 3 refers to the possibility for the 'parties concerned' to agree to a specific solution regarding matters of succession to the consequence of responsibility. One important question is therefore to determine who are the 'parties concerned' which may agree to adopt any such specific solution. Article 3 covers those agreements concluded between the parties that are in the position to decide the consequences of the commission of an internationally wrongful act. In fact, two kinds of agreement must be distinguished, depending on the parties to them. First, these parties may be, on one side, the predecessor or the successor State, and, on the other side, a third State (or subject), which can either be the author of the wrong or the one injured by that act. Second, Article 6 deals with another specific kind of agreement: 'devolution agreements'. They are concluded between the predecessor and the successor State(s) (or another subject that is in a position to engage the successor State).[113] As further explained below, one important characteristic of these 'devolution agreements' is the fact that they always involve the predecessor State as one of the parties. The specific nature of 'devolution agreements' and their effect are analysed below.[114]

70.   For the purposes of Article 3, the expression 'the parties concerned' is therefore not limited to the predecessor and the successor State(s) only, but covers also the other party to the relationship resulting from the commission of an internationally wrongful act. In fact, there can be three (or even more) States concerned in this kind of situation: the predecessor and the successor State(s), and the State (or other subject) the author of, or injured by, the internationally wrongful act. The following paragraphs briefly explain some of the possible combinations of the 'parties concerned' to such agreements.

71.   One typical example of an agreement covered by Article 3 are those concluded between the successor State and the *injured* State (i.e. the victim of a wrongful act committed before the date of succession). In his First Report, the ILC Special Rapporteur refers to such agreements as 'claims agreements'.[115] In his study on the question, the co-author of this Commentary provides a number of illustrations of such agreements:

-       Two treaties entered into by the successor State with the injured States (France and the United Kingdom) in the context of the unification of the United Arab Republic (1958);[116]

112   Article 13, *Vienna Convention on Succession of States in Respect of Treaties*; Articles 15(4) and 38(2), *Vienna Convention on Succession of States in Respect of State Property, Archives and Debts*.

113   For the same definition, see: ILC Special Rapporteur, First Report, 2017, paras. 96, 99.

114   See commentary to Article 6.

115   ILC Special Rapporteur, First Report, 2017, paras. 100ff.

116   *Accord général entre le gouvernement de la République française et le gouvernement de la République arabe unie*, in: *La documentation française*, 18 October 1958, no. 2473; (1958) *RGDIP* 738ff; *Agreement between the Government of the United Kingdom of Great Britain and Northern Ireland and the Government of the United Arab Republic Concerning Financial and Commercial Relations and British Property in Egypt*, in: (1959) UKTS no. 35 (Cmd. 723); 343 UNTS 159; (1958) 14 *Rev.*

- A 1992 agreement between the injured State (United States) and the successor State (Germany) in the context of the incorporation of the German Democratic Republic into the Federal Republic of Germany (1990);[117]

- In the context of the dissolution of the Union of Colombia (1829–1831), the three different successor States (Venezuela, Ecuador and New Grenada) entered into separate agreements with the injured State (United States of America);[118]

- A 1926 agreement between Panama and the injured State (United States) following the secession of the former from Colombia in 1903.[119]

72.   Article 3 also covers agreements in which a party is a non-State actor. This can be the case of an agreement between a successor State with a foreign company. The above-mentioned study provides one example of such an agreement in the context of the creation of the United Arab Republic, which was the result of the unification of Egypt and Syria in 1958.[120] The example concerns acts of nationalisation of the Société Financière de Suez by Egypt (the predecessor State) in 1956 before the date of succession.[121] After the unification, an agreement was entered into on 13 July 1958 between the United Arab Republic (the successor State) and the private corporation under which the former undertook, inter alia, to pay some EGY£ 28.3 million to the shareholders of the latter for wrongful acts which had been committed by Egypt (the predecessor State).[122]

73.   Other examples of agreements covered under Article 3 include those concluded between the State concerned and individuals victims of international law breaches (in the field of human rights, for example). Another possibility is that of an agreement between a national liberation movement and a State *other* than the predecessor State.[123] Under such an agreement, a national liberation movement may, for instance, agree in advance (i.e. before the date of succession) to take over the consequence of responsibility after the

Égyptienne d.i. 364; (1960) 54 *AJIL* 511–519. The examples are examined in: Dumberry, *State Succession to International Responsibility*, 93.

117 *Agreement between the Government of the Federal Republic of Germany and the Government of the United States of America Concerning the Settlement of certain Property Claims*, 13 May 1992, in: TIAS no. 11959; also in: Jan Klappers (ed.), *State Practice Regarding State Succession and Issues of Recognition* (The Hague: Kluwer Law International, 1999), at 240. The example is examined in: Dumberry, ibid., 91.

118 *Protocol between the United States of America and Venezuela* (1 May 1852, Caracas), in: William M. Malloy, *Treaties, Conventions, International Acts, Protocols and Agreements between the United States of America and other Powers, 1776–1909*, vol. II (Washington: US Govt., 1910), 1842. Both treaties signed by the United States with Ecuador and New Grenada can be found in: William M. Malloy, ibid., vol. I, at 319 and 432. The example is examined in: Dumberry, ibid., 106.

119 *Claims Convention between the United States and Panama*, signed on 28 July 1926, ratified on 3 October 1931, in: 138 LNTS 120–126; 6 UNRIAA 301. The example is examined in: Dumberry, ibid., 164.

120 Dumberry, ibid., 96.

121 L. Focsaneanu, 'L'accord ayant pour objet l'indemnisation de la compagnie de Suez nationalisée par l'Egypte' (1959) *AFDI* 161–204.

122 UN Doc. A/3898, S/4089, 23 September 1958.

123 As further explained below (see analysis of Article 6), an agreement concluded between the predecessor State and a national liberation movement is considered a 'devolution agreement'.

establishment of the newly independent State. Finally, another type of agreement which could be foreseen in this context is one between a national liberation movement and a foreign investor whereby the former would ensure that the new State will provide reparation after independence.

74.   As mentioned above, another specific type of relevant agreement in this field ('devolution agreements') will be examined below when analysing Article 6.

ARTICLE 4:

Invocation of responsibility for an internationally wrongful act committed by the predecessor State before the date of succession of States

1.   International responsibility arising from an internationally wrongful act committed before the date of succession of States by a predecessor State falls on this State.

2.   If the predecessor State continues to exist, the injured State or subject of international law may, even after the date of succession, invoke the international responsibility of the predecessor State for an internationally wrongful act committed by that State before the date of succession of States and request from it reparation for the injury caused by that internationally wrongful act.

3.   In conformity with the following Articles, the injured State or subject of international law may also or solely request reparation from a successor State for the injury caused by an internationally wrongful act of the predecessor State.

Commentary

75.   Articles 4 and 5 were added to the text of the Resolution following the release of the Final Report in order to clarify one of its most important aspects.[124] They address the situation when the predecessor State continues to exist after the date of succession. They deal with two distinct situations. First, Article 4 concerns the situation when an internationally wrongful act has been committed *by* the predecessor State before the date of succession. Second, Article 5 deals with the different situation of an act committed *against* the predecessor State before that date. In other words, while Article 4 focuses on the issue of succession to *obligations* arising from the commission of a wrongful act, Article 5 is concerned with succession to *rights* arising from such an act.

76.   The first paragraph of Article 4 expresses the basic principle which is mentioned at Article 1 of the ILC's Articles on Responsibility of States for Internationally Wrongful Acts: 'Every internationally wrongful act of a State entails the international responsibility

---

124 Institut de Droit international, Session de Tallinn – 2015, PVPL plénière n° 1, 4e séance plénière, 14ème Commission, in: (2015) 76 *Annuaire de l'Institut de Droit international*, at 638ff.

of that State.'[125] According to ILC Special Rapporteur Crawford, this provision 'affirms the basic principle that each State is responsible for its own wrongful conduct'.[126] In other words, only the State which has actually committed an internationally wrongful act should engage its responsibility for it.

77.   This basic principle does not create any difficulty whenever the predecessor State continues to exist after any changes affecting its territory and population have occurred. As further examined in detail below, such situations include those of 'transfer of part of the territory of a State' (Article 11) and 'separation of parts of a State' (Article 12). The situation of newly independent States (Article 16), although different, can be assimilated to these two. In these situations, the predecessor State should *remain* responsible for *its own* internationally wrongful acts, including those committed *before* the date of succession. Thus, in situations where the predecessor State continues to exist, the general rule is that the injured State (or another subject of international law) can invoke the responsibility of the predecessor State. This State continues to be responsible for obligations arising from the internationally wrongful acts in which it was involved before the date of succession. The ILC Special Rapporteur's Second Report also follows this general principle.[127] The term 'continuing' State is often used by scholars to refer to the predecessor State in the situation just described.[128] In its 2007 final judgment in the *Bosnia and Herzegovina Genocide Convention* Case, the ICJ, however, used the expression 'continuator' State.[129] Both terms can be used and have the same meaning.

78.   Under Article 4(2), the victim of an internationally wrongful act committed by the predecessor State before the date of succession can invoke the international responsibility of *that State* and request reparation for the injury caused by the act. Such a claim can be made *after* the date of succession even if the event took place before that date. The provision further adds that the victim of such an act can be either a State or another 'subject of international law'.[130]

79.   The following sections provide several examples of State practice and judicial decisions where the basic principle set out at Article 4 has been consistently applied. There

125 ILC, Titles and Texts of the Draft Articles on Responsibility of States for Internationally Wrongful Acts Adopted by the Drafting Committee on Second Reading, 26 July 2001, U.N. Doc. A/CN.4/L.602/Rev.1, (2001) II(2) *Yearbook ILC*, p. 30.
126 ILC, 'First Report on State Responsibility (addendum no. 4)', by Mr James Crawford, Special Rapporteur, 26 May 1998, U.N. Doc. A/CN.4/490/Add.4, at para. 110. It should be noted that the ILC Articles envisage two *exceptional* cases where an internationally wrongful act committed by a State entails the responsibility of another State (see Article 17 dealing with cases where a State directs and controls another State in the commission of an internationally wrongful act and Article 18 concerning cases where a State exerts coercion on another).
127 ILC Special Rapporteur, Second Report, 2018, paras. 45–47.
128 See, for instance: Dumberry, *State Succession to International Responsibility*, 16–17.
129 *Application of the Convention on the Prevention and Punishment of the Crime of Genocide (Bosnia and Herzegovina v. Serbia and Montenegro)*, Judgment 26 February 2007, ICJ Rep. 2007, paras. 71, 75, 80, 81, 106, 130, 131.
130 See the analysis above regarding Article 2(1), explaining which non-State actors can be envisaged as a 'subject of international law' under this provision.

is also wide support among scholars for this principle,[131] which is also followed by the ILC Special Rapporteur.[132] It should be added that one recent study examining the question of State succession to cultural property also provides a number of examples supporting the general solution adopted by the Resolution.[133]

80.   This provision is also telling about the structure followed by the Resolution. Thus, Article 4(2) provides the *general rule* that the predecessor State, when it continues to exist after the date of succession, should remain responsible for *its own* internationally wrongful acts committed before that date and bears the obligation to repair. The same principle is also expressed in specific provisions dealing with transfer of territory (Article 11(1)); separation (Article 12(2)); and newly independent States (Article 16(1)). Yet, as explained in detail below, these provisions also contain a number of exceptional circumstances where a *different solution* should apply and when the obligations arising from an internationally wrongful act –but not responsibility for the commission of that act – should, in fact, pass to the successor State.[134] This should be the case even though the predecessor State, author or victim of the wrongful act, continues to exist. Such situations include the following:

-    When the author of the wrongful act was an organ of a territorial unit of the predecessor State that has later become an organ of the successor State;[135]

-    when the successor State accepts responsibility for the commission of a wrongful act and the conditions set out in Article 6 are met.[136]

81.   The existence of these specific circumstances explains the presence of the third paragraph of Article 4. Thus, the injured State (or another subject of international law) as a result of an internationally wrongful act committed by the predecessor State before the date of succession can sometimes request reparation to the successor State. The provision also envisages the situation where the responsibility can be invoked against both the

---

131   See several writers mentioned in: Dumberry, *State Succession to International Responsibility*, 143–144, referring to: B. Stern, 'Responsabilité internationale et succession d'Etats', 335–336; Czapliński, 'State Succession and State Responsibility' 357; W. L. Gould, *An Introduction to International Law* (New York: Harpers & Brothers, 1957), 428; Monnier, 'La succession d'Etats en matière de responsabilité internationale', 67; K. Marek, *Identity and Continuity of States in Public International Law* (Geneva: Librairie Droz, 1968), 11; Volkovitsch, 'Righting Wrongs: Toward a New Theory of State Succession to Responsibility of International Delicts', 2200; Peterschmitt, *La succession d'Etats et la responsabilité international*, 54; Atlam, *Succession d'Etats et continuité en matière de responsabilité internationale*, 258; Sir R. Jenning & Sir A. Watts, *Oppenheim's International Law*, vol. I (Peace: Introduction and Part 1) (London: Longman, 1996), 224; H. Kelsen, 'Théorie générale du droit international public. Problèmes choisis' (1932) 42 *Rec. des Cours* 327, 333–334. See also, more recently: Mikulka, 'Succession of States in Respect of Rights of an Injured State', 292.
132   ILC Special Rapporteur, First Report, 2017, para. 17 ('The common point in those two articles [Arts 4 and 5] is the continuing existence of the predecessor State. It reflects a general rule of non-succession if the predecessor State continues to exist').
133   See Jakubowski, *State Succession in Cultural Property*, 265–267. See also examples mentioned at 194–198 and 198ff.
134   The same approach is also adopted in: ILC Special Rapporteur, Second Report, 2018, para. 48.
135   Articles 11(3) and 12(3). It should be added that a similar provision exists for the conduct of national liberation movements in the context of the creation of newly independent States (Article 16(3)).
136   See the commentary to Article 6 below.

predecessor State and the successor State. The first words of this provision ('In conformity with the following Articles') makes it clear that any such request to the successor State will however only be possible when a number of specific circumstances are present. These circumstances are examined in detail below.[137]

ARTICLE 5:

Invocation of responsibility for an internationally wrongful act committed against the predecessor State before the date of succession of States

1.   The predecessor State which after the date of succession of States continues to exist may invoke the international responsibility of another State or subject of international law for an internationally wrongful act committed against it before that date by that State or subject and may request reparation for the injury caused by this act.

2.   If the injury caused by an internationally wrongful act committed before the date of succession of States against a predecessor State affected the territory or persons which, after this date, are under the jurisdiction of a successor State, the successor State may request reparation for the injury caused by such act, as provided in the following Articles, unless reparation was already obtained in full before the date of succession of States.

Commentary

82.   As mentioned above, while Article 4 focuses on international wrongful acts committed by the predecessor State before the date of succession, Article 5 deals with the situation in which the internationally wrongful act was committed against the predecessor State before the date of succession.

83.   The first paragraph explains that in situations where the predecessor State continues to exist, it is that State which continues to enjoy rights arising from internationally wrongful acts in which it was involved before the date of succession. The predecessor State can therefore invoke the international responsibility of the 'perpetrator' (i.e. another State or a subject of international law) for such an act and request reparation for the injury caused. The provision adds that this can be done by the 'victim' (i.e. the predecessor State) after the date of succession even if the event took place before that date.

84.   The first paragraph of Article 5 therefore provides the general rule whereby the right to reparation remains that of the predecessor State which continues to exist. The second paragraph of Article 5 provides for an exception to that general principle. This is the situation where the internationally wrongful act committed against a predecessor State 'affect[s] the territory or persons' which, after the date of succession, are under the jurisdiction of the successor State(s). These exceptional circumstances are dealt with in

---

137   These circumstances are mentioned at Articles 11(2) and (3), 12(2), (3) and (4) and 16(3) and (4).

other provisions in the context of transfer of territory (Article 11(2)), separation (Article 12(2)) and newly independent States (Article 16(2)). Thus, these provisions indicate that the rights arising from an internationally wrongful act committed against the predecessor State pass to the successor State(s) if there exists a 'direct link between the consequences of this act and the territory or the population' of the same.[138] Under Article 5(2), whenever this is the case, the successor State may request reparation from the perpetrator for the injury caused by such act. The framework and the general solution adopted by the Resolution have been supported by scholars[139] and by the ILC Special Rapporteur.[140]

85.　　Article 5(2) further explains that the successor State(s) cannot request such reparation in the event that reparation 'was already obtained in full' before the date of succession. The reason is quite clear: the fact that reparation has already been obtained by the victim means that the consequences of that internationally wrongful act no longer exists after the date of State succession. The Resolution does not apply in such a case.

ARTICLE 6:

Devolution agreements and unilateral acts

1.　　Devolution agreements concluded before the date of succession of States between the predecessor State and an entity or national liberation movement representing a people entitled to self-determination, as well as agreements concluded by the States concerned after the date of succession of States, are subject to the rules relating to the consent of the parties and to the validity of treaties, as reflected in the Vienna Convention on the Law of Treaties. The same principle applies to devolution agreements concluded between the predecessor State and an autonomous entity thereof that later becomes a successor State.

2.　　The obligations of a predecessor State arising from an internationally wrongful act committed by it against another State or another subject of international law before the date of succession of States do not become the obligations of the successor State towards the injured State or subject only by reason of the fact that the predecessor State and the successor State have concluded an agreement, providing that such obligations shall devolve upon the successor State.

3.　　The obligations of a predecessor State in respect of an internationally wrongful act committed by it against another State or another subject of international law before the date of succession of

---

138　Under Article 11(2), such a direct link must exist with the territory transferred or the population concerned by the transfer of territory.

139　Jakubowski, *State Succession in Cultural Property*, 265–266 (indicating that it 'reflects a general rule of non-succession if the predecessor State continues to exist').

140　ILC Special Rapporteur, First Report, 2017, para. 17. The question of succession to the right to reparation will be examined by the Special Rapporteur in his upcoming Third Report (not yet published at the time of writing).

States do not become the obligations of the successor State towards the injured State or subject only by reason of the fact that the successor State has accepted that such obligations shall devolve upon it.

4.   Where the injured State or subject of international law does not accept the solution envisaged by the devolution agreement or unilateral act, good faith negotiations must be pursued by the States or subjects concerned. If these negotiations do not succeed within a reasonable period of time, the solution envisaged by the relevant Article of Chapter III of the present Resolution is applicable.

Commentary

86.   Article 3 highlights the subsidiary character of the guiding principles contained in the Resolution. Thus, as explained above, these principles only apply in the absence of any different solution agreed upon by the parties concerned by a situation of succession and the author or injured State. The question of who are the 'parties concerned by a situation of succession of States' under Article 3 has been examined above.[141] Article 6 deals specifically with possible solutions envisaged by the parties to the succession relationship, either through agreement, called a 'devolution agreement', or through unilateral acts.

87.   Paragraphs 1 and 2 of Article 6 explain the nature and the effect of devolution agreements. Paragraphs 3 and 4 of Article 6 deal with the different question of unilateral acts. As further discussed below, the main purpose of Article 6 is to preserve the interests of the victim of an illegal conduct, which could be affected by a devolution agreement concluded between the parties in a State succession relationship or by an unilateral act by one of them.

88.   Devolution agreements will be examined first (Section 1). An analysis of unilateral acts will follow (Section 2).

1   Devolution Agreements

89.   The expression 'devolution agreement' is defined at Article 1 of the Resolution:

'Devolution agreement' means an agreement, concluded by the predecessor State and the successor State or a national liberation, insurrectional or other movement, or an entity or organ that later becomes the organ of the successor State, providing that rights and/or obligations of the predecessor State shall devolve upon the successor State.

90.   Devolution agreements are problematic. First, there are difficulties regarding the question of the nature of the parties that can conclude such agreements. These agreements are concluded by either the author of a wrongful act or the injured State (which is in both cases always the predecessor State) and another party. The latter can be an entity claiming

---

141   See discussion in the context of the analysis of Article 3.

to engage the future successor State or the successor State itself. This question is examined at Section 1.1. Second, in some cases, these agreements are concluded before the independence of a State in circumstances in which the negotiating power of the parties may be unbalanced. In such a case, the validity of an agreement may be questioned. This issue, addressed in paragraph 1 of Article 6 is examined in Section 1.2 below. Third, another crucial question is that of the effect of devolution agreements. Thus, what happens when devolution agreements take a stance as to which of the predecessor or successor State(s) will enjoy the rights and/or accept the obligations arising from wrongful acts committed before the date of succession? Is the decision taken by these parties in such agreements opposable to the other actors involved in the responsibility relationship (either the author or the injured State)? These questions are examined in Section 1.3.

1.1   THE PARTIES TO DEVOLUTION AGREEMENTS

91.   The first paragraph of Article 6 identifies two different types of devolution agreement: those concluded *before* and *after* the date of succession. When the successor State is a new sovereign entity (such as, for instance, in situations of separation, dissolution and newly independent States), only those agreements concluded after the date of succession are considered as agreements entered into between sovereign States. Devolution agreements concluded before the date of succession necessarily involve a non-State actor as one of the parties. If a situation of State succession relates to the transfer of territory from one State to another, or the incorporation of one State into another existing one, devolution agreements dealing with responsibility matters are concluded between sovereign States. In the case of a transfer of part of the territory from one State to another, they can be concluded either before or after the date of succession. These different situations will be examined separately at sections 1.1.1 and 1.1.2.

1.1.1   *Agreements Concluded before the Date of Succession*

92.   Article 6 expressly envisages different possibilities of combination of parties to agreements concluded *before* the date of succession

93.   The first possibility considered is that of an agreement concluded before the date of succession between, on the one hand, the predecessor State, and, on the other hand, an 'entity' or 'a national liberation movement representing a people entitled to self-determination'.

94.   Article 1, defining the term 'devolution agreement', explains who these 'entities' are. It first refers to an 'insurrectional or other movement'. This is a reference to movements in the context of a separation of part of the territory of the predecessor State which succeeds in establishing a new State. One example of this type of agreement is the Comprehensive Peace Agreement concluded on 9 January 2005 between the Government of Sudan and the Sudan People's Liberation Movement that set the basis for the independence of South Sudan on 9 July 2011.[142]

---

142   South Sudan was admitted to the United Nations on that date, see: GA Res. 65/308, 25 August 2011.

95.   Another category of 'entities' envisaged by the definition of devolution agreements embodied in Article 1 consists of an 'organ that later becomes the organ of the successor State' or an 'autonomous entity' which later becomes a successor State (such as in the context of separation).[143] One illustration is the *Agreement regarding the Separation of Singapore from Malaysia as an Independent and Sovereign State* of 7 August 1965, which was concluded between the Federal Government of Malaysia and the Government of Singapore, while the latter was still a member of the former State.[144]

96.   These different scenarios are specifically envisaged in the context of transfer of territory from one State to another (Article 11(3)), separation (Article 12(3)) and dissolution (Article 15(3)).

97.   In the context of the creation of newly independent States, dealt with at Article 16 of the Resolution, devolution agreements are those concluded between the predecessor State and the entity or national liberation movement representing the people entitled to self-determination. One example of such an agreement is the Evian Accords concluded on 19 March 1962 between France and the National Liberation Front (FLN) in the context of the independence of Algeria.[145]

98.   Finally, reference should be made to a second possibility included in the definition of 'devolution agreement' at Article 1: an agreement concluded *before* the date of succession between the predecessor State and the successor State. One example of such an agreement is the *Treaty on the Establishment of German Unity* signed between the GDR and the FRG on 31 August 1990 providing for the 'unification' of the two States by 3 October 1990.[146] On that date, the GDR ceased to exist as an independent State and its territory comprising five *Länder* was *integrated* into the already existing FRG. Article 24(1) of the Treaty indicates that Germany will endorse claims of third States regarding 'claims and liabilities' arising from 'the performance of State tasks' by the GDR.[147] This provision has been interpreted by many in doctrine as the acceptance by Germany of obligations arising from internationally wrongful acts committed by the former East Germany.[148]

---

143   See Final Report, para. 45, in: (2015) 76 *Annuaire de l'Institut de Droit international*, 531.
144   *Agreement relating to the Separation of Singapore from Malaysia as an Independent and Sovereign State*, signed at Kuala Lumpur, on 7 August 1965, 563 UNTS 89, No. 8206.
145   Text in French at: www.legifrance.gouv.fr/jo_pdf.do?id=JORFTEXT000000498172&pageCourante=03019#.
146   *Vertrag zwischen der Bundesrepublik Deutschland und der Deutschen Demokratischen Republik über die Herstellung der Einheit Deutschlands* [Treaty between the Federal Republic of Germany and the German Democratic Republic on the Establishment of German Unity], 31 August 1990, (1990) II BGBl. 885; (1991) 30 ILM 463.
147   It should be noted that ILC Special Rapporteur, First Report, 2017, paras. 105–106, does not include this agreement in the category of devolution agreements, but rather as an example of 'other agreements' since it was adopted outside the context of decolonisation. The scope and content of this provision is further discussed below when analysing Article 14.
148   See the analysis in: Dumberry, *State Succession to International Responsibility* 86, for a long list of writers, including: S. Oeter, 'German Unification and State Succession' (1991) 51(2) *ZaöRV* 381; Volkovitsch, 'Righting Wrongs: Toward a New Theory of State Succession to Responsibility of International Delicts', 2177; B. Stern, 'Responsabilité internationale et succession d'Etats', 352; See also: Crawford, *State Responsibility: The General Part*, 449–450; Šturma, 'State Succession in Respect of International Responsibility', 668. *Contra*: F. Drinhausen, *Die Auswirkungen der Staatensukzession*

99.   In sum, the combination of Articles 1 and 6 provides that devolution agreements can be concluded *before* the date of succession between the predecessor State and the following five actors:

-     a national liberation movement or another entity representing a people entitled to self-determination;

-     an insurrectional or another movement which succeeds in creating a new State;

-     an organ of the territorial unit of the predecessor State that has later become an organ of the successor State;

-     the successor State.

1.1.2   Agreements Concluded after the Date of Succession

100.   Article 6 also refers to devolution agreements concluded *after* the date of succession. By definition, a post-succession devolution agreement can only be concluded between the predecessor State and the successor State(s). This situation can occur in the context of transfer of territory, separation and the creation of newly independent States. Two illustrations of such agreements are the following:

-     Article 38 of the 1947 *Paris Peace Treaty* in the context of the cession of the Dodecanesian Islands from Italy to Greece;[149]

-     *Agreement between the Republic of the Sudan and the Republic of South Sudan on Certain Economic Matters* (2012).[150]

101.   Finally, it should be added that an agreement concluded between successor States themselves is not considered as a 'devolution agreement'. The reason is that the predecessor State (i.e. the entity which is making the 'devolution' of rights and obligations) is not a party to such an agreement. In his First Report, the ILC Special Rapporteur referring to the *Agreement on Succession Issues* in the context of the break-up of Yugoslavia comes to the same conclusion.[151] The predecessor State must be a party to the agreement for it to be considered as a 'devolution agreement'.

I.2   PRESERVATION OF THE VALIDITY OF THESE AGREEMENTS

102.   The first paragraph of Article 6 indicates that devolution agreements 'are subject to the rules relating to the consent of the parties and to the validity of treaties' contained in

---

auf Verträge eines Staates mit privaten Partnern (Frankfurt: Peter Lang, 1995), 151; U. Fastenrath, 'Der deutsche Einigungsvertragim Lichte des Rechts der Staatennachfolge' (1992) 44 *ÖZöRV* 39; P.E. Quint, 'The Constitutional Law of German Unification' (1991) 50 *Md. L.Rev.* 534.

149   *Paris Peace Treaty*, signed on 10 February 1947 at Paris, entered into force on 15 September 1947, in: 49 UNTS 126; (1948) UKTS no. 50 (Cmd. 7481). The example is examined in: Dumberry, *State Succession to International Responsibility*, 129.

150   See Articles 5.1.1 and 5.1.4. This example is referred to in: ILC Special Rapporteur, First Report, 2017, para. 107. It should be noted that he does not refer to this agreement as a devolution agreement, but rather as an example of 'other agreements'.

151   ILC Special Rapporteur, First Report, 2017, para. 110.

the Vienna Convention on the Law of Treaties. The Final Report explains the importance of this provision for devolution agreements concluded by the predecessor State with subjects other than States:

> Since these kinds of agreements are not governed by the Vienna Convention on the Law of Treaties or by customary law applicable to inter-State relations, it is important to explicitly indicate in the Resolution [...] that the so-called devolution agreements concluded with non-State actors must also respect the rules relating to the validity of treaties and consent of the parties.[152]

103.   The question of the validity of devolution agreements concluded before the date of succession is of particular importance for newly independent States. Given the factual power imbalance between the predecessor State (the administering power) and the representatives of the future independent State, it must be ensured that proper consent by the latter has been appropriately given, without the former imposing any conditions for the achievement of independence. Other rules relating to the validity of treaties must also be taken into account. This matter has been discussed in the framework of the cases concerning the Chagos Archipelago, both in the arbitration on the *Chagos Marine Protected Area* under Annex VII of the United Nations Convention on the Law of the Sea[153] and in the advisory opinion proceedings on the *Legal consequences of the separation of Chagos from Mauritius in 1965* before the ICJ.[154]

104.   The scope and content of Article 6(1) has been endorsed by the ILC Special Rapporteur in his First Report.[155]

I.3   THE EFFECT OF DEVOLUTION AGREEMENTS ON THE INJURED STATE OR SUBJECT

105.   Agreements covered under Article 6 may provide for the devolution to the successor State of rights and/or obligations arising from wrongful acts committed before the date of succession against or by the predecessor State. It should be added that these agreements can also provide for the opposite, i.e. that such rights and/or obligations remain with the predecessor State notwithstanding the event of State succession. Paragraph 2 of Article 6 deals with the effect and the consequences that such agreements have on a *third* party,

---

152   Final Report, para. 45, in: (2015) 76 *Annuaire de l'Institut de Droit international*, 531.

153   *In the Matter of the Chagos Marine Protected Area Arbitration (Mauritius v. United Kingdom)*, PCA Case no. 2011-03. See: Memorial of Mauritius, 1 January 2012, paras. 2.40, 3.68; Counter-Memorial of the United Kingdom, 15 July 2013, paras. 2.54–2.66; Reply of Mauritius, 18 November 2013, para. 2.36; Rejoinder of the United Kingdom, 17 March 2014, para. 2.52; arbitral award of 18 March 2015, paras. 418–428; Dissenting and Concurring Opinion of Judges Kateka and Wolfrum, paras. 74–79.

154   *Legal consequences of the separation of Chagos from Mauritius in 1965 (Request for Advisory Opinion)*, Written Statement of Mauritius, paras. 3.111–3.112; Written Statement of the United Kingdom, paras. 3.51–3.53.

155   ILC Special Rapporteur, First Report, 2017, para. 93, noting that 'the content of paragraph 1 seems to be generally acceptable', and adding that other questions regarding devolution agreements concerning national liberation movements, insurgents and other non-State entities would be examined at a later stage of the work of the ILC.

i.e. the injured State (or another subject of international law) in cases of internationally wrongful acts committed by the predecessor State. The goal of this provision is the preservation of the rights of the *victim* of the internationally wrongful act. As further explained below, this is an important point which explains why Article 6 is silent with respect to the different situation when the third State is in fact the author of that illegal act. The following sections deal with a number of questions related to the effect of devolution agreements:

- the scope of Article 6(2) (Section 1.3.1);

- the goal of this provision, which is to protect the interests of the injured State (Section 1.3.2); and

- the applicable procedure whenever the injured State rejects the solution adopted in the agreement (Section 1.3.3).

1.3.1   The Scope of Article 6(2)

106.   Article 6(2) acknowledges that the parties to a devolution agreement may agree that the obligations of a predecessor State arising from an internationally wrongful act committed against another State or another subject of international law before the date of succession will devolve upon the successor State. Article 3(1) of the draft proposed by the ILC Special Rapporteur in his First Report contains the exact same language as Article 6(2). His Report indicates that 'many devolution agreements concluded by the former dependent territories of the United Kingdom of Great Britain and Northern Ireland also provide for the continuity of delictual responsibility of the new States'.[156]

107.   Yet, Article 6(2) goes further. The underlying rationale behind the adoption of this provision is that the parties to the State succession relationship cannot solely decide on their own about which of them will bear the obligation to repair. The victims must be allowed to take position on the matter. Thus, as mentioned in the Final Report, 'the victims may fix their position in the case of an agreement between or among successor States deciding which of them will bear the obligation to repair'.[157]

108.   Two basic remarks should be made at this juncture.

109.   First, Article 6(2) only covers agreements dealing with the transfer of *obligations*. It does *not* cover any accord between the parties providing for the transfer of the *rights* of a predecessor State arising from an internationally wrongful act committed by another State. The provision therefore follows the general pattern guiding the entire Resolution: the basic need to protect the interests of the injured State or subject who is the *victim* of an internationally wrongful act. Thus, if the injured State or subject is a third party to a devolution agreement, it cannot be imposed a change of debtor of the obligation to repair. The injured State or subject needs to consent to the transfer of the obligation to repair from the predecessor State to the successor State. There might be situations where the injured State

---

156   ILC Special Rapporteur, First Report, 2017, para. 40. See also para. 96.
157   Final Report, para. 26, in: (2015) 76 *Annuaire de l'Institut de Droit international*, 524.

would prefer, for different reasons, to be given proper reparation by the same State having committed the internationally wrongful act (i.e. the predecessor State). This is just the application of the *pacta tertiis nec nocent nec prosunt* rule, as discussed below.

110.   The situation is obviously quite different in the event where the third State or subject is, on the contrary, the *author* of the internationally wrongful act. Whenever this is the case, the third State or subject has the obligation to repair. This basic fact is not altered in any way by the existence of a devolution agreement concluded between the predecessor and the successor State(s). The only impact of any such agreement would be to change the identification of the State to whom the third State should provide proper reparation. Importantly, the third State or subject's obligation to repair remains unaffected by any such agreement.

111.   In contrast, the impact of any changes regarding who is the holder of the obligation to repair is substantially different. In the event that the obligation to repair is transferred to the successor State, the victim may, for instance, consider less likely the possibility of ever receiving any reparation. The victim may prefer, for whatever reasons, that the predecessor State remains the bearer of this obligation. In his First Report, the ILC Special Rapporteur adopted a different approach by adding a provision (Article 3(2)) dealing with the transfer of *rights*, which reads as follows:

> The *rights* of a predecessor State arising from an international wrongful act owed to it by another State before the date of succession of States do not become the rights of the successor States towards the responsible State only by reason of the fact that the predecessor State and the successor State have concluded an agreement providing that such rights shall devolve upon the successor State.[158]

112.   Thus, according to this provision, the perpetrator of the wrongful act would have to consent for any such rights to be transferred to the successor State. The risk associated with Draft Article 3(2) is that the wrongdoer may find comfort in such a provision if it intends to delay the accomplishment of its obligation to repair. Ultimately, Draft Article 3(2), as proposed by the ILC Special Rapporteur, seems designed to protect the interests of the wrongdoer, and not the victim.

113.   The second remark regarding Article 6(2) is the fact that it only covers those agreements providing for the transfer of obligations to the successor State. It does not cover any other accords whereby the parties would agree that the continuing State remains responsible for obligations arising from acts committed before the date of succession.[159] The reason is quite simple. In such a case, there is no change in the original responsibility relationship between the parties and consequently no succession to obligations arising from the internationally wrongful act committed before the date of succession.

---

158   ILC Special Rapporteur, First Report, 2017, para. 111 (emphasis added).
159   More generally, the situation where the predecessor State continues to be responsible for acts committed before the date of succession is already covered by Article 4(2).

1.3.2   The Goal is to Protect the Interests of the Injured State

114.   Article 6(2) makes it clear that obligations do not become those of the successor State towards the injured State (or another subject of international law) 'only by reason of the fact' that the parties have entered into a devolution agreement to that effect. In other words, the existence of any such agreement between the parties is not sufficient by itself for the successor State to automatically take over the obligation to repair. The Resolution follows the same rule established at Article 8(1) of the 1978 Vienna Convention with regard to treaties.[160] As mentioned above, the aim of Article 6(2) is to protect the interests of the injured State or the injured subject of international law. Thus, as noted in the Final Report, 'in the case of succession to the obligations arising from an internationally wrongful act committed by the predecessor State, any agreement with regard to the successor State that holds the obligation or to the apportionment of the obligation among the successor States must require the consent of the victim'.[161] Moreover, just like the injured State, 'the victim individuals or human groups' must also 'have the opportunity to fix their position vis-à-vis the devolution agreement'.[162]

115.   The Final Report explains that a devolution agreement 'must respect the rights of the third States or individuals or human groups concerned by these agreements'.[163] The Report further adds that 'if the predecessor State continues to exist after the date of State succession, the victim must have the possibility to express its view on the question of the holder of the obligation in its favour'.[164] In other words, the injured State (or subject) must have a say in the determination of which of the predecessor State or the successor State should be responsible for the consequences of the commission of a wrongful act.[165] The same is true in the context of dissolution where the injured State (or subject) must consent to any allocation of obligations between the successor States themselves. This is the case even if such an agreement is not considered as a devolution agreement.[166] This is in

---

160   For an analysis, see: A. Garrido-Muñoz, 'Article 8', in: G. Distefano, G. Gaggioli & A. Hêche (eds.), *La Convention de Vienne de 1978 sur la succession d'États en matière de traités: Commentaire article par article et études thématiques* (Brussels: Bruylant, 2015), 261ff.

161   Final Report, para. 51, in: (2015) 76 *Annuaire de l'Institut de Droit international*, 533.

162   Ibid., para. 26, at 524.

163   Ibid., para. 47, at 532.

164   Ibid., para. 48, at 532.

165   The same position is adopted in: ILC Special Rapporteur, First Report, 2017, paras. 95–96 (mentioning that in the context of such agreements between the predecessor State and the successor State 'it is clear that the *pacta tertiis* rule applies') (see also at para. 99).

166   It should be noted that the ILC Special Rapporteur, First Report, 2017, para. 111, seems to have taken a different position on the matter. As mentioned above, he rightly qualified the *Agreement on Succession Issues* in the context of the break-up of Yugoslavia *not* as a devolution agreement (see ibid., para. 108). This is because this agreement was concluded between the successor States themselves, and did not involve the predecessor State. He mentioned the agreement in his section dealing with 'other agreements'. Importantly, on the effect of these agreements on third parties, he stated that 'While devolution agreements are subject to the *pacta tertiis* rule and require consent of the third States, other agreements have full effects according to their provisions and the rules of the law of treaties.' Draft Article 3(3) he proposed also provides for the same solution: 'Another agreement than a devolution agreement produces full effects on the transfer of obligations or rights arising from State responsibility. Any agreement is binding upon the parties to it and must be performed by them in good faith.' Yet, paragraph 4 of the provision mentions that 'The preceding paragraphs are without prejudice to

accordance with Article 34 of the Vienna Convention on the Law of Treaties, whereby 'a treaty does not create either obligations or rights for a third State without its consent'.[167] Thus, a devolution agreement is only binding on the parties to this instrument.[168] It is not binding on the injured State, who is not a party to the agreement.

116.   The fundamental importance of the solution adopted by the Resolution regarding the protection of the interests of the injured State or subject is clear whenever the parties have agreed to the extinction of any obligation arising from the commission of a wrongful act.[169] Thus, as noted in the Final Report, 'what is clear is that the predecessor and the successor State cannot decide on their own that the obligations emerging from an internationally wrongful act committed by the former State will cease with its disappearance, and will not pass to the successor State without the consent of the third injured State'.[170] In other words, the injured State (or subject) must necessarily consent to any such annihilation of its right to reparation. As noted by the Final Report, a devolution agreement 'cannot by itself relieve the State author of the internationally wrongful act of its obligation to repair'.[171]

117.   In his First Report, the ILC Special Rapporteur explains the effect of devolution agreements regarding 'third States' as follows:

> To sum up provisionally, devolution agreements are agreements between the predecessor State and the successor State, therefore the *pacta tertiis* rule applies. They mostly relate to succession in respect of treaties. However, they also address the transfer of obligations and responsibilities arising from their application. They may nevertheless have certain impact on the third States. Concerning such possible effects, rules in articles 35 and 36 of the Vienna Convention on the Law of Treaties should be taken into account. When it

the applicable rules of the law of treaties, in particular the *pacta tertiis* rule, as reflected in articles 34 to 36 of the Vienna Convention on the Law of Treaties.' The addition of this last fourth paragraph is confusing. Thus, it is not clear whether the *pacta tertiis* rule actually applies to these 'other agreements' (i.e. those not considered as devolution agreements). The passage mentioned above (at para. 111) suggests that the *pacta tertiis* rule *does* not apply to an agreement concluded between the successor States in the context of a dissolution and that, consequently, the injured State (or subject) would *not* have to consent to any allocation of obligations between the successor States.

167   Vienna Convention on the Law of Treaties, 1155 UNTS 331.
168   See: K. Zemanek, 'State Succession after Decolonization' (1965) 116 *Rec. des cours*, 221; C.J. Tams, 'State Succession to Investment Treaties: Mapping the Issues' (2016) 31(2) *ICSID Rev.* 314–343, 333; A. Zimmermann and J.G. Devaney, 'Succession to Treaties and the Inherent Limits of International Law', in: C.J. Tams, A. Tzanakopoulos, & A. Zimmermann (eds.), *Research Handbook on the Law of Treaties* (London: Edward Elgar, 2014), 536; E. Lagrange, 'Les successions d'États: pratiques françaises' (2003) 63 *La. L.Rev.*, 1224ff; C. Binder, '*Sanum Investments Limited v The Government of the Lao People's Democratic Republic*' (2016) 17 *J. World Invest. & Trade* 292; O.G. Repousis, 'On Territoriality and International Investment Law: Applying China's Investment Treaties to Hong Kong and Macao' (2015) 37(1) *Michigan JIL* 186.
169   See also: ILC Special Rapporteur, First Report, 2017, para. 91, indicating that agreements between States on that matter may 'limit or exclude' the transfer of obligations arising from State responsibility of the predecessor State and that this 'is why consent of the third States is important and cannot be presumed in all cases'.
170   Final Report, para. 49, in: (2015) 76 *Annuaire de l'Institut de Droit international*, 533.
171   Ibid., para. 26, at 524.

comes to rights of third States, their assent may be presumed. A transfer of obligations from State responsibility to the successor State may be viewed so as to accord rights to the third injured State. However, it is also possible that succession will bring some obligations for third States. Then it is required that the third State expressly accepts such obligations.[172]

118. Rather than distinguishing the effect of a devolution agreement on third States (or subjects) based on the consideration of whether it is the victim or the author of the wrongful act, the ILC Special Rapporteur focuses instead on the general question as to whether the agreement creates rights or obligations for that State (or subject).

119. The IDI Resolution adopts a different position on the matter. It establishes a specific rule: the *consent* of the injured State or subject is *required* whenever a devolution agreement provides for the transfer of the obligation to repair from the predecessor State to the successor State.

1.3.3   When the Injured State Rejects the Agreement's Solution

120. In the event that the injured State (or subject) *accepts* the solution adopted in the devolution agreement, it goes without saying that this is the allocation of obligations which should actually prevail between the parties concerned. In other words, the different solutions set out under Chapter III of the Resolution should *not* apply in this situation. This reflects the subsidiary character of the guiding principles set out under Chapter III (see Article 3).

121. Article 6(4) explains what happens when the injured State (or subject) does not accept the solution adopted in a devolution agreement: 'good faith negotiations must be pursued' by the States or subjects 'concerned'. Article 8 of the Resolution explains which are the States or other subject of international law concerned. In principle, at least at first, these negotiations should be undertaken between, on the one hand, the successor State and, on the other hand, the injured State (or subject). However, in the event that the victim insists on the obligation to repair being performed by the predecessor State, the participation of the latter in these negotiations would become indispensable.

122. Under Article 6(4), if 'these negotiations do not succeed within a reasonable period of time, the solution envisaged by the relevant Article of Chapter III of the present Resolution is applicable'.[173] Chapter III thus provides for the application of specific solutions to different categories of State succession. Again, this reflects the subsidiary character of the guiding principles set out under Chapter III, which only apply in the absence of any other solution adopted by the parties concerned (Article 3).

---

172   ILC Special Rapporteur, First Report, 2017, para. 99.
173   Different solutions are envisaged under Chapter III of the Resolution depending on the types of succession involved.

2   Unilateral Acts by the Successor State

123.   While paragraphs 1, 2 and 4 of Article 6 deal with devolution agreements, paragraphs 3 and 4 concern unilateral acts by the successor State. Article 6(3) deals with the situation where the successor State has *unilaterally accepted* to take over the obligations arising from an internationally wrongful act committed by the predecessor State against another State (or another subject of international law).

124.   As mentioned above, Article 4(2) establishes the general rule whereby when the predecessor State continues to exist after the date of succession, it should remain responsible for its own wrongful acts. Thus, in the context of transfer of territory, separation and newly independent States (Articles 11, 12 and 16, respectively) the guiding principle established under the Resolution (with a number of exceptions) is that the obligations arising from an internationally wrongful act committed before the date of succession by the predecessor State do *not* pass to the successor State. While Article 6(2) envisages an agreement for the transfer of the obligation to repair from the predecessor to the successor State, Article 6(3) deals with another possibility: a unilateral decision by the successor State.

125.   As a matter of principle, a unilateral decision by the *predecessor* State to transfer its obligation to repair to the successor State is inconceivable or, at least, should be considered as having no binding effect. But nothing prevents a successor State from freely accepting such obligations. This possibility is recognised at Article 6(3). The fact that a successor State can decide to succeed to the consequences arising from the commission of an internationally wrongful act by the predecessor State has been recognised by scholars.[174] The question remains, however, whether this unilateral decision can be imposed on the third State or subject of international law involved in the responsibility relationship with the predecessor State.

126.   The following sections will first examine a number of examples of State practice and judicial decisions involving unilateral acts by a successor State (Section 2.1), which will be followed by an analysis of the legal effect of that State's acceptance of any such responsibility (Section 2.2).

---

174   Stern, 'Responsabilité internationale et succession d'Etats', 350; Šturma, 'State Succession in Respect of International Responsibility', 669. See also: Dumberry, *State Succession to International Responsibility*, 215, referring to the following writers: M. Udina, 'La succession des Etats quant aux obligations internationals autres que les dettes publiques' (1933) 44 *Rec. des Cours*, 768; H. Lauterpacht, *Oppenheim's International Law*, vol. I (London: Longmans Green & Co., 1955), 162; Jenning and Watts, *Oppenheim's International Law*, 218; J. O'Brien, *International Law* (London: Cavendish Publ. Ltd, 2001), 605; P.M. Dupuy, *Droit international public*, 4th ed. (Paris: Dalloz, 1998), 54; J. Crawford, *Brownlie's Principles of Public International Law*, 8th ed. (Oxford: OUP, 2013), 424; Monnier, 'La succession d'Etats en matière de responsabilité internationale', 67, 90; Volkovitsch, 'Righting Wrongs: Toward a New Theory of State Succession to Responsibility of International Delicts', 2199–2200; N. Ronzitti, *La succession internazionale tra stati* (Milan: Dott. A. Giuffrè, 1970), 221; J. Dugard, *International Law; a South African Perspective*, 2nd ed. (Kenwyn: Juta, 2000), 232–233; H. Booysen, 'Succession to Delictual Liability: A Namibian Precedent' (1991) 24 *Comp. & Int'l L.J. S. Afr.* 207; T.S.N. Sastry, *State Succession in Indian Context* (New Delhi: Dominant Publ. & Dist., 2004), 209.

2.1 EXAMPLES OF SUCCESSOR STATES ACCEPTING TO TAKE OVER THE CONSEQUENCES OF RESPONSIBILITY

127. The basic principle underlying Article 6(3) has been affirmed by the ICJ in the *Gabčíkovo-Nagymaros Project* case.[175] The Special Agreement between the parties to the case recognised that the Slovak Republic, as one of the two successor States to Czechoslovakia, was the 'sole successor state in respect of rights and obligations relating to the Gabčíkovo-Nagymaros Project'. It should be mentioned here that this is an agreement between a successor State (Slovakia) and the other State regarding a responsibility relationship in a case in which the predecessor State had ceased to exist. Yet, the other successor State (the Czech Republic) did not (at least officially) take part in this decision. For this reason, the position adopted by Slovakia can be considered as a unilateral act. The Court did not question whether the Slovak Republic could freely decide to be held responsible for the consequences of an internationally wrongful act committed by the predecessor State; it simply accepted this position, which was agreed by the successor State (Slovakia) and the party to the responsibility relationship (Hungary).[176] It should be added that this solution adopted by the parties was no doubt influenced by the geographic location of the project, which only concerns the territory of Slovakia and not that of the Czech Republic.

128. Another example examined by scholars[177] is Article 140(3) of the Namibian Constitution, stating that anything done in accordance with the South African laws by South African organs prior to the date of independence of Namibia shall be deemed to have been done by the Government of Namibia.[178] Importantly, this provision also reserves the right for the new State to repudiate (by an act of legislation) the internationally wrongful acts committed by South Africa. The scope and content of this provision were analysed

---

175 *Case Concerning the Gabčíkovo-Nagymaros Project* (Hungary v. Slovakia), Judgment of 25 September 1997, ICJ Rep. 1997, 3.

176 Ibid., para. 151. See: Crawford, *State Responsibility: The General Part*, 446.

177 See H.A. Strydom, 'Namibian Independence and the Question of the Contractual and Delictual Liability of the Predecessor and Successor Governments' (1990) 15 *South African YIL* 111–121; Dumberry, *State Succession to International Responsibility*, 192ff; ILC Special Rapporteur, First Report, 2017, para. 117.

178 Constitution of Namibia, adopted by the Constituent Assembly of Namibia on 9 February 1990, entered into force on 21 March 1991, U.N. Doc. S/20967/Add.2. The provision reads as follows: '(1) Subject to the provisions of this Constitution, all laws which were in force immediately before the date of Independence shall remain in force until repealed or amended by Act of Parliament or until they are declared unconstitutional by a competent Court. (2) Any powers vested by such laws in the Government, or in a Minister or other official of the Republic of South Africa shall be deemed to vest in the Government of the Republic of Namibia or in a corresponding Minister or official of the Government of the Republic of Namibia, and all powers, duties and functions which so vested in the Government Service Commission, shall vest in the Public Service Commission referred to in Article 112 hereof. (3) Anything done under such laws prior to the date of Independence by the Government, or by a Minister or other official of the Republic of South Africa shall be deemed to have been done by the Government of the Republic of Namibia or by a corresponding Minister or official of the Government of the Republic of Namibia, unless such action is subsequently repudiated by an Act of Parliament, and anything so done by the Government Service Commission shall be deemed to have been done by the Public Service Commission referred to in Article 112 hereof, unless it is determined otherwise by an Act of Parliament.'

in the cases of *Mwandinghi v. Minister of Defence, Namibia*[179] before the High Court of Namibia and that of *Minister of Defence, Namibia v. Mwandinghi*[180] before the Supreme Court of Namibia.

129. The *Mwandinghi* case involved damages arising from the shooting of Mr Mwandinghi, a Namibian national, by elements operating for the South African Defence Forces in 1987. Before independence, the plaintiff submitted a claim for damages against the Minister of Defence of South Africa. Upon independence, he sought to substitute the Minister of Defence of Namibia as defendant based on Article 140(3) of the new Namibian Constitution. He applied to the High Court by notice of motion for an order to allow the substitution. In its judgment, the High Court (comprised of one sitting Judge) indicated that Article 140 of the Constitution was an 'acceptance by the new government of all that was previously done under those laws in the exercising of the powers conferred thereby'[181] and that it was wide enough to cover the claim of the plaintiff for 'delicts' committed by the South African Defence Forces. The Minister of Defence of Namibia submitted that under international law 'a new State does not succeed to delicts committed by its predecessor and consequently, applying art. 145(1)(b), the Minister of Defence of Namibia is not liable and cannot be substituted for the wrong committed by the Minister of Defence of the Republic of South Africa'.[182] The sitting Judge seems to have accepted this argument, as a matter of principle, and stated that '[F]or the purpose of this case, I shall accept that in international law a new State is not liable for the delicts committed by its predecessor'.[183] However, in the concrete situation of the present case, he had already concluded that Article 140(3) expressed the acceptance by the new State of the internationally wrongful acts committed by the predecessor State.[184] The Judge thus stated that 'in the present case the new State chose to accept liability, subject to its right to repudiate, and is therefore liable'.[185] He further maintained that 'I know of no principle whereby international law can step in and undo such an acceptance by a State'.[186] The Judge therefore decided that the Minister of Defence of Namibia was substituted as the defendant in the present case to the Minister of Defence of the Republic of South Africa. The Supreme Court later confirmed the decision (and made a number of controversial statements regarding the question of succession to responsibility[187]). This case will be further examined below when dealing with newly independent States.[188]

---

179 *Mwandinghi v. Minister of Defence, Namibia*, 14 December 1990, in: 1991 (1) *SA* 851 (Nm); 91 ILR 343.
180 *Minister of Defence, Namibia v. Mwandinghi*, 25 October 1991, in: 1992 (2) *SA* 355 (NmS); 91 ILR 358.
181 *Mwandinghi v. Minister of Defence, Namibia*, High Court, at 346.
182 Ibid., at 353.
183 Ibid.
184 Ibid., at 354: 'The question whether in international law delicts committed by a predecessor State become the delicts of a successor Sate or not is no longer relevant. By its acceptance of such debts, in this case in terms of the Constitution, the debt became that of the new State in terms of the municipal law of the State and is according to municipal law principles justiciable in the courts of the land.
185 Ibid., at 355.
186 Ibid., at 354–355.
187 See analysis in: Dumberry, *State Succession to International Responsibility*, 198; Crawford, *State Responsibility: The General Part*, 453–454.
188 See section examining Article 16, below.

130.   In his First Report, the ILC Special Rapporteur provides a number of other examples of unilateral declarations by the successor States in the context of the dissolution of Czechoslovakia.[189]

2.2   THE EFFECT OF ANY SUCH ACCEPTANCE BY THE SUCCESSOR STATE

131.   Article 6(3) explains the legal effect of a unilateral declaration made by the successor State accepting to take over the obligations arising from an internationally wrongful act committed by the predecessor State against another State (or another subject of international law). The important feature of this provision is that, as pointed out in the Final Report, the declaration 'does not automatically produce the effect desired by the successor State'.[190] A unilateral act is thus not sufficient by itself for the successor State to automatically take over such obligations towards the injured State.[191] The provision is based on Article 9(1) of the 1978 Vienna Convention.[192] Scholars have long recognised that in the context of succession to treaties, a unilateral statement made by a new State cannot by itself create rights and obligations for other States.[193]

132.   The position of the injured State (or subject of international law) on the matter is fundamental.[194] The injured party must be given the possibility to accept or reject the solution unilaterally adopted by the successor State regarding the devolution of obligations. The goal is to protect the right of the injured State (or subject) to receive proper reparation for the damage suffered. As indicated in the Final Report, 'any unilateral act of the predecessor or successor State cannot by itself relieve the State author of the internationally wrongful act of its obligation to repair.'[195] Thus, 'the acceptance of this undertaking by the other party to the responsibility relationship – the injured State or another victim subject – is required'.[196]

---

189   ILC Special Rapporteur, First Report, 2017, paras. 118–120.
190   Final Report, para. 68, in: (2015) 76 *Annuaire de l'Institut de Droit international*, 538.
191   Ibid.: 'a unilateral undertaking by the successor State to the effect that it will succeed to the obligations stemming from a tort committed before the date of the succession will not be enough for succession to apply with respect to that tort'.
192   *Vienna Convention on Succession of States in Respect of Treaties*, Art. 9(1): 'Obligations or rights under treaties in force in respect of a territory at the date of a succession of States do not become the obligations or rights of the successor State or of other States parties to those treaties by reason only of the fact that the successor State has made a unilateral declaration providing for the continuance in force of the treaties in respect of its territory.' On this provision, see: A. Kolliopoulos, 'Article 9', in: G. Distefano, G. Gaggioli & A. Hêche (eds.), *La Convention de Vienne de 1978 sur la succession d'États en matière de traités: Commentaire article par article et études thématiques* (Brussels: Bruylant, 2015), 295ff.
193   Tams, 'State Succession to Investment Treaties', 332–333; Zimmermann and Devaney, 'Succession to Treaties and the Inherent Limits of International Law', 536; Kolliopoulos, 'Article 9', 329.
194   The expression 'injured subject' refers to situations where the victim of a wrongful act is a non-State actor which is a subject of international law. See the analysis above in the section dealing with Article 2(1).
195   Final Report, para. 26, in: (2015) 76 *Annuaire de l'Institut de Droit international*, 524.
196   Ibid., para. 68, at 538.

133.   The question of the injured State's consent is important whenever the predecessor State continues to exist after the date of succession. In this context, the solution adopted under Article 6(3) is essentially the same as regarding devolution agreements examined above. The situation is not different in the context of dissolution. Thus, the decision to take over the consequences of responsibility cannot be unilateral either. The injured State (or subject) must have its say about which of the successor States should fulfil the obligation to repair.

134.   The ILC Special Rapporteur has taken a different position.[197] Draft Article 4(2) proposed in his First Report is identical to Article 6(3) of the IDI Resolution, with the following addition at the end of the provision: 'unless its unilateral declaration is stated in clear and specific terms'.[198] The language is borrowed from Principle 7 of the 'Guiding Principles applicable to unilateral declarations of States capable of creating legal obligations'.[199] Generic unilateral declarations of succession would therefore not be considered as clear enough to have any legal effect. Only a specific unilateral declaration made by the successor State of its engagement to comply with the obligation stemming from an internationally wrongful act committed by the predecessor State would produce such legal effect.

135.   In fact, the addition of these words at ILC Draft Article 4(2) has the effect of diluting the goal of this provision. As a result of the wording used under this provision, the question of whether or not a unilateral declaration has a binding effect solely depends on the degree of specificity and clarity of the declaration.

136.   It should be recalled here that the aim of Article 6(3) of the Resolution is to protect the interests of the injured State or subject. As a result of the wording used under ILC Draft Article 4(2), the injured party would not have the possibility of accepting or rejecting the solution unilaterally adopted by the successor State whenever such declaration is considered to be clear and specific enough. The goal of Article 6(3) is to give the injured State such a possibility to take position regarding unilateral declarations made by a successor State, no matter whether these acts are general, vague or unclear or, on the contrary, specific and clear.

137.   Just like Article 6(2) mentioned above, Article 6(3) only deals with the situation where the successor State has unilaterally accepted the *obligations* arising from an internationally wrongful act committed by the predecessor State before the date of succession. The provision does *not* cover the different situation of the unilateral acceptation of *rights* arising from such an act. As mentioned above, this is because the goal of this provision is to protect the interests of the injured State or subject. As explained above, the interests of the

---

197 ILC Special Rapporteur, First Report, 2017, para. 113.
198 Ibid., para. 132.
199 Ibid., para. 130, referring to the 'Guiding Principles applicable to unilateral declarations of States capable of creating legal obligations', GA Resolution 61/34 of 4 December 2006, (2006) II(2) *Yearbook ILC*, paras. 176–177. It should be added that the ILC Special Rapporteur Draft Article 4(3) further adds: 'Any unilateral declarations by a successor State and their effects are governed by rules of international law applicable to unilateral acts of States'.

injured State or subject are in fact only relevant in the context of the transfer of *obligations* to the successor State, not when the third State (or subject) is the wrongdoer.

138.   Draft Article 4(1) proposed by the ILC Special Rapporteur follows a different pattern and includes a reference to unilateral declarations of the successor State claiming to be the holder of the *right* to reparation for an internationally wrongful act committed against the predecessor State. Draft Article 4(1) reads as follows:

> The rights of a predecessor State arising from an internationally wrongful act committed against it by another State or another subject of international law before the date of succession of States do not become the rights of the successor State by reason only of the fact that the successor State has made a unilateral declaration providing for its assumption of all rights and obligations of the predecessor State.[200]

139.   The explanation given by the ILC Special Rapporteur for the adoption of this provision is the following: 'the rights arising from State responsibility cannot be assumed by the successor State only by way of its unilateral declaration (as it implies obligations of other States)'.[201] In other words, when the successor State unilaterally takes over the right to reparation this results in the creation of obligations for 'other States'. The above-mentioned quote suggests that the purpose of this clause would be the protection of the interests of these 'other States'. But, it should be recalled that in the context of an internationally wrongful act committed by a State against the predecessor State, the only 'obligation' at stake is that of the wrongdoer to repair the damages suffered by the injured State. The provision therefore seems to suggest that the perpetrator of the internationally wrongful act should be given the opportunity to accept (or not) the successor State's unilateral acceptance of rights arising from such act.

140.   Finally, Article 6(4) of the Resolution sets out what happens when the injured State or subject does not accept the solution adopted by the successor State under Article 6(3). As mentioned above regarding devolution agreements, in such a case 'good faith negotiations must be pursued' by the States or subjects 'concerned'. Article 8 explains that negotiations should be undertaken between, on the one hand, the successor State having made the declaration and, on the other hand, the injured State (or other injured subject of international law) concerned. As mentioned before regarding devolution agreements, if the predecessor State continues to exist and the injured State (or subject) insists on the performance of the obligation to repair by the predecessor State, the participation of that State in these negotiations will be required. In the event that 'these negotiations do not succeed within a reasonable period of time, the solution envisaged by the relevant Article of Chapter III of the present Resolution is applicable'. Again, this reflects the subsidiary character of the guiding principles set out under Chapter III, which only apply in the absence of any other solution adopted by the parties concerned (Article 3).

---

200   ILC Special Rapporteur, First Report, 2017, para. 132.
201   Ibid., para. 131.

ARTICLE 7:

Plurality of successor States

1.   In case of succession in which it is not possible to determine a single successor State, all the successor States will enjoy the rights or assume the obligations arising from the commission of an internationally wrongful act in an equitable manner, unless otherwise agreed by the States or subjects of international law concerned.

2.   In order to determine an equitable apportionment of the rights or obligations of the successor States, criteria that may be taken into consideration include the existence of any special connections with the act giving rise to international responsibility, the size of the territory and of the population, the respective contributions to the gross domestic product of the States concerned at the date of succession, the need to avoid unjust enrichment and any other circumstance relevant to the case.

3.   Negotiations in good faith must be pursued by the successor States, with the goal of reaching a solution within a reasonable time.

Commentary

141.   Article 7 concerns situations where there is a plurality of successor States. It applies when the application of the provisions of the Resolution with regard to particular cases does not result in identifying specifically the State that should be the holder of the rights or obligations arising from an internationally wrongful act which occurred before the date of succession.

142.   The typical situation where Article 7 may find application is that of a dissolution of a State when the predecessor State ceases to exist and several new successor States emerge. Cases of dissolution of States are specifically examined at Article 15. Another situation of a plurality of successor States may exist in cases of separation of parts of a State, examined at Article 12. This would be the case when more than one new State separates from the predecessor State which continues to exist. The purpose of Article 7 is to fill any potential gap resulting from the application of Articles 10(3) (applicable in the context of diplomatic protection), 12 and 15 as to the identification of which successor States should inherit the rights or obligations arising from the responsibility relationship.

143.   The solution proposed at Article 7 is of a subsidiary nature. Whenever it is not possible to identify a single successor, all successor States will enjoy the rights or assume the obligations emerging from the responsibility relationship, in an equitable manner. Importantly, this solution only applies if 'the States or subjects of international law concerned' have not themselves agreed to a different outcome. The provision is another illustration of the subsidiary character of the guiding principles of the Resolution, as set out, more generally, at Article 3.

144.   The expression 'equitable manner' is used at Article 7(1) and the term 'equitable apportionment' at Articles 7(2) and 12(5). Equity has been described as 'the key ... to the entire problem of State succession'.[202] According to the 1983 *Vienna Convention on Succession of States in Respect of State Properties, Archives and Debts*, in cases of dissolution of a State, separation, cession and transfer of territory, the debts of the predecessor State 'pass to the successor State[s] in an equitable proportion, taking into account, in particular, the property, rights and interests which pass to the successor State[s] in relation to that State debt'.[203] The Institute's Resolution on 'State Succession in Matters of Property and Debts' adopted in 2001 also indicates at its Article 8 that 'the result of the apportionment of property and debts must be equitable'.[204] Stern even speaks of a 'customary international rule requiring the equitable distribution of the national debts' of the predecessor State.[205] The notion of equity is thus generally used for the establishment of 'equitable criteria of repartition' of rights and obligations between the different States involved.[206] The Badinter Arbitration Commission in its *Opinion no. 1* also stated that 'the outcome of succession should be equitable, the States concerned being free to settle terms and conditions by agreement.'[207]

145.   Scholars have recognised that the concepts of equity and fairness should also be used for the allocation of rights and obligations arising from the consequences of the commission of wrongful acts.[208] The equitable allocation of rights and obligations was indeed central to the 2001 *Agreement on Succession Issues* which was entered into by the successor States in the context of the dissolution of the SFRY. The preamble indicates that the Agreement was reached after discussions and negotiations 'with a view to identifying and determining the equitable distribution among themselves of rights, obligations, assets and liabilities of the former Socialist Federal Republic of Yugoslavia'.[209]

146.   Paragraph 2 of Article 7 establishes what criteria must be taken into consideration in order to determine an equitable apportionment of rights and obligations among the successor States. The non-exhaustive list of criteria includes the following:

-       Whether there exists 'any special connections' between one or more successor States 'with the act giving rise to international responsibility';

-       'The size of the territory and of the population';

202   D.P. O'Connell, *The Law of State Succession* (Cambridge: CUP, 1956), 268.
203   See Articles 37, 40 and 41, *Vienna Convention on Succession of States in respect of State Property, Archives and Debts*.
204   Institut de Droit international, 'State Succession in Matters of Property and Debts'.
205   B. Stern, 'General Concluding Remarks', in: Brigitte Stern (ed.), *Dissolution, Continuation and Succession in Eastern Europe* (The Hague: Martinus Nijhoff Publ., 1998), 204. See also B. Stern, 'La succession d'Etats' (1996) 262 *Rec. des cours*, 171.
206   V.D. Degan, 'Equity in Matters of State Succession', in: R.S.J. Macdonald (ed.), *Essays in Honour of Wang Tieya* (Dordrecht: Martinus Nijhoff, 1993), 207.
207   International Conference on the Former Yugoslavia, Arbitration Commission, Opinion No 1, 29 November 1991, in: (1993) 92 ILR (under letter 1(e)).
208   W. Czaplinski, 'Equity and Equitable Principles in the Law of State Succession', in: M. Mrak (ed.), *Succession of States* (The Hague: Martinus Nijhoff Publ., 1999), at 72; Dumberry, *State Succession to International Responsibility*, 279ff; Degan, 'Equity in Matters of State Succession', 207.
209   *Agreement on Succession Issues*, 29 June 2001.

- 'The respective contributions to the gross domestic product of the States concerned at the date of succession';

- The 'need to avoid unjust enrichment'.

147. The basic logic behind Article 7(2) is the simple fact that (apart from the existence of any 'special connection' between one successor State and the wrongful act), the allocation of rights and obligations between the different successor States should be proportionate to their overall weight and the relative importance just before the date of succession when they were still part of the predecessor State. The relevant elements mentioned under Article 7(2) for such a determination are the size of the territory and the population and the respective contributions to the gross domestic product of the States concerned at the date of the succession. In his commentary to a similar formula employed in Article 11 of the 2001 IDI Resolution on State succession in matters of property and debts, Rapporteur Georg Ress gave the following explanation:

> Les critères en usage au 19ème siècle, la redistribution des dettes *per capita* (en proportion de la population) ou en proportion de l'extension du territoire de l'État successeur, ne reflètent pas les conditions d'équité à la fin du 20ème siècle. L'étendue du territoire fut peut-être importante dans la société encore agraire du 19ème siècle. Aujourd'hui, c'est plutôt le développement du capital humain et le niveau technologique qui sont décisifs.[210]

148. Another criterion which may be taken into account to determine an 'equitable apportionment of the rights or obligations' among the successor States is the 'need to avoid unjust enrichment'.[211] Under Article 7(2), the relevant question to be asked is which of the successor States has enriched itself as a result of an act committed before the date of succession.[212] The provision follows the solution adopted at Article 8 of the Institute's Resolution on the question of 'State Succession in Matters of Property and Debts' indicating that the result of the apportionment of property and debts should be equitable and that 'unjust enrichment shall be avoided'.[213]

149. The concept of unjust enrichment is intrinsically abstract. This, however, is, no reason, in itself, to refrain from making use of it. Thus, as explained by O'Connell, 'the concept of unjust enrichment may not be notably articulate in practice, but once one perceives that practice corresponds roughly to its fundamental requirements, that, with

210 Institut de Droit international, 'State Succession in Matters of Property and Debts', 163.
211 The same position is followed by ILC Special Rapporteur, Second Report, 2018, para. 106 ('it is advisable to follow the Institute of International Law resolution, which does not treat unjust enrichment as an independent basis for succession to responsibility. The need to avoid unjust enrichment should be taken into consideration as one of criteria and circumstances relevant to the case'.
212 It should be noted that Article 16 concerning newly independent States does *not* contain a similar provision whereby the unjust enrichment is one of the criteria to determine the appointment of rights and obligations between the predecessor State and the new State. The same is true regarding Article 15(2) on dissolution.
213 Institut de Droit international, 'State Succession in Matters of Property and Debts'. See also Articles 11 and 13.

a consideration of the relevant social and ethical factors, suffices'.[214] Because of its very abstract nature, one needs to 'take into account all the circumstances of each specific situation' to determine whether any unjust enrichment has occurred.[215] The obligation for reparation based on unjust enrichment does not arise directly from the commission of an act but derives from a state of fact, which may be caused by a legal or an illegal act. In the context under scrutiny, the concept is linked to the outcome of an equitable share of the consequences arising from an internationally wrongful act among the successor States. In order for a situation to qualify as an unjust enrichment, not only does the consequence of such situation needs to (i) result in a given State's enrichment, but also such enrichment needs to (ii) be 'unjust' and, finally, (iii) be detrimental to another State.[216] These different requirements were expressed as follows by the Iran–U.S. Claims Tribunal in the case of *Sea-Land Service, Inc. v. The Islamic Republic of Iran, et al.*:

> There are several instances of recourse to the principle of unjust enrichment before international tribunals. There must have been an enrichment of one party to the detriment of the other, and both must arise as a consequence of the same act or event. There must be no justification for the enrichment, and no contractual or other remedy available to the injured party whereby he might seek compensation from the party enriched.[217]

150. The use of the concept of unjust enrichment in the specific context of State succession to responsibility was analysed by one of the authors of this Commentary,[218] indicating that reference has been made to the concept by some international tribunals and municipal courts.[219] One of the most vocal advocates of the use of the principle of unjust enrichment to deal with questions of State succession is O'Connell.[220] As noted above, for him, the principle is in fact central to the whole question of succession, noting that it has a

214 O'Connell, *The Law of State Succession*, 274.
215 *Sea-Land Service, Inc. v. The Islamic Republic of Iran, et al.*, Award No. 115–33–1, 22 June 1984, in: 6 *Iran-U.S. C.T.R.*, 149, at 168–169.
216 These criteria are examined in: Dumberry, *State Succession to International Responsibility*, 264ff. For the application of the concept of unjust enrichment to the question of succession to State contracts, see: P. Dumberry, *A Guide to State Succession in International Investment Law* (London: Elgar Publ., 2018, 382ff); P. Dumberry, 'State Succession to State Contracts: A New Framework of Analysis for an Unexplored Question' (2018) 19 *J. World Invest. & Trade* 595–627.
217 *Sea-Land Service,* at 168–169.
218 Dumberry, *State Succession to International Responsibility*, 263–279; P. Dumberry, 'The Use of the Concept of Unjust Enrichment', 506–528.
219 See Dumberry, *State Succession to International Responsibility*, 269ff, examining the following cases: *Emeric Koranyi & Mme. Ernest Dengcjel (née Koranyi) v. Romanian State* case, Hungary-Romania Mixed Arbitral Tribunal, Award of 27 February 1929, in: 8 *Recueil des decisions des tribunaux arbitraux mixtes*, 980; in: (1929–1930) *Annual Digest* 64; *Lighthouse Arbitration* case, at 81; *Zilberszpic v. (Polish) Treasury*, Supreme Court of Poland, First Division, 14 December 1928, in: (1928) *Zb. O.S.N.*, no. 190, reported in: 4 (1927–1928) *Annual Digest* 82; *Niedzielskie v. (Polish) Treasury*, Supreme Court of Poland, 13 October 1926, in: *Rw.* III, 1485/26/I; 3 (1925–1926) *Annual Digest* 74, and 4 (1927–1928) *Annual Digest* 83.
220 O'Connell, *State Succession in Municipal Law*, 266–267, 348–349, 352; O'Connell, 'Recent Problems of State Succession', 140.

'special significance in the solution of problems of State succession when one of the parties to a legal relationship has disappeared'.[221] In his view, 'the juridical justification for the obligation to pay compensation is to be found in the concept of unjustified enrichment.'[222] Writers are generally favourable to the use of the principle of unjust enrichment to solve problems of State succession,[223] including regarding the question of State succession to the consequences of responsibility.[224]

151. Finally, paragraph 3 of Article 7 was included at the request of some members of the Institute to stress the need that negotiations between successor States in order to determine the equitable apportionment of rights and obligations must be conducted in good faith, with the goal of reaching a solution within a reasonable time. The aim of this provision is to discourage conduct which could lead to endless negotiations and prevent any final outcome.

ARTICLE 8:

States or subjects of international law concerned

For the purposes of Articles 6 and 7, "States or subjects of international law concerned" are:

a)   in the case of an internationally wrongful act committed by the predecessor State, the injured State or subject of international law and all the successor States;

b)   in the case of an internationally wrongful act committed against the predecessor State, all the successor States.

Commentary

152. This provision explains the meaning of the expression 'States or subjects of international law concerned' used at Articles 6 and 7. The provision has been examined above in the context of these two provisions. It should be recalled that for the purposes of Article 6, only Article 8a) is applicable and that the notion of 'States concerned' may also include the predecessor State if it continues to exist after the date of succession and in the event that the injured State or subject wishes that this State – and not the successor State – provide proper reparation for the consequences of the internationally wrongful act. For the purposes of Article 7, both a) and b) of Article 8 are applicable.

---

221   O'Connell, *State Succession in Municipal Law*, 34; see also: 266–267, 348–349, 352; O'Connell, 'Recent Problems of State Succession', 140.
222   O'Connell, *The Law of State Succession*, 273. He also mentions that this principle 'is the norm behind the doctrine of respect for acquired rights in the law of State succession'.
223   See the list of writers mentioned in: Dumberry, *State Succession to International Responsibility*, 263.
224   For instance: Volkovitsch, 'Righting Wrongs: Toward a New Theory of State Succession to Responsibility of International Delicts', 2210–2211; P.M. Eisemann, 'Emprunts russes et problèmes de succession d'États', in: P. Juillard & B. Stern (eds.), *Les emprunts russes et le règlement du contentieux financier franco-russe* (Paris: Cedin Cahiers internationaux, 2002), 62.

*Internationally wrongful acts having a continuing or
composite character performed or completed after the
date of succession of States*

1.   When a successor State continues the breach of an international
obligation constituted by an act of the predecessor State having a continuing character, the international responsibility of the successor
State for the breach extends over the entire period during which the
act continues and remains not in conformity with the international
obligation.

2.   When a successor State completes a series of actions or
omissions initiated by the predecessor State defined in the aggregate as
a breach of an international obligation, the international responsibility
of the successor State for the breach extends over the entire period
starting with the first of the actions or omissions of the series and lasts
for as long as these actions or omissions are repeated and remain not in
conformity with the international obligation.

3.   The provisions of the present Article are without prejudice to
any responsibility incurred by the predecessor State if it continues to
exist.

Commentary

153.   Article 9 deals with one particular set of circumstances which must be examined
generally under Chapter II of the Resolution because the very nature of the internationally wrongful act at stake can be present irrespective of the category of State succession
concerned. This is the situation where an act has a continuing or a composite character
and is completed *after* the date of succession. It is worth stressing at the outset that Article
9 refers to the *responsibility* of the successor State that has continued or completed these
acts. The distinction is important. Thus, in other cases where the internationally wrong-
fully act entirely occurred and was completed *before* the date of succession, the question
at issue is *not* that of the 'responsibility' of the successor State. In such cases, relevant
for the analysis of other provisions of the Resolution, the question is whether there is
any succession by the successor State to the *obligations* arising from the commission
of an internationally wrongful act by the predecessor State. As further discussed below,
Article 9 deals with the different question of the successor State's *responsibility* for
wrongful acts.

154.   The following sections will first distinguish between internationally wrongful acts
which have a continuing character from those that have a composite character (Section
1). The next section will examine the question of which State(s) should be responsible for
which portion of the wrongful act (Section 2).

1   Distinction between Continuing and Composite Wrongful Acts

155.   The ILC Articles on State Responsibility distinguish between different types of acts from a temporal perspective.[225]

156.   An instantaneous act takes place at the moment when it occurs. Other acts will lapse during a certain period of time and terminate at some later point. In both situations, the act will be completed at some point in time. The moment when the act is considered to be completed can take place either before or after the date of succession. This temporal element is fundamental for the scope of application of the Resolution. The Resolution only takes into consideration internationally wrongful acts occurring *before* the date of State succession.[226] Once succession has occurred, the question becomes which State should be accountable for the rights and obligations arising from such an act. The Resolution is only concerned with situations where the consequence of a wrongful act remains pending and unsettled after the date of succession. It does *not* address the different situation where appropriate reparation has already been provided by one State to another at the date of succession.

157.   Another important distinction is between acts which may have a *continuing* or a *composite* character. These acts occur over a given period of time and constitute a wrongful act during that period. Acts having a continuing or a composite character are relevant for the purpose of the Resolution when they occur in a process taking place both *before* and *after* the date of succession.[227]

158.   Article 9 distinguishes between acts having a *continuing* and a *composite* character. The first paragraph refers to the situation where a successor State 'continues the breach of an international obligation constituted by an act of the predecessor State having a continuing character'. The second paragraph of Article 9 concerns the different situation when a successor State 'completes a series of actions or omissions' after the date of succession which were 'initiated by the predecessor State' before that date. The provision specifies that these actions or omissions must be 'defined in the aggregate as a breach of an international obligation'. One example of an act having a continuous character is the taking of hostages starting from the capture until the moment the individual is finally released.[228]

---

225 See Articles 14 and 15 of the ILC Articles on Responsibility of States for Internationally Wrongful Acts.

226 The question of what happens to acts committed *after* the date of succession is not addressed by the Resolution. This is because the successor State should logically be held responsible for its *own* acts which were committed after that date.

227 Continuing and composite acts which take place either fully *before* or *after* the date of succession are not relevant for Article 9.

228 ILC Special Rapporteur, Second Report, 2018, para. 56, refers to other examples: 'unlawful detention of a foreign official or unlawful occupation of embassy premises of another State, maintenance by force of colonial domination or unlawful occupation of part of the territory of another State'. He also refers to forced disappearance and expropriation as examples of other types of violations which 'can also be qualified as continuing wrongful acts, depending on the circumstances of the given case' (at para. 57).

One example of a wrongful act having a composite character is the crime of genocide. Such a crime is not committed until the series of acts defined in the aggregate as wrongful are completed or have reached the threshold or the conditions imposed by law to constitute the wrongful act.

2   Allocation of Responsibilities for Different Portions of the Wrongful Act

159.   Acts having a continuing or a composite character require the determination of which State(s) should be responsible for the obligations arising from such acts.

160.   In its commentary to Article 11 of the Articles on State responsibility, the ILC envisages situations where a successor State acknowledges and adopts the conduct in question as its own: '[I]f the successor State, faced with a continuing wrongful act on its territory, endorses and continues that situation, the inference may readily be drawn that it has assumed responsibility for it.'[229] Article 9 of the Resolution follows and further elaborates the general solution adopted by the ILC.

161.   One fundamental question is to determine which State (the predecessor or the successor) should be responsible for which part of the act having a continuing or a composite character. As explained by the Final Report, there are three possibilities:

-        A joint responsibility shared by both the predecessor State (if it continues to exist) and the successor State for the consequences arising from the act;

-        Each State is only responsible for the relevant period of time in which it actually committed the wrongful act (i.e. the predecessor State is responsible for the portion of the act taking place before the date of succession and the successor State for the part occurring after that date); or

-        The successor State continuing or completing an act is responsible for the consequence of the *entire* act (i.e. both before and after the date of succession).[230]

162.   In the following sections, the question of the allocation of responsibility will be examined by first looking at wrongful acts having a *continuing* character (Section 2.1), which will then be followed by an analysis of those acts having a *composite* character (Section 2.2). It should be added that although the ILC Special Rapporteur distinguishes the two concepts in his Second Report, he nevertheless proposed one provision using the umbrella term 'continuing' acts which is meant to also cover composite acts.[231]

---

229   ILC, 'Commentaries to the Draft Articles on Responsibility of States for Internationally Wrongful Acts', analysing Article 11, at 119, para. 3.

230   Final Report, para. 112, in: (2015) 76 *Annuaire de l'Institut de Droit international*, 551.

231   ILC Special Rapporteur, Second Report, 2018, paras. 63ff, 72 ('the reference to the continuing breach also includes the case of a breach consisting of a composite act'), 74. See Draft Article 6(3).

2.1 WRONGFUL ACTS HAVING A CONTINUING CHARACTER

163. With respect to acts having a continuing character, Article 9(1) provides that the successor State is responsible for its own conduct since the date of succession and for the whole period during which the act continues and remains not in conformity with the international obligation concerned. The same solution has been adopted by the ILC Special Rapporteur.[232]

164. In fact, this is a situation not involving any problem related to State succession. Thus, it only deals with conduct taking place *after* the date of succession.[233] The provision is concerned with the simple question of the attribution of an internationally wrongful act to its author and its responsibility arising from such conduct.

165. Article 9(1) does not provide for any general solution with respect to the question of succession to obligations for the portion of the continuing act which took place *before* the date of succession. The Final Report explains that 'the specific rules for each category' of Part III of the Resolution should apply.[234] The same approach was also adopted by the ILC Special Rapporteur in his Second Report.[235] The next paragraphs will briefly expose the practical outcome for acts having a continuing character in the context of different types of succession of States.

166. As mentioned above, under Article 4(2), when the predecessor State continues to exist after the changes affecting its former territory have occurred, that State should remain *responsible* for *its own* internationally wrongful act committed *before* the date of succession. This basic rule is applied in Chapter III for situations of transfer of territory (Article 11(1)), separation (Article 12(1)) and newly independent States (Article 16(1)). In such a case, the predecessor State should remain responsible for the portion of the continuing wrongful act which took place *before* the date of succession. As a matter of principle, that solution should prevail *even if* the act is subsequently continued by the successor State after the date of succession.[236]

167. It should be added, however, that in the context of the transfer of territory from one State to another and that of separation of States, Articles 11(3) and 12(3) provide for an exception to this general rule of non-succession when the author of the wrongful act was an organ of a territorial unit of the predecessor State that has later become an organ of the

---

232 ILC Special Rapporteur, Second Report, 2018, para. 59. See Draft Article 6(3).
233 Final Report, paras. 113–114, in: (2015) 76 *Annuaire de l'Institut de Droit international*, 551.
234 Ibid., para. 112, at 551.
235 ILC Special Rapporteur, Second Report, 2018, para. 59, explaining that 'The breach of an international obligation having a continuing character entails the responsibility of a successor State, if such State continues in the act commenced before the date of succession', adding that 'Yet the question remains whether it is the sole responsibility of the successor State or a shared responsibility with the predecessor State'. According to him, the answer to that question 'is contingent on several factors to be addressed in special draft articles' (para. 73). In other words, also following the stance of the IDI Resolution, the answer is to be found in specific provisions dealing with each different type of succession. See Draft Article 6(4).
236 See analysis of Dumberry, *State Succession to International Responsibility*, 222.

successor State.[237] Under these provisions, the obligations arising from the commission of the internationally wrongful act can pass to the successor State. Whenever the successor State is continuing such a wrongful act, it should be accountable for the consequences arising from the portion of the act which was initially committed by that organ *before* the date of succession. One important point to mention in this specific context is the fact that the successor State would be accountable for the *consequences* arising from the commission of the pre-succession portion of the act. In contrast, the successor State would be *responsible* for the continuation of the illegal act occurring *after* the date of succession. This is an illustration of the distinction between, on the one hand, 'responsibility' for wrongful acts and, on the other hand, rights and obligations arising from the commission of such an act. As explained above,[238] this fundamental distinction is at the core of the Resolution. In his Second Report, the ILC Special Rapporteur also adopts the same distinction when examining acts having a continuing character.[239]

168.   Another related point is the fact that Paragraph 3 of Article 9 indicates that this solution is 'without prejudice to any *responsibility* incurred by the predecessor State if it continues to exist'. In other words, the fact that the successor State may be accountable for the *consequences* arising from the commission of the *pre*-succession portion of a wrongful act committed by an organ does not prevent the predecessor State from being *responsible* for the same portion of the act.

169.   In the context of dissolution, the general rule is that obligations arising from the commission of an internationally wrongful act by the predecessor State pass to the successor States (Article 15(1)). Under Article 15(2) and (3), one of the factors which will be relevant to determine which of the successor States should become the bearer of the obligation to repair is the 'existence of a direct link between the consequences of the internationally wrongful act committed against the predecessor State and the territory or the population' of one of the successor States. In the event that one of the successor States continues the breach of an international obligation initially committed by the predecessor State, it could indeed be argued that there exists such a 'direct link' between that new State and the wrongful act. This would be the case, for instance, in the event of the continuation by the new State of an act of expropriation initially committed by the predecessor State. Thus, after the date of succession, the new State would clearly benefit from having on its territory some property for which no compensation was paid. This is a situation where the consequences of a wrongful act committed *by* the predecessor State is clearly linked to the territory of the new State.[240] For that reason, that State should bear the obligation to repair arising from the commission of the portion of the continuing act which took place *before* the date of succession. In accordance with Article 9(1), the successor State is *responsible* for the portion of the wrongful act it continues after that date. Another clear

---

237   Article 16(3) provides for a similar solution of succession for newly independent States for conduct of national liberation movements before the date of succession.
238   See comments in the context of the analysis of Article 2(1).
239   ILC Special Rapporteur, Second Report, 2018, paras. 51, 59 and 74. See Draft Article 6(3) referring to the 'attribution' of the wrongful act to the successor State.
240   The question is examined in the context of international investment law in: Dumberry, *A Guide to State Succession in International Investment Law*, 374, 393ff.

situation in the context of dissolution where the successor State continuing a wrongful act should be responsible for the consequences arising from the portion of the act which took place *before* the date of succession is when the author of the act was an organ of the predecessor State that later became an organ of the new State. This solution is akin to that provided for at Article 15(3), describing it as 'a relevant factor' to determine 'which of the successor States becomes bearer of the obligations' to repair. The solution of succession should a fortiori find application in the context of the continuation of a wrongful act by the new State.

170. Interestingly, the solution of continuation of responsibility in the context of dissolution was adopted by Hungary in its pleadings in the *Gabčíkovo-Nagymaros Project* case.[241] Thus, to the 'well-established principle that there is in general no succession to international responsibility',[242] Hungary maintained that there was one 'key exception': when 'a successor State, by its *own* conduct, has acted in such a way as to assume the breaches of the law committed by its predecessor'.[243] The argument developed by Hungary in its Memorial indicates that by endorsing and continuing the internationally wrongful act (i.e. the unilateral derivation of the Variant C project), Slovakia was not only responsible for the damage resulting from its own illicit act committed upon its creation in January 1993, but also for the consequences arising from the act committed by the predecessor State. Thus, Hungary mentioned that Slovakia must 'assume the obligations, as operator of variant C, to repair damage caused by *present and prior breaches of international law*'.[244]

171. Finally, it should be added that Article 7 (regarding 'plurality of successor States') deals with the specific situation where two (or more) successor States in the context of a dissolution are continuing a wrongful act which was initially started by the predecessor State.[245]

2.2 WRONGFUL ACTS HAVING A COMPOSITE CHARACTER

172. Article 9(2) deals with the situation of a breach consisting of *composite* acts, which are a series of actions or omissions defined in the aggregate as wrongful. Examples of such composite acts include the obligations concerning genocide, apartheid or crimes against humanity. In accordance with Article 15 of the ILC Articles on State Responsibility, the breach only occurs when a given act is accomplished and is, taken together with the other acts or omissions, sufficient to constitute the wrongful act. However, the breach extends over the entire period starting with the first acts or omissions of the series, and lasts for as long as they are repeated and remain not in conformity with an international obligation.

---

241 *Case Concerning the Gabčíkovo-Nagymaros Project*, 3. See: *Reply of the Republic of Hungary*, vol. I, 20 June 1995, at para. 3.163; *Memorial of the Republic of Hungary*, vol. I, 2 May 1994, at paras. 8.05, 8.06; Oral Pleadings, 7 March 1997, CR 97/6, 54, paras. 6–7, Dupuy (Hungary).
242 *Reply of the Republic of Hungary*, vol. I, 20 June 1995, at para. 3.163.
243 Ibid. (emphasis in the original text). The argument is also described in: Oral Pleadings, 7 March 1997, CR 97/6, 54, paras. 6–7, Dupuy (Hungary).
244 *Memorial of the Republic of Hungary*, vol. I, 2 May 1994, at para. 8.05 (emphasis added). See also at para. 8.06.
245 The question has already been examined above in the analysis of Article 7.

173.   Article 9(2) provides that when a successor State completes a series of actions or omissions initiated by the predecessor State, in the sense that the composite wrongful act is performed, it bears international responsibility for the *entire* period (including, importantly, for what happened *before* the date of succession).[246]

174.   The solution adopted under Article 9(2) whereby the successor State is responsible for the entire period logically applies to cases where the predecessor State cease to exists (such as dissolution). The same solution also finds application when the predecessor State continues to exist after the date of succession (such as in the context of transfer of territory, separation and newly independent States).

175.   In this context, it is important to recall the third paragraph of Article 9 indicating that the solution just described under Article 9(2) is 'without prejudice to any responsibility incurred by the predecessor State if it continues to exist'. In other words, even if the successor State bears an international responsibility for the *entire* period, there may be circumstances where the predecessor State could *also* be held accountable for its portion of actions/omission which took place *before* the date of succession. Thus, the fact that the composite wrongful act is only perpetrated once the entire series of acts defining it is completed and that the successor is responsible for the composite wrongful act does not in itself deprive the predecessor State of its own responsibility. This would be the case in the event where the individual acts committed by the predecessor State are also illegal (even though they do not constitute the typology of the composite act).[247] One example would be, for instance, in the context of the commission of a crime of genocide, which is the end result of a series of acts, which are individually considered illegal. While the successor State would be responsible for the composite wrongful act of genocide covering the entire period, under Article 9(3) the predecessor State could also be considered responsible for the commission of each individual illegal act.

ARTICLE 10:

Diplomatic protection

1.   A successor State may exercise diplomatic protection in respect of a person or a corporation that is its national at the date of the official presentation of the claim but was not a national at the date of injury, provided that the person or the corporation had the nationality of the predecessor State or lost his or her previous nationality and acquired, for a reason unrelated to the bringing of the claim, the nationality of the successor State in a manner not inconsistent with international law.

2.   A claim in exercise of diplomatic protection initiated by the predecessor State may be continued after the date of succession of States

---

246   Final Report, para. 114, in: (2015) 76 *Annuaire de l'Institut de Droit international*, 551.

247   The same position has been adopted by the ILC Special Rapporteur: 'Let us suppose a typical situation where a series of actions or omissions commenced before the date of succession and was accomplished after that date. Provided that the obligation in question was binding on both States at the time when the act occurred, both the predecessor and the successor State would incur international responsibility for the breach consisting of a composite act' (Second Report, 2018, para. 71).

by the successor State under the same conditions set out in paragraph 1 of this Article.

3.   A claim in exercise of diplomatic protection initiated by a State against the predecessor State may be continued against the successor State if the predecessor State has ceased to exist. In the case of a plurality of successor States, the claim shall be addressed to the successor State having the most direct connection with the act giving rise to the exercise of diplomatic protection. When it is not possible to determine a single successor State having such a direct connection, the claim may be continued against all the successor States. The provisions of Article 7 apply *mutatis mutandis*.

4.   Where the predecessor State continues to exist and the individual or corporation possesses the nationality of both the predecessor and the successor States, or the nationality of a third State, the question is governed by the rules of diplomatic protection concerning dual or multiple nationality.

Commentary

176.   This provision deals with the interaction between the question of succession to the rights and obligations arising from the commission of an internationally wrongful act and the international law rules relating to diplomatic protection.

177.   The provision deals with three distinct situations:

-      Whether or not a successor State can exercise diplomatic protection in respect of one of its nationals in the event that this person (or a corporation) did *not* have its nationality at the date of injury, which occurred before the date of succession (Article 10(1));

-      Whether or not the successor State can continue a claim in exercise of diplomatic protection which was first initiated *by* the predecessor State (Article 10(2));

-      Whether or not a State can continue against the successor State(s) a claim in exercise of diplomatic protection which was first initiated *against* the predecessor State (Articles 10(3)).

178.   Article 10(1) focuses on the situation where the successor State initiates *for the first time* (after the date of succession) a claim of diplomatic protection on behalf of one of its 'new' nationals. This question is examined at Section 2. The other paragraphs of the provision set out what happens to claims of diplomatic protection which had already *been* initiated by the predecessor State (Article 10(2)), or against that State (Article 10(3)), before the date of succession. These two questions will be examined at Section 3. Before examining in detail these three distinct questions, we will first analyse the diplomatic protection rule of 'continuous nationality' and its problematic application in the context of State succession (Section 1).

1   The Problematic Application of the Continuous Nationality Rule in the Context of State Succession

179. One controversial question addressed by the ILC in its Articles on Diplomatic Protection concerned the application of the continuous nationality rule. According to that rule, a State is only entitled to exercise diplomatic protection in respect of persons who have their nationality continuously from the date of the injury until the date of the presentation of the claim by the State. The ILC has considered this to be a general rule, but has also rightly included some important exceptions that are examined below. This had also been the attitude adopted by the Institute of International Law in its 1965 Warsaw Resolution on 'the national character of an international claim raised by a State by reason of an injury suffered by individuals'.[248]

180. Support for the rule of continuous nationality is, however, far from being unanimous.[249] The application of the rule of continuous nationality is especially problematic in the particular context of State succession. By limiting the possibility for the predecessor State and the successor State to submit claims on behalf of persons injured as a result of internationally wrongful acts committed before the date of succession, it ends up allowing this illegal conduct to remain without consequences. In fact, two situations must be distinguished depending on whether or not the predecessor State ceases to exist after the date of succession.[250]

181. First, in cases where the predecessor State *ceases to exist* (such as incorporation, unification and dissolution), nationals of the predecessor State will become nationals of the successor State(s) at the date of succession. Since at the time of the commission of the internationally wrongful act by the third State the individuals injured possessed the nationality of the predecessor State and not that of the successor State(s), the rule of continuous nationality would prevent the successor State from exercising its diplomatic protection on behalf of its 'new' nationals.

182. Second, in the other situation where the predecessor State *does not cease to exist* (such as in cases of separation, newly independent States and transfer of territory), the successor State would also not be able to exercise diplomatic protection for its 'new' nationals since, at the time of the commission of the internationally wrongful act by the third State, the individuals injured did not possess its nationality but only the nationality of the predecessor State. This situation is largely acknowledged by scholars.[251]

---

248   Institut de Droit international, 'Le caractère national d'une réclamation internationale présentée par un État en raison d'un dommage subi par un individu', in: (1965) 51-II *Annuaire de l'Institut de Droit international*, 260–261.

249   See on this question: E. Wyler, *La règle dite de la continuité de la nationalité dans le contentieux international* (Paris: PUF, 1990). See also: Dumberry, *State Succession to International Responsibility*, 338ff.

250   See the analysis in: Dumberry, ibid., 340ff; Dumberry, 'Obsolete and Unjust', 153–183.

251   Stern, 'Responsabilité internationale et succession d'États', 354; Dupuy, *Droit international public*, 54; P. Guggenheim, *Traité de Droit international public*, vol. I (Geneva: Librairie de l'Université, 1953) 474; Šturma, 'State Succession in Respect of International Responsibility', 671.

183. The conclusion reached by the Permanent Court of International Justice (PCIJ) in the *Panevezys-Saldutiskis* case supports the application of the rule of continuous nationality.[252] In that case, in 1937 Estonia (a new State since 1918) exercised diplomatic protection on behalf of an Estonian railway company which had been expropriated in 1919 by Lithuania (also a new State since 1918). The problem was that at the time when the act was committed the company was still a Russian company and only became Estonian a few years later. The Court therefore rejected the claim by applying the rule of continuous nationality.

184. It has been suggested by writers that in such cases where the predecessor State continues to exist, it should be the one exercising diplomatic protection.[253] Indeed, this is true when there exists a right of option of nationality, and when the person injured before the date of succession decides to keep the nationality of the predecessor State. In such a case, the continuing State may espouse the claim of such person, as there is no break in the chain of nationality. However, such a right of option is not always available, and even in cases where it does exist, a person may decide not to exercise it (and, in such a case, the rule applicable is that of the acquisition of the new nationality). In this last scenario, the individual injured before the date of succession would become a national of the successor State at the date of succession. The predecessor State could therefore not exercise diplomatic protection for such person for the simple reason that he/she is no longer its national at the time the claim is submitted. Thus, the rule of continuous nationality would prevent the predecessor State from exercising diplomatic protection for individuals who used to be its nationals, but have since the date of succession become nationals of the successor State.

185. A good illustration of the practical implication of the situation just described in the previous paragraph is the *Henriette Levy* case, which was decided by a U.S.-France Commission in 1881.[254] This case dealt with the claim by Mrs. Henriette Levy, the widow of Mr. Jacob Levy, for the seizure by US forces in Louisiana in 1863 of cotton belonging to Mr. Levy and some associates of his firm. Mr. Levy was a French national at the time the damage occurred. He subsequently moved with his family to the city of Strasbourg (France), where he died in 1871. Following the cession of the territories of Alsace-Lorraine by France to Germany, Mrs. Levy did not make use of her right of option to keep her French nationality pursuant to Article II of the *Frankfurt Treaty* and therefore became a German national in 1871. In its 1881 decision, the Commission dismissed the claim based on the ground that it did not have jurisdiction over claims of individuals who were no longer French nationals at the time the proceedings were filed.

186. In sum, the application of the rule of continuous nationality in the context of State succession would result in *neither* the predecessor State nor the successor State being able to exercise diplomatic protection on behalf of an individual injured as a result of an

---

252   *Panevezys-Saldutiskis Railway Case*, 16–17. The case is examined in detail in: Dumberry, *State Succession to International Responsibility*, 390ff.
253   See, for instance, Dumberry, ibid., 356.
254   This case is discussed in: John Bassett Moore, *History and Digest of the International Arbitrations to which the United States has been a Party*, vol. III (Washington: US Govt., 1898), at 2514ff. See also: Dumberry, ibid., 404ff.

internationally wrongful act committed before the date of succession.[255] This is clearly an unsatisfactory outcome requiring a more suitable and just solution.

2   The Right for the Successor State to Claim Reparation on Behalf of its New Nationals for Internationally Wrongful Acts Committed before the Date of Succession

187.   Many scholars argue that the application of the rule of continuous nationality may lead to unjust results when changes of nationality are *involuntary*, such as in cases of State succession.[256] It would thus result in nationals of the successor State being left without any possible redress for internationally wrongful acts suffered at the time they were nationals of another State. The fact that the application of this rule, in the context of State succession, would ultimately deprive of a remedy 'large numbers and extensive categories of persons' has been described as 'offensive to the modern conception of the role of international law in protecting the individual'.[257]

188.   The work of the Institute of International Law[258] and the International Law Association (ILA)[259] also support the proposition that the rule is not appropriate in the context of State succession. The same position has been adopted by several ICJ judges in their individual and dissenting opinions,[260] and also by arbitral tribunals in the *Pablo Nájera*[261] and *Administrative Decision No. V* cases.[262] The traditional rule of continuous nationality

255   Dumberry, ibid., 408.
256   C. Rousseau, *Droit international public*, vol. V (Paris: Sirey, 1983), 119; A. de Lapradelle & N. Politis, *Recueil des arbitrages internationaux*, vol. III, 1872–1875 (Paris: Pedone, 1954), 99–100 (fn 1); M. Mendelson, 'The Runaway Train: The Continuous Nationality Rule from the Panevezys-Saldutiskis Railway Case to Loewen', in: T. Weiler (ed.), *International Investment Law and Arbitration: Leading Cases from the ICSID, NAFTA, Bilateral Treaties and Customary International Law* (London: Cameron May 2005), 19; John Dugard, 'Continuous Nationality', in: *Max Planck Encyclopedia of Public International Law* (OUP, online edn, 2006) para. 11; J.H.W. Verzijl, *International Law in Historical Perspective*, vol. V (Leiden: A.W. Sijthoff, 1973), 449; O'Connell, *State Succession in Municipal Law*, 537–539; Fastenrath, 'Der Deutsche Einigungsvertrag im Lichte des Rechts der Staatennachfolge', 39; R. Donner, *The Regulation of Nationality in International Law*, 2nd ed. (Ardsley, NY: Transnational Publ., 1994), 252.
257   O'Connell, *State Succession in Municipal Law*, 538–539.
258   Institut de Droit international, 'La protection diplomatique des individus en droit international. La nationalité des réclamations', Session of Warsaw, 1965, in: (1965) 51-II *Annuaire de l'Institut de Droit international*, 157ff. See the analysis in: Dumberry, *State Succession to International Responsibility*, 352ff, 357 (fn 81).
259   ILA, 'The Changing Law of Nationality of Claims, Interim Report', Francisco Orrego Vicuña, Committee on Diplomatic Protection of Persons and Property, Interim Report (2000), 35–36.
260   *Case Concerning the Barcelona Traction, Light and Power Company, Limited (Second Phase) (Belgium v. Spain)*, Judgment, 5 February 1970, ICJ Rep. 1970, individual opinions of Judge Fitzmaurice, at 100–101, and Judge Jessup, at 203.
261   *Pablo Nájera (France) v. United Mexican States*, France-Mexico Claims Commission, Decision no. 30-A, 19 October 1928, *obiter dictum* by President Verzijl, 5 UNRIAA 488; (1927–1928) *Annual Digest* 52.
262   *Administrative Decision No. V*, US-German Mixed Claims Commission, 31 October 1924, 7 UNRIAA 141–143.

was firmly criticised by Judge van Eysinga in his dissenting opinion in the *Panevezys-Saldutiskis Railway* case before the PCIJ:[263]

> [T]he question arises whether it is reasonable to describe as an unwritten rule of international law a rule which would entail that, when a change of sovereignty takes place, the new State or the State which has increased its territory would not be able to espouse any claim of any of its new nationals in regard to injury suffered before the change of nationality. It may also be questioned whether indeed it is any part of the Court's task to contribute towards the crystallization of unwritten rules of law which would lead to such inequitable results.[264]

> [I]t is difficult to see why a 'claim' against a third State arising out of an unlawful act should not also pass from the old to the new State. Regarded from this aspect of the law of State succession – there is nothing surprising in the fact that Estonia should have had the right to take up a case which previously only Russia could have espoused. Such a 'succession' is an absolutely characteristic and even essential feature of the law of State succession. The successor State is continually exercising rights which previously belonged exclusively to the old State, and the same holds good as regards obligations. Accordingly it would be quite normal that in this case the successor State should have protected both diplomatically and before the Court a company the diplomatic protection of which formerly fell to Russia alone.[265]

189.   In the following sections, we will first examine the principle set out at Article 10(1) whereby the traditional rule of continuous nationality does not apply in the context of changes to nationality resulting from State succession (Section 2.1). This analysis will be followed by a survey of several examples of State practice and court decisions illustrating the concrete application of this principle (Section 2.2).

2.1   ARTICLE 10(1) PROVIDES FOR THE NON-APPLICATION OF THE CONTINUOUS NATIONALITY RULE IN THE CONTEXT OF STATE SUCCESSION

190.   The work of the ILC on diplomatic protection has clearly adopted the position that the traditional rule of continuous nationality should not apply in the context of changes to nationality resulting from State succession.[266] For its Special Rapporteur John Dugard, the rule of continuous nationality 'may cause great injustice where the injured individual has undergone a *bona fide* change of nationality, unrelated to the bringing of an international claim, after the occurrence of the injury, as a result, *inter alia*, of … cession of territory or succession of States'.[267] For this reason, the ILC decided that there should be a 'basic

---

263   *Panevezys-Saldutiskis Railway Case*, at 16, 35.
264   Ibid., 35.
265   Ibid., 16–17.
266   See the analysis in: Dumberry, *State Succession to International Responsibility*, 348ff.
267   ILC, 'Addendum to First Report on Diplomatic Protection', by Mr. John R. Dugard, Special Rapporteur, 20 April 2000, UN Doc. A/CN.4/506/Add.1, at para. 1.

exception' to the rule of continuous nationality to deal with cases of 'involuntary changes of nationality of the protected person, arising from succession of States' and another one for 'situations where it would be impossible to apply the rule of continuity owing to, for example, the disappearance of the State of original nationality through dissolution or dismemberment'.[268]

191.   The ILC therefore adopted Article 5(2) providing for an exception to the traditional rule of continuous nationality in the context of changes of nationality resulting from State succession:

A State may exercise diplomatic protection in respect of a person who is its national at the date of the official presentation of the claim but was not a national at the date of injury, provided that the person had the nationality of a predecessor State.[269]

192.   The IDI Resolution follows exactly the same approach as the ILC. Thus, under Article 10(1), a successor State may exercise diplomatic protection in respect of a person (or a corporation) who is its national at the date of the official presentation of the claim, even if he/she was not at the date of injury.[270] The position is supported by many scholars.[271]

193.   It is important to note that under Article 10(1), the successor State can exercise diplomatic protection on behalf of persons under the circumstances described in the previous paragraph in two distinct situations.

194.   First, the successor State can exercise diplomatic protection on behalf of a person by the mere fact that he/she had the nationality of the predecessor State before the date of succession. This situation includes *involuntary* changes of nationality. Persons (and corporations) may lose their nationality simply as a result of a succession of States over a given territory. The ILC Special Rapporteur on diplomatic protection also mentions other situations where the changes of nationality could also be involuntary: 'adoption and marriage when a change of nationality is compulsory'.[272] In relation to his work on diplomatic protection, the ILC Special Rapporteur stated that the aim of Article 5(2) is to 'limit exceptions to the continuous nationality rule to cases involving compulsory imposition of nationality, such as those in which, the person has acquired a new nationality as a necessary consequence of factors such as marriage, adoption or the succession of States'.[273]

268   ILC, 'Report of the International Law Commission on the Work of its Fifty-Third Session', 23 April to 1 June and 2 July to 10 August 2001, ILC Report, UN Doc. A/56/10, 2001, chp. VII, 507ff, at para. 177.
269   ILC, 'Draft Articles on Diplomatic Protection with commentaries' (2006) II(2) *Yearbook* ILC, 23.
270   Final Report, para. 120, in: (2015) 76 *Annuaire de l'Institut de Droit international*, 553.
271   Dumberry, 'Obsolete and Unjust'; Dumberry, *State Succession to International Responsibility*, 355; Ian Brownlie, *Principles of Public International Law*, 5th ed. (Oxford: Clarendon Press, 1998) 661; Wyler, *La règle dite de la continuité de la nationalité dans le contentieux international*, 117; Šturma, 'State Succession in Respect of International Responsibility', 669ff, 677; ILC, Working-Group Recommendations, 409.
272   ILC, 'Draft Articles on Diplomatic Protection with commentaries', 38
273   ILC, 'Report of the International Law Commission on the Work of its Fifty-Fourth Session', 29 April–7 June and 22 July–16 August 2002, ILC Report, A/57/10, 2002, chp. V, 120ff, at 180, paras. 7, 8.

195.   Second, the successor State can exercise diplomatic protection on behalf of persons in the different scenario where they have changed their nationality *voluntarily*. As mentioned in the ILC Articles on Diplomatic protection, the 'fear that a person may deliberately change his or her nationality in order to acquire a State of nationality more willing and able to bring a diplomatic claim on his or her behalf is the basis for the rule of continuous nationality'.[274] The aim of Article 10(1) of the Resolution is to address this fear. Thus, in the context of *voluntary* changes of nationality, Article 10(1) requires that the person or the corporation must have lost that previous nationality and acquired the new one (of the successor State) for 'reason unrelated to the bringing of the claim' and in a 'manner not inconsistent with international law'. This is exactly the same language employed at Article 5(2) of the ILC Articles on diplomatic protection.[275] Thus, the individual for whom the new successor State espouses the claim needs to have changed his/her nationality for *bona fide* reasons unrelated to the bringing of an international claim.[276]

2.2   EXAMPLES OF STATE PRACTICE AND JUDICIAL DECISIONS SUPPORTING THIS PRINCIPLE

196.   In his study on the question, one of the authors of this Commentary refers to four examples of international judicial decisions where the traditional rule of continuous nationality was *not* applied in the specific context of State succession.[277] These four examples will be briefly examined in the following paragraphs.

197.   The first example is the 1928 *Pablo Nájera* case decided by the France-Mexico Claims Commission.[278] It arose from incidents which took place in 1916 in Mexico, when an Ottoman national (Mr. Nájera, born in Lebanon in 1860) was injured as a result of the action of Mexican revolutionaries (during the Mexican Revolution, which started in 1910). At the time, Mr. Nájera was still formally a national of the Ottoman Empire even though France had traditionally exercised diplomatic protection for protected Lebanese and Syrians abroad before the end of the First World War (and the break-up of the Ottoman Empire). After the War, France became the Mandatory Power of both Syria and Lebanon, in the framework of Article 22 of the Covenant of the League of Nations. In 1926 France filed a complaint on behalf of Mr. Nájera, whom it considered to be a French national, before the Claims Commission which was set up in 1923–1924 to examine claims for losses by French nationals against Mexico. President Verzijl of the Tribunal held that Mr. Nájera was included in the term 'French protégés' under Article III of the *Compromis* at the time France espoused his claim and submitted its Memorial.[279] Yet, when the damage occurred, Mr. Nájera was an Ottoman national and not a French national. For President Verzijl, the rule of continuous nationality should not apply in this case because it was the intention of the parties when they were negotiating the setting up of the Commission

274   ILC, 'Draft Articles on Diplomatic Protection with commentaries', 39.
275   ILC, 'Report of the International Law Commission on the Work of its Fifty-Fourth Session', 120ff.
276   See analysis in: Dumberry, *State Succession to International Responsibility*, 346, 360ff.
277   Ibid., 367ff. See also: Šturma, 'State Succession in Respect of International Responsibility', 672ff.
278   *Pablo Nájera* case, at 487–488. See analysis in: Dumberry, *State Succession to International Responsibility*, 367ff.
279   *Pablo Nájera* case, at 487–488.

to consider Lebanese living abroad as 'French protégés' *retroactively*. Mexico strongly objected that this was ever its intention. The Mexican Commissioner refuted the position taken by President Verzijl and maintained that the rule of continuous nationality should have found application to prevent France from espousing the claim.[280]

198.   The second example is the 1934 Arbitral Award in the case of the *Claim of Finnish Shipowners against Great Britain in respect of the Use of Certain Finnish Vessels During the War*.[281] This is a case where a claim was submitted by Finland against Great Britain for damage suffered by Finnish nationals before the First World War. At the time of the commission of the internationally wrongful act, Finland was not yet an independent State (it became one after the Russian Revolution of 1917) and the victims had Russian nationality. In this case, the respondent (the United Kingdom) did not invoke the traditional rule of continuous nationality to deny the jurisdiction of the Sole Arbitrator over the case. By not rejecting its own jurisdiction over the dispute, the Sole Arbitrator implicitly endorsed the validity of the proposition that a new State may be entitled to reparation for damage which occurred at a time when the person (in this case, a corporation) for which it claims did not have its nationality.

199.   The third and fourth examples are the consistent approaches adopted by the Mixed Arbitral Tribunals established after the First World War[282] and the United Nations Compensation Commission (UNCC) set up after the Gulf War (1990–1991).[283] In both cases, it was deliberately decided to exclude the application of the rule of continuous nationality to prevent the unjust consequences created after these two conflicts whereby nationals of new States could not seek redress for the damage they suffered during the war. The new States were thus allowed to claim reparation on behalf of their new nationals which did not have such nationality at the time the damage occurred. The above-mentioned solution was applied, for instance, by UNCC Panels in the context of the dissolution of Czechoslovakia.

200.   In his study, one of the authors of this Commentary has also found several examples of State practice where reparation was provided to the successor State to compensate its nationals, even if they did not have its nationality at the time when the damage occurred.[284] Even if they also raise other problems, in these four examples (further discussed in the next paragraphs), the State responsible for the internationally wrongful act committed before the date of succession did not advance any objection based on the continuous nationality rule to such claims submitted by successor States on behalf of their new nationals.

201.   The first example is the 1952 Agreement on reparation between the Federal Republic of Germany (FRG) and Israel calling for the former to provide annual fixed instalments

---

280   Ibid., at 503.
281   *Claim of Finnish Shipowners against Great Britain in respect of the Use of Certain Finnish Vessels During the War (Finland v. United Kingdom)*, Award of Dr. Bagge, 9 May 1934, 3 UNRIAA 1481. See Dumberry, *State Succession to International Responsibility*, 370.
282   See several cases examined in: Dumberry, ibid., 370.
283   Ibid., 379.
284   Ibid., 382. See also: Šturma, 'State Succession in Respect of International Responsibility', 677ff.

of goods and services to the Jewish State over the next 11 to 13 years in compensation for the internationally wrongful acts committed by the Third Reich against Jewish people before and during the Second World War.[285] The Agreement provided for the amount of DM3 billion (US$715 million) to be paid in reparation by Germany to Israel. In two separate but parallel instruments (the *Hague Protocols*), the FRG also committed to the amount of DM450 million to be paid to Israel for the Conference on Jewish Material Claims against Germany (or 'Claims Conference', a Jewish organisation) to compensate Nazi victims.[286] It also called for Germany to enact laws to compensate Jewish victims of Nazi persecution.[287] At the time of the commission of the internationally wrongful acts by the Third Reich, the victims were nationals of European States or had become stateless. They were not nationals of the State of Israel, which did not yet exist. This situation did not prevent the new State of Israel from seeking reparation against Germany on behalf of its new nationals (as well as on behalf of non-Israeli Jews). This is one example of State practice where the traditional rule of continuous nationality was not applied by the parties concerned in the context of State succession.

202. The second example of State practice is the 1982 Agreement between the United Kingdom and Mauritius. In 1966, before Mauritius became an independent State (in 1968), the United Kingdom, the colonial power, separated the Chagos Islands from Mauritius and ceded (for a first period of 50 years, with an extension option) one of these islands (the Island of Diego Garcia) to the United States, which eventually built a military base there. The local population which lived on the Island of Diego Garcia (some 2,000 Ilois) were moved essentially to Mauritius. This situation created a dispute which is still unsettled to this day.[288] Equally, individuals of Chagossian origin had raised claims before British tribunals seeking redress to their situations. A treaty was entered into force between the United Kingdom and Mauritius in 1982 with the desire to 'settle certain problems which have arisen concerning the Ilois who went to Mauritius on their departure or removal from the Chagos Archipelago after November 1965'.[289] This is a case of State practice (it should be noted, however, *between* the predecessor and the successor State) where the strict rule of continuous nationality was not applied. The United Kingdom did not object to the fact that Mauritius could enter an agreement with regard to a group of people who did not have

---

285 *Agreement between the State of Israel and the Federal Republic of Germany on Compensation*, in: 162 UNTS 205; (1953) II(5) BGBl 37. The example is discussed in Dumberry, *State Succession to International Responsibility*, 383ff.

286 *Protocol II between the Federal Republic of Germany and the Conference on Jewish Material Claims against Germany*, in: 162 UNTS 205; (1953) II(5) BGBl 85.

287 *Protocol I between the Federal Republic of Germany and the Conference on Jewish Material Claims against Germany*, in: ibid. The different laws enacted by West Germany to compensate Nazi victims are examined in Dumberry, *State Succession to International Responsibility*, 387ff.

288 Based on its competence over questions of decolonisation, the UN General Assembly requested an advisory opinion to the ICJ on the Legal Consequences of the Separation of Chagos from Mauritius in 1965 (UN GA Resolution 71/292 of 22 June 2017).

289 *Agreement between the Government of the United Kingdom of Great Britain and Northern Ireland and the Government of Mauritius*, of 7 July 1982 (in force on 28 October 1982), in: (1983) UKTS no. 6 (Cmnd. 8785); also in: Burns H. Weston, Richard B. Lillich & David J. Bederman, *International Claims: Their Settlement by Lump Sum Agreements, 1975–1995* (Ardsley, N.Y., Transnational Publ., 1999), 283.

its nationality at the time when the damage occurred. Indeed, those individuals had the nationality of the United Kingdom at that time.

203. A third example of State practice are the bilateral agreements entered into force by Austria with Central and Eastern European States in the context of the 2000 Austrian Reconciliation Fund Law, which was created with money from both the government and the private sector to provide compensation for persons who were deported from their home countries by the Nazi regime to work as forced or slave labour in the territory of the Republic of Austria during the Second World War.[290] Some of these bilateral treaties were concluded with new States (Belarus, Czech Republic and Ukraine) even if, when the damage occurred, the individuals injured were not nationals of these new successor States. This did not prevent Austria from providing compensation to the new successor States on behalf of these victims.[291]

204. Finally, in August 2000, the FRG passed the Law on the Creation of a Foundation 'Remembrance, Responsibility and Future'.[292] The legislation established a fund of approximately US$5.2 billion to compensate persons who performed forced labour in concentration camps or in another place of confinement (outside Austria) or a ghetto 'under comparable conditions'. Under this law, the German government and German companies each provided half the funds for the Foundation. In the context of the Final Plenary Meeting concluding the preparation of the Foundation, a Joint Statement was signed by Germany, the United States, Belarus, the Czech Republic, Ukraine, Israel, Poland, Russia, the Foundation Initiative of German Enterprises and the Claims Conference (a Jewish organisation).[293] It is noteworthy that this statement was entered into by Germany and several States which did not exist at the time the internationally wrongful acts were committed. Germany did not invoke the rule of continuous nationality; it accepted that these States could negotiate a reparation agreement on behalf of individuals which did not have their nationality at the time when the damage occurred. This is another example of State practice where the rule of continuous nationality was not applied by the parties concerned.

205. In sum, the examples of judicial decisions and State practice mentioned in the previous paragraphs show that the rule of continuous nationality was *not* considered by the State responsible for the internationally wrongful act as an *obstacle* preventing the successor State from receiving reparation.[294] There is, in fact, *very limited* support in case law and State practice for the application of the strict rule of continuous nationality in the context of State succession. In the study cited above, its author found *only one case* where the classic rule of continuous nationality was endorsed by a judicial body, therefore preventing the successor

---

290 Bundesgesetz über den Fonds für freiwillige Leistungen der Republik Österreich an ehemalige Sklaven- und Zwangsarbeiter des nationalsozialistischen Regimes (Versöhnungsfonds-Gesetz) (Federal Law Concerning the Fund for Voluntary Payments by the Republic of Austria to Former Slave Labourers and Forced Laborers of the National Socialist Regime (the 'Reconciliation Fund Law')), signed on 8 August 2000, entered into force on 27 November 2000, in: ÖBGBl., I No. 74/2000.

291 See analysis in: Dumberry, *State Succession to International Responsibility*, 386.

292 Gesetz Zur Errichtung Einer Stiftung 'Erinnerung; Verantwortung Und Zukunft', in: (2000) I BGBl. 1263. See analysis in: Dumberry, ibid., 387ff.

293 The Joint Statement was issued on 17 July 2000, in: (2000) II BGBl. 1383ff.

294 Dumberry, *State Succession to International Responsibility*, 410.

State from claiming reparation on behalf of its new national. This is the 1939 *Panevezys-Saldutiskis Railway* case.[295]

206. However, the reasoning of the Permanent Court in this case does not constitute the most solid foundation in support of the application of the traditional rule in the context of State succession.[296] Thus, the Permanent Court's reasoning on the question is limited to one sentence where it simply stated that Estonia 'must prove that at the time when the injury occurred ... the company suffering the injury possessed Estonian nationality'.[297] The Court does not provide any explanation as to the origin, the content or the application of the rule. In fact, the only clear support for the application of the rule of continuous nationality can be found in one paragraph of the common individual opinion of Judge De Visscher and Count Rostworowski.[298] In his dissenting opinion, Judge van Eysinga, on the contrary, concluded that the new successor State of Estonia should have been given the right to exercise diplomatic protection on behalf of the company even if it did not have its nationality when the damage occurred.[299] Article 10(1) of the Resolution takes the position that this should have indeed been the case.

3   The Continuous Right for States to Exercise Diplomatic Protection for Claims Already Initiated at the Date of Succession

207. Articles 10(2) and 10(3) deal with the situation where a claim in exercise of diplomatic protection has *already* been initiated at the date of succession. While Article 10(2) focuses on claims initiated *by* the predecessor State, Article 10(3) concerns claims initiated *against* the predecessor State.

---

295 *Panevezys-Saldutiskis Railway* case.
296 Dumberry, *State Succession to International Responsibility*, 390–402, 410.
297 *Panevezys-Saldutiskis Railway* case, at 16–17.
298 Ibid., at 24, 27. They argued that the claim submitted by Estonia should have been rejected on the ground of the lack of the 'bond of nationality required by international law': 'The Estonian Government has tried to prove that the rule of law underlying the objection is subject to various qualifications, but it has not claimed that in 1919 the interests damaged by the seizure had already acquired Estonian character. On its own admission, the First Russian Company, which is said to have survived the nationalization decrees, was only transformed into an Estonian company as a result of the Treaty of Tartu of February 2nd, 1920, and, to quote the words of the Estonian Agent: "at the time and by the fact of the treaty of peace" (oral statement of the Agent for the Estonian Government, June 14th, 1938; Oral Statements, 40). Accordingly, even it could be agreed that the change of nationality dates back to the Treaty of Tartu, the change could still not operate in regard to a fact which the Parties agree in dating 1919. Finally, either the interests affected by the seizure were at that time still represented by the Russian company, according to the Estonian Government's theory of survival, or they were no longer represented by any company at all, according to the argument of the Lithuanian Government to the effect that the nationalization decrees destroyed the Company's legal personality. In either case – and this fact is alone decisive – there was in 1919 no Estonian company, and therefore the bond of nationality required by international law to have existed at the time the injury was suffered, was manifestly lacking.'
299 Ibid., at 35.

208.   Article 10(2) concerns the situation where the *predecessor State* had initiated before the date of succession a diplomatic protection claim on behalf of one of its nationals and the matter remained unsettled at the time of the event of succession. In this case, Article 10(2) provides that the claim may be continued by the successor State under the same conditions set out at Article 10(1). Thus, for the successor State to be allowed to continue such a claim, the person on behalf of whom the claim was submitted must have had the nationality of the predecessor State or lost that nationality and acquired, for a reason unrelated to the bringing of the claim, the nationality of the successor State in a manner not inconsistent with international law.

209.   Article 10(3) deals with the different situation of a claim in exercise of diplomatic protection which was initiated by a *third State* (the injured State) *against* the predecessor State on behalf of one of its nationals before the date of succession. In this situation, the question is whether or not such a claim may be continued (after the date of succession) by that State *against a successor State*. Under Article 10(3), such a claim can be pursued against the successor State in the event that the predecessor State has ceased to exist (such as in situations of incorporation, unification and dissolution). Any claim in exercise of diplomatic protection initiated by a third State against a predecessor State which continues to exist after the date of succession (such as in situations of transfer of territory, separation and newly independent States) is simply unaffected.

210.   In the context of a dissolution of State one complex question arises: against which of the different successor States may a claim be pursued by the injured State? Under Article 10(3), in such a case of a plurality of successor States, the claim shall be addressed to the successor State 'having the most direct connection with the act giving rise to the exercise of diplomatic protection'. The provision also mentions that 'when it is not possible to determine a single successor State having such a direct connection, the claim may be continued against all the successor States'.

211.   Article 10(3) further adds that 'The provisions of Article 7 apply *mutatis mutandis*.' Under Article 7(1), the successor States will assume the obligations arising from the commission of an internationally wrongful act in an 'equitable manner'. Article 7(2) provides for the criteria to be taken into account to achieve this equitable distribution of obligations among all the different successor States.[300] Importantly, Article 7(1) mentions one exception to this general principle: when the 'States or subjects of international law concerned' have *agreed otherwise*.

212.   Two observations should be made regarding the application of Article 7. First, as mentioned already above, the solution proposed under this provision is of a subsidiary nature.[301] It only applies if 'the States or subjects of international law concerned' have not themselves agreed to a specific outcome. Second, as in other situations already analysed, an agreement exclusively concluded by the successor States will not be enough if the situation is one in which the diplomatic protection claim was raised by virtue of a wrongful

---

300   See the analysis above examining Article 7.
301   The provision is another illustration of the subsidiary character of the guiding principles of the Resolution, as set out, more generally, at Article 3.

act committed by the predecessor State. The injured State is clearly one of the 'States or subjects of international law concerned' by such a situation. The parties to the State succession relationship cannot solely decide on their own about which of them will bear the obligation to repair. The victim must be allowed to take a position on the matter. The injured State will therefore need to approve any outcome of allocation of obligations decided by other States.

213.   Finally, Article 10(4) deals with the specific situation of persons having dual nationality. According to this provision, in cases where the predecessor State continues to exist and the individual or corporation possesses both the nationality of the predecessor and the successor State, the question is governed by general rules of diplomatic protection concerning dual or multiple nationality.[302] Articles 6 and 7 of the ILC Articles on diplomatic protection deal with these situations. Under Article 7 of the ILC Articles, 'A State of nationality may not exercise diplomatic protection in respect of a person against a State of which that person is also a national unless the nationality of the former State is predominant, both at the date of injury and at the date of the official presentation of the claim'.

D   Chapter III: Provisions Concerning Specific Categories of Succession of States

PRELIMINARY OBSERVATIONS

214.   Chapter III examines the different solutions to the question of succession to the consequences of international responsibility which should prevail for different types of succession of States. It should be recalled that under Article 3, the different principles (and exceptions) set out under Chapter III only apply in the event that the relevant parties have not themselves agreed to any other specific solution.

215.   The importance of distinguishing between the different types of succession of States is recognised by writers and international tribunals.[303] In fact, as mentioned above, Article 4 recognises the basic distinction between cases where the predecessor State *ceases to exist* from those other situations where it continues to exist. The two Vienna Conventions on State succession distinguish between four basic types of succession: a) cession, that is, the transfer of part of the territory of one State to another State;[304] b) separation of a part of a State's territory,[305] which includes not only cases of secession/devolution but also the different category of dismemberment/disintegration of a State; c) the uniting of two or more existing States;[306] and d) succession in the context of decolonisation (newly

---

302   Final Report, para. 123, in: (2015) 76 *Annuaire de l'Institut de Droit international*, 554.
303   See for instance: *Lighthouse Arbitration* case, at 91, 93.
304   Article 15, *Vienna Convention on Succession of States in Respect of Treaties*; Article 14(1), *Vienna Convention on Succession of States in Respect of State Property, Archives and Debts.*
305   Article 34(1), *Vienna Convention on Succession of States in Respect of Treaties*; Article 30(1), *Vienna Convention on Succession of States in Respect of State Property, Archives and Debts.*
306   Article 31(1), *Vienna Convention on Succession of States in Respect of Treaties*; Article 16, *Vienna Convention on Succession of States in Respect of State Property, Archives and Debts.*

independent States). As noted in the Final Report, the classification adopted by the Vienna Conventions 'does not fully or accurately depict the different hypotheses of State succession'.[307] Moreover, the 1978 Vienna Convention does not even distinguish between situations of separation and dissolution, providing for the same rules in both cases.[308] It thus departs from the ILC's proposal made in 1972 to distinguish between these two different concepts.[309] These distinctions must be made. This is also the position since then adopted by the ILC Special Rapporteur.[310]

216.   The Resolution has adopted the general framework of the two Conventions, but improves its content by adding some further essential distinction between these different categories. The Resolution specifically distinguishes between six categories of State succession:

-       Transfer of part of the territory of a State to another State (Article 11);

-       Separation of parts of a State to form a new State (Article 12);

-       Merger of States aiming at the creation of a new State (Article 13);

-       Incorporation of a State into another existing State (Article 14);

-       Dissolution of a State (Article 15); and

-       Newly independent States in the context of decolonisation (Article 16).

217.   The distinction between these different types of State succession and the terminology used is discussed in the following sections. It should be added that the Resolution does not contain any rule on how to determine whether a specific situation falls within one category of State succession or another. This is a matter of interpretation or application of the relevant rules of State succession.

218.   The following sections examine the applicable rules set out for these six categories of succession with regard to the question of succession to rights and obligations stemming from an internationally wrongful act.

ARTICLE II:

Transfer of part of the territory of a State

1.   With the exception of the situations referred to in the following paragraphs, the rights and obligations arising from an internationally wrongful act in relation to which the predecessor State has been either the author or the injured State do not pass to the successor State when part of the territory of the predecessor State, or any territory for the

---

307 Final Report, para. 39, in: (2015) 76 *Annuaire de l'Institut de Droit international*, 529.
308 See Article 34, *Vienna Convention on Succession of States in Respect of Treaties*.
309 Draft Articles 27 and 28 in: ILC, 'Fifth Report on Succession in Respect of Treaties, prepared by the Special Rapporteur, Sir Humphrey Waldock', A/CN.4/256 and Adds 1–4, 10 April, 29 May and 8, 16 and 28 June 1972, A/8710/Rev.1, in: (1972) II *Yearbook ILC*, at 292–298.
310 ILC Special Rapporteur, First Report, 2017, para. 25.

international relations of which this State is responsible, becomes part
of the territory of the successor State.

2.   The rights arising from an internationally wrongful act
committed against the predecessor State pass to the successor State if
there exists a direct link between the consequences of this act and the
territory transferred and/or its population.

3.   If particular circumstances so require, the obligations arising
from an internationally wrongful act pass to the successor State when
the author of this act was an organ of the territorial unit of the predecessor State that has later become an organ of the successor State.

Commentary

219.   This provision deals with the question of succession to rights and obligations arising
from the commission of an internationally wrongful act in the context of a transfer of part
of the territory of *one* State to *another* State. The term 'cession' is sometimes used to refer
specifically to cases where the territorial change is made pursuant to a treaty, while the
term 'transfer' applies to situations where there is no explicit agreement between the predecessor State and the successor State. The Resolution adopts the generic term 'transfer'
to include both situations. It should be added that treaties of cession generally include
provisions regarding questions of State succession, including sometimes those related to
the consequences of wrongful acts.

220.   Transfer of territory is a distinct type of State succession for many reasons. It must be
distinguished from the situation of 'incorporation' of a State. Thus, while Article 11 deals
with cases of transfer of *part* of the territory of one State, Article 14 concerns the incorporation of the *whole territory* of one State which is integrated into another already existing
State. Another important distinction with incorporation is that in the case of transfer, the
predecessor State continues to exist after such transfer of part of its territory to another
State. On the contrary, in the context of incorporation the predecessor State will cease to
exist. Finally, transfer of territory is a unique type of State succession insofar as it results
neither in the extinction of a State nor in the creation of a new State.[311] These particular
features make transfer of territory a clearly distinct type of State succession, which has
been recognised as such by scholars[312] and by the ILC since it started working on matters
of State succession.[313]

221.   Article 11 also covers the situation where a State bears the responsibility for the
international relations of a territory, without being its sovereign, and transfers that territory,
or part of it, to another State. Thus, Article 11(1) uses the expression 'or any territory for
the international relations of which this State is responsible'. The wording employed under

---

311   Dumberry, *State Succession to International Responsibility*, 21.
312   Stern, 'La succession d'Etats', 105.
313   Article 15, *Vienna Convention on Succession of States in Respect of Treaties*; Article 14(1), *Vienna
Convention on Succession of States in Respect of State Property, Archives and Debts.*

this clause is similar to that of Article 15 of the 1978 Vienna Convention.[314] One example of this situation is the transfer to Morocco of the territory of Ifni, a non-self-governing territory (under Chapter XI of the UN Charter and General Assembly Resolution 1514 (XV)), which was until then under the administration of Spain.[315]

222.   Article 11(1) sets out the solution which should generally prevail (discussed in Section 1), while the second and third paragraphs deal with two exceptions (see Section 2).

1   Principle: No Transfer of Rights and Obligations to the Successor State

223.   Under Article 11(1), the rights and obligations arising from an internationally wrongful act in relation to which the predecessor State has been either the author or the injured State do *not* pass to the successor State when part of the territory of the former is transferred to the latter. The principle of non-succession is adopted in this situation for the simple reason that the predecessor State continues to exist following the transfer of part of its territory to another State. The predecessor State should therefore remain the holder of rights and obligations arising from wrongful acts which took place before the date of succession. This solution is in fact an illustration of the basic principle applicable under Articles 4 and 5 to cases where the predecessor State continues to exist after the date of succession.

224.   This general solution of non-succession for cases of transfer of territory is supported by writers.[316] It is also followed by ILC Special Rapporteur at Draft Article 9(1).[317] Many municipal law cases, a few cases decided by international arbitral tribunals and examples of State practice also support this solution.[318] These examples are briefly examined in the next paragraphs.

On this provision, see: A. Tanzi & L. Iapichino, 'Article 15', in: G. Distefano, G. Gaggioli & A. Hêche (eds.), *La Convention de Vienne de 1978 sur la succession d'États en matière de traités: Commentaire article par article et études thématiques* (Brussels: Bruylant, 2015), 543ff.

315 See Resolution 2428 (XXIII) of 18 December 1968.

316 See analysis in: Dumberry, *State Succession to International Responsibility*, 123ff, referring to the position of scholars, at 124, including: Jennings & Watts, *Oppenheim's International Law*, vol. I, 227; Brownlie, *Principles of Public International Law*, 632; Philippe Drakidis, 'Succession d'Etats et enrichissements sans cause des biens publics du Dodécanèse' (1971) 24 *RHDI* 72–123.

317 ILC Special Rapporteur, First Report, 2017, para. 17; ILC Special Rapporteur, Second Report, 2018, para. 139. See Draft Article 9(1): 'Subject to the exceptions referred to in paragraphs 2 and 3, the obligations arising from an internationally wrongful act of the predecessor State do not pass to the successor State when part of the territory of the predecessor State becomes part of the territory of the successor State'.

318 These cases are examined in: Dumberry, *State Succession to International Responsibility*, 126ff; ILC Special Rapporteur, Second Report, 2018, paras. 140ff. One example of State practice is Article 14 of the 1947 *Paris Peace Treaty* in the context of the cession of the Dodecanese Islands from Italy to Greece: Paris Peace Treaty, signed on 10 February 1947 at Paris, entered into force on 15 September 1947, in: 49 UNTS 126; UKTS 1948, no. 50 (Cmd. 7481). The case is discussed in: Drakidis, 'Succession d'États et enrichissements sans cause des biens publics du Dodécanèse'; Dumberry, *State Succession to International Responsibility*, 129; ILC Special Rapporteur, Second Report, 2018, para. 141.

225.   Examples of decisions by municipal courts of successor States supporting the solution of non-succession include the cases of *Mordcovici v. P.T.T.*,[319] *Sechter*[320] and *Vozneac*,[321] all decided by the Court of Cassation of Romania in the context of the transfer of the territory of Bessarabia from Soviet Russia to Romania in 1918.[322] Other examples include the cases of *Alsace-Lorraine Railway v. Ducreux es-qualité*[323] and *Kern v. Chemin de fer d'Alsace-Lorraine*, decided by French courts in the context of the retrocession of Alsace-Lorraine to France after the First World War.[324] The same solution of non-succession was also affirmed by the French–German Mixed Arbitral Tribunal in a series of awards, including the case of *Levy v. German State*, in the same context involving Alsace-Lorraine.[325]

226.   It should be added that the principle of non-succession was also adopted by one municipal court of a *predecessor* State (from which the ceded territory was detached) in the case of *Kalmar v. Hungarian Treasury* before the Supreme Court of Hungary in the context of the cession of Transylvania to Romania after the First World War.[326] A different solution was adopted, however, in one domestic court case.[327] A German court concluded that the FRG (the predecessor State) could not be held liable to compensate the plaintiff for internationally wrongful acts committed before the transfer of the territory of Upper Silesia to Poland after the Second World War. One important point to mention is the fact that none of these municipal law cases involves 'real' questions of succession to the consequences arising from international responsibility.[328] In these cases, the wrongful acts were indeed committed by the predecessor State not against another State (or a national of another State) but against *its own nationals* which became nationals of the successor State after the date of succession.

227.   The *Lighthouse Arbitration* case is, on the contrary, a good illustration of the principle that the predecessor State should remain responsible for *its own* internationally wrongful acts committed before the date of succession in the context of a transfer

---

319   *Mordcovici v. P.T.T.*, Romania, Court of Cassation, 29 October, 1929, in: *Buletinul deciziunilor Inaltei Curti de Casatie*, LXVI (1929), Part 2, 150, in: (1929–1930) *Annual Digest* 62.

320   *Sechter v. Ministry of the Interior*, Romania, Court of Cassation, 1929, in: *Jurisprudenta Română a Inaltei Curti de Casatiesi Justitie*, XVII, N°. 4 (1930), 58, in: (1929–1930) *Annual Digest*, case no. 37.

321   *Vozneac v. Autonomous Administration of Posts and Telegraphs*, Romania, Court of Cassation, 22 June 1931, in: *Jurisprudenta Română a Inaltei Curti de Casatiesi Justitie*, 1932, 36–38; (1931–1932) *Annual Digest*, case no. 30.

322   See analysis in: Dumberry, *State Succession to International Responsibility*, 126ff.

323   *Alsace-Lorraine Railway v. Ducreux Es-qualité*, French Court of Cassation, Civil Chamber, 30 March 1927, in: (1928) 55 *JDI* 1034; (1928) *Sirey* Part. I, 300; (1927–1928) *Annual Digest* 85.

324   *Kern v. Chemin de fer d'Alsace-Lorraine*, Cour de Colmar (Première Ch, civile), 16 May 1927, in: (1929) 56 *JDI* 446ff. See analysis in: Dumberry, *State Succession to International Responsibility*, 127–128.

325   *Levy v. German State*, French-German Mixed Arbitral Tribunal, Award of 10 July 1924, in: 4 *Recueil des décisions des tribunaux arbitraux mixtes* 726; (1923–1924) *Annual Digest*, case no. 27. See analysis in: Dumberry, ibid., 127; ILC Special Rapporteur, Second Report, 2018, para. 140.

326   *Kalmar v. Hungarian Treasury*, Supreme Court of Hungary, 24 March 1929, case no. P.VI.5473/1928, in: *Maganjog Tara*, X, no. 75; (1929–1930) *Annual Digest* 61.

327   *Personal Injuries (Upper Silesia) Case*, Court of Appeal of Cologne, FRG, 10 December 1951, in: (1952) 5 *NJW* 1300; (1951) ILR 67ff. The case is discussed in: Dumberry, *State Succession to International Responsibility*, 133.

328   The point is further examined in: Dumberry, ibid., 125.

of territory.[329] The case involved concession rights obtained in 1860 by a French company from the Ottoman Empire for maintaining lighthouses in Crete, a territory then under Ottoman sovereignty that became Greek later on. Several claims (contractual and delictual) were brought by the French owner of the concession (*la Société Collas et Michel*) against Greece after the transfer of the territory by the Ottoman Empire to Greece in 1913. Greece had expropriated the concession during the First World War. One such claim (Claim no. 12–a) was submitted by France against Greece (the successor State) for acts allegedly entirely committed by the Ottoman Empire (the predecessor State). The alleged internationally wrongful act was the unauthorised removal by the Ottoman Empire of a buoy belonging to the French company. The Arbitral Tribunal ruled that the Ottoman authorities had not committed any internationally wrongful act and that the acts were legitimate for reasons of security. In an *obiter dictum*, the Arbitral Tribunal nevertheless indicated that even if the Ottoman Empire had committed an internationally wrongful act, Greece could not have been held liable for it. It is Turkey (the continuing State of the Ottoman Empire[330]) which would be liable for its 'own' acts committed before the loss of a substantial portion of its territory.[331] This solution was in accordance with Article 9 of Protocol XII of the *Lausanne Peace Treaty* of 24 July 1923.[332] As further examined in the next section, the reasoning of the Tribunal regarding another claim illustrates the existence of an exception to this general rule of non-succession.

2   Exception: Situations Calling for the Transfer of Rights and Obligations to the Successor State

228.   To the general principle of non-succession set out at Article 11(1), the second and third paragraphs of this provision provide for two exceptions. While the first exception (at Article 11(2)) deals with the question of succession to *rights* arising from the commission of a wrongful act (Section 2.1), the second one (Article 11(3)) concerns succession to *obligations* (Section 2.2).

2.1   THE EXISTENCE OF A 'DIRECT LINK' BETWEEN THE CONSEQUENCES OF A WRONGFUL ACT AND THE TERRITORY TRANSFERRED AND/OR ITS POPULATION

229.   The first exception is mentioned at Article 11(2). It concerns the specific situation of the existence of a 'direct link' between the consequences of an internationally wrongful

---

329   *Lighthouse Arbitration* case, 81. This case is examined in: Dumberry, ibid., 130ff; ILC Special Rapporteur, Second Report, 2018, paras. 142ff.
330   On the question whether or not Turkey should be considered as the same State as the Ottoman Empire under international law, see, inter alia: P. Dumberry, 'Is Turkey the "Continuing" State of the Ottoman Empire under International Law?' (2012) 59(2) *Netherlands ILR* 235–262; P. Dumberry, 'Turkey's International Responsibility for Internationally Wrongful Acts Committed by the Ottoman Empire' (2012) 42, *Revue générale de droit* 562–589.
331   See also the reasoning of the Tribunal regarding Claim no. 11.
332   Treaty of Peace of Lausanne, signed on 24 July 1923, in: (1923) UKTS No. 16 (Cmd. 1929); 28 LNTS 11; (1924) 18 *AJIL* Supp., 4.

act committed *against* the predecessor State before the date of succession and the territory transferred and/or the population of that territory.[333] Whenever there exists such a
link the *rights* arising from the act pass to the successor State. In other words, after the
date of succession, the successor State becomes the holder of any right arising from the
consequences of the commission of a wrongful act which has directly affected the territory
transferred (and/or its population). Article 11(2) is a concrete illustration in the specific
context of transfer of territory of the general principle set out at Article 5(2).

230.   As highlighted in the Final Report, the question of where a wrongful act took place
is, in general, not 'necessarily decisive'.[334] The Report explains why this is so:

> Acts committed within or in relation to a given territory can be the result of
> centrally controlled organs, and not necessarily those of the territorial unit in
> which those acts were performed. Moreover, internationally wrongful acts
> can be committed inside or outside the territory of the author or the injured
> State, and the place where the acts were committed is irrelevant, unless the
> spatial element forms part of the elements of the primary obligation that has
> been violated'. What is essential in the field of international responsibility is
> the personal or subjective element – i.e. the attribution of an illegal conduct to
> a State or other subject of international law – and not the spatial element. An
> exception would be the violation of obligations related to territorial regimes,
> which, by definition, includes rights and obligations attached to a given ter-
> ritory. This is probably the clearest example in which the primary obligation
> contains a spatial element.[335]

231.   In the past, while some writers have emphasised the importance of where an internationally wrongful act was actually committed to determine which State should bear the
responsibility for it,[336] others have rejected such position.[337] One of the authors of this
Commentary explained the reason why the importance of the spatial element is relative:

> There is no principle under positive international law whereby the successor
> State is *automatically* responsible for obligations arising from internation-
> ally wrongful acts committed by the predecessor State before the date of
> succession *solely based* on the fact that such acts took place on what is now
> its territory. In other words, the fact that an internationally wrongful act took
> place on the territory of the new State before its independence should not, *in
> itself*, be a ground for finding this State responsible for such act. The question
> of where an internationally wrongful act was committed is in fact *only one*

---

333 As further examined below, the expression 'direct link' is also used in Articles 12(2) (separation), 16(2)
     (newly independent States), and 15(2) (dissolution).
334 Final Report, paras. 57–58, in: (2015) 76 *Annuaire de l'Institut de Droit international*, 535.
335 Ibid.
336 See, for instance, Charles Cheney Hyde, *International Law Chiefly as Interpreted and Applied by the
     United States*, 2nd ed., vol. I (Boston, MA: Little, Brown & Co., 1945), 437–438.
337 Udina, 'La succession des Etats quant aux obligations internationales autres que les dettes publiques',
     690, 767; Monnier, 'La succession d'Etats en matière de responsabilité internationale', 88–89.

relevant element out of many which need to be taken into account in determining which State should be responsible for such act.

Any general theory to the contrary would anyway be quite limited in its scope of application, as it would not be able to deal with internationally wrongful acts committed *outside* the territory of the predecessor State. The concrete application of such general theory could also lead, in certain circumstances, to unfair results. Such would certainly be the case whenever an internationally wrongful act is committed before the date of succession in the territory of a new State but with which that new State had nothing to do and for which it received no benefit or advantage. In such circumstances, it would seem unfair to transfer to the new State the obligations arising from the commission of the act only based on the fact that it took place on what is now its territory.[338]

232. It should be added, however, that there is one specific area where the territorial element is truly central and explains the existence of the exception under Article 11(2). This is the case of violations of territorial regime obligations.[339] The special importance of territorial regime is recognised by the Final Report mentioning that 'an exception would be the violation of obligations related to territorial regimes, which, by definition, includes rights and obligations attached to a given territory'.[340] One clear example of such a situation, although not concerning a case of transfer of territory, is the *Gabčíkovo-Nagymaros Project* case. The case involved an agreement concerning the construction and joint operation of a large barrage system along the Danube river concluded between Hungary and Czechoslovakia in 1977.[341] On the Czechoslovakian side, the project was located on Slovakian territory. After the dissolution of Czechoslovakia in 1992, Slovakia solely took over the rights and obligations stemming from the conduct of the predecessor State. According to the Court, the 1977 Treaty had established the navigational regime for the Danube and created a situation where the interests of other users of the Danube were affected. The Treaty being of a 'territorial character', the rights and obligations which were 'attached' to part of the Danube were therefore unaffected by the succession of States. For that reason, Slovakia was bound by the Treaty.[342]

233. In any event, what matters (apart from the special case of territorial regimes) is not *where* the wrongful act took place, but rather to identify the *consequences* arising from such an act. What is relevant, according to the Final Report, is the 'existence of a direct link between the *consequences* of the internationally wrongful act and the

---

338 Dumberry, *State Succession to International Responsibility*, 287 (emphasis in the original).
339 See the analysis in: ibid., 288ff.
340 Final Report, para. 58, in: (2015) 76 *Annuaire de l'Institut de Droit international*, 535, adding: 'Wrongful acts whose core element is territory, such as in the case of violations of obligations stemming from territorial regimes or in relation to acts that must essentially be accomplished within a given territory, for its benefit or as a burden to it (for example, works benefitting a specific area, rights of passage on a given territory, fishing rights in a given waterway), deserve an exceptional treatment' (at para. 61).
341 *Gabčíkovo-Nagymaros Project* case, 7.
342 Ibid., para. 123.

territory or the population that becomes part of the territory or the population of the successor State'.[343]

234.   There are many possible examples illustrating the existence of such territorial direct link. For instance, this should be the case whenever the act is affecting *one* territory specifically, such as in the context of pollution and other forms of environmental damage. One could also think of the destruction of property located in the territory transferred to the successor State. Another example would be illegal fishing and other violations of the law of the sea committed within the territorial sea or the internal waters of the territory transferred. What matters is that the consequences of these wrongful acts are felt in the territory of *that* successor State (not in that of others) or, in the context of Article 11(2), in *that* territory transferred.

235.   Regarding the existence of a direct link between the consequences of a wrongful act and a population concerned, the Final Report indicates that 'if the population directly concerned by the wrongful act becomes the population of the successor State, the situation also deserves to constitute an exception to the non-succession rule in cases in which the predecessor State continues to exist.'[344] One illustration of this principle would be, for instance, any wrongful acts targeting the population in one specific area of the predecessor State which later becomes the territory of the successor State.[345]

236.   Finally, it should be noted that the Resolution only recognises the importance of the existence of a direct link between the consequences of an internationally wrongful act and the territory transferred and/or the population of that territory in the specific context of *succession to rights*. The situation is different for *obligations* arising from an internationally wrongful act committed by the predecessor State. In such a case, the author of the act is the State through its organs and not its population, irrespective of the place where the act was committed. Hence, the 'direct link' exception under Article 11(2) is not applicable when the internationally wrongful act was committed *by* the predecessor State.[346] In such a case, the solution of non-succession identified at Article 11(1) should therefore generally prevail.

237.   Nevertheless, it may be argued that in some situations the consequences of an internationally wrongful act committed *by* the predecessor State will be directly linked to the *territory* transferred to the successor State. This would be the case, for instance, in the event of an expropriation without compensation taking place in that territory. In such a

---

343   Final Report, para. 60, in: (2015) 76 *Annuaire de l'Institut de Droit international*, 536 (emphasis added).
344   Final Report, para. 62, in: (2015) 76 *Annuaire de l'Institut de Droit international*, 536.
345   It should be noted that Draft Article 9(3) proposed by ILC Special Rapporteur, Second Report, 2018, does not refer to 'population', but only to the link with the territory of the successor State.
346   As further discussed in the following paragraphs, a different approach has been adopted in: ILC Special Rapporteur, Second Report, 2018, para. 144. See Draft Article 9(3). The other question regarding succession to the right to claim reparation will be examined in the Special Rapporteur's Third Report (see para. 21) (not yet published at the time of writing).

case, the predecessor State has benefited from the act of expropriation before the date of succession for the simple reason that it did not pay any compensation to the owner of the property expropriated. Thus, in the event where the property expropriated is located in the territory transferred to the successor State, different options are available. It may be that the successor State will not continue the illegal conduct and recognises the foreign property. If, on the contrary, the successor State continues the illegal expropriation, the situation is then covered by Article 9 of the Resolution.

238.   In his First Report, the ILC Special Rapporteur provides the following example of State practice involving a situation where there is a direct link between the consequences of an internationally wrongful act and the territory transferred to the successor State:

> The transfer of responsibility was also invoked in the case of cession of the Tarapacá region by Peru to Chile in 1883. In the view of Italy, 'the action taken with respect to the Tarapacá nitrate mines by the Peruvian Domain (action which is to be still to be [*sic*] considered as a disguised form of forced expropriation) was *Government action*, responsibility for which has now passed from the old to the new ruler of the province, from Peru to Chile'.[347]

239.   In his Second Report, ILC Special Rapporteur refers to Claim no. 4 decided by the *Lighthouse Arbitration* case[348] as one example of a situation where there also exists such a 'direct link between the consequences of this act and the territory transferred'.[349]

240.   In fact, ILC Draft Article 9(3) specifically refers to the existence of such a linkage as one situation where the succession solution could prevail in the context of the transfer of the *obligation* to repair.[350] Yet, it should be added that the provision is drafted only as a possible exception (it uses the expression 'if particular circumstances so require'). Another important feature of this provision is the fact that it envisages the assumption of the obligation to repair to *both* the predecessor and the successor State.[351]

---

347   ILC Special Rapporteur, First Report, 2017, para. 45 (emphasis in the original), quoting the Observations from the Government of Italy, in: United Nations, Legislative Series, Materials on Succession of States in Respect of Matters other than Treaties, ST/LEG/SER.B/17 (United Nations publication, Sales No. E/F.77.V.9), 126.

348   See analysis under Section 2.2 below.

349   ILC Special Rapporteur, Second Report, 2018, para. 145.

350   Ibid., see Draft Article 9(3): 'If particular circumstances so require, the obligations arising from an internationally wrongful act of the predecessor State, where there is a direct link between the act or its consequences and the territory of the successor State or States, are assumed by the predecessor and the successor State'. As mentioned above, the provision does not refer to 'population', but only to the link with the territory of the successor State.

351   ILC Special Rapporteur, Second Report, 2018, para. 145, provides the following explanation: 'Another aspect may be a direct link between the consequences of this act and the territory transferred. The last aspect could be even more relevant if the injured State or subject required not just a financial compensation but restitution, which would clearly be outside of powers of the predecessor State after the cession of the territory in question. At the same time, this possible exception is limited, as the financial compensation for damage caused before the date of succession can also be required from the predecessor State.'

2.2 THE AUTHOR OF THE WRONGFUL ACT WAS AN ORGAN OF THE PREDECESSOR STATE THAT LATER BECAME AN ORGAN OF THE SUCCESSOR STATE

241. Article 11(3) provides for a second exception to the principle of non-succession. This exception concerns the specific situation where the author of a wrongful act was an 'organ of the territorial unit of the predecessor State that has later become an organ of the successor State'.[352] When this is the case, the *obligations* arising from such an act may pass to the successor State. This is also the solution followed by the ILC Special Rapporteur at Draft Article 9(2).[353]

242. Yet, according to the Final Report, this is a 'possible' exception which can apply only if 'particular circumstances so require'.[354] The same approach has also been adopted by the ILC Special Rapporteur.[355] The wording used under Article 11(3) reflects a rather restrictive approach, which is in accordance with the general position adopted by the Resolution under Article 4. Under that provision, a State is responsible for its own acts; if the predecessor State author of the wrongful act continues to exist after the date of succession, it must face its own responsibility. In other words, in normal circumstances, the obligation to repair should remain with the predecessor State in accordance with Article 11(1). The exceptional solution envisaged at Article 11(3) will only find application in 'particular circumstances'. The concrete application of the exception under Article 11(3) will ultimately depend on the prevailing circumstances of each case, as explained in the Final Report:

> if the author of the internationally wrongful act was the organ of an administrative unit of the predecessor State that later becomes the organ of the new State, the possibility *might* exist that the latter succeeds to the obligations stemming from that act. One circumstance could be the existence of some benefit derived from the internationally wrongful act. However, different circumstances which it is not possible to determine beforehand may lead to the opposite solution.[356]

243. Article 12(3), dealing with cases of separation of parts of a State, follows the same restrictive approach. Similarly, under Article 15(3), dealing with dissolution of a State, the 'organ' exception is just one 'relevant factor' among others to be taken into account

---

352 On this question, see the analysis in: Dumberry, *State Succession to International Responsibility*, 136.
353 ILC Special Rapporteur, First Report, 2017, paras. 144–145; ILC Special Rapporteur, Second Report, 2018, para. 139. See Draft Article 9(2): 'If particular circumstances so require, the obligations arising from an internationally wrongful act of the predecessor State will transfer to the successor State when the act was carried out by an organ of a territorial unit of the predecessor that has later become an organ of the successor State'.
354 Final Report, para. 63, in: (2015) 76 *Annuaire de l'Institut de Droit international*, 536.
355 Draft Article 9(2) uses the expression if 'particular circumstances so require'. See also: ILC Special Rapporteur, Second Report, 2018, para. 144, referring to 'possible exceptions to the general rule of non-succession'.
356 Final Report, para. 65, in: (2015) 76 *Annuaire de l'Institut de Droit international*, 537 (emphasis in the original).

in determining which of the different successor States should take over the obligation to repair.[357]

244.   One exceptional circumstance where the solution set out at Article 11(3) could find application is a situation similar to that involving acts committed by insurrectional or national liberation movements in their struggle for independence.[358] As further examined below, under Article 12(6) of the Resolution in the context of separation, these acts are attributed to the new State. We explain below[359] that the basic reason why a new State should take over responsibility for acts committed by an insurrectional movement is because there is a *structural continuity* between the new State and the actual wrongdoer. The same logic may also apply more generally when there exists the same type of organic and structural continuity between that new State and an organ of the territorial unit of the predecessor State which committed the wrongful act before the date of succession.[360] Article 11(3) envisages the possibility that the same circumstances may also prevail in the context of a transfer of territory.

245.   Case law supports the solution envisaged at Article 11(3). One example is the decision taken by the Court of the Aegean Islands (Greece) in the *Samos (Liability for Torts) case* in the context of the cession of the Aegean Islands by the Ottoman Empire to Greece in 1913.[361] It concerned damage allegedly caused by customs officials of the Island of Samos at the time when it was still under Ottoman rule.[362] The Court held that Greece substituted the former Principality of Samos and that it must be deemed to be responsible for the injurious acts complained about which took place before the cession of territory. In other words, it held that as the successor State, Greece should be held accountable for internationally wrongful acts committed before the date of succession. The reason why this succession solution was adopted by the Court is because of the autonomous status which the island enjoyed prior to its formal cession to Greece in 1913.[363]

246.   Another relevant example is the decision of the Arbitral Tribunal in the *Lighthouse Arbitration* case already mentioned above.[364] Claim no. 4 dealt with tax exemptions granted to a Greek shipping company and its ship (the *Haghios Nicolaos*) by a law proclaimed by the local authorities of Crete in 1908, at the time when the island was still under Ottoman sovereignty. After 1913, when the island became officially part of Greece, the law remained

---

357   Importantly, the situation is entirely different for newly independent States whereby under Article 16(3) the conduct of the national liberation movement 'shall be considered the act of the new State'.
358   Dumberry, *State Succession to International Responsibility*, 260.
359   See below analysis of Article 12(6).
360   The same position is adopted in: ILC Special Rapporteur, Second Report, 2018, para. 112: 'The very same argument [as those used under ILC Article 10(2)] could be used also for State organs of the predecessor that evolved into State organs of the successor, especially if they consist of the same personnel, which is the case in many situations'.
361   *Samos (Liability for Torts) Case*, Greece, Court of the Aegean Islands, 1924, N° 27, in: 35 *Thémis* 294; (1923–1924) *Annual Digest* 70.
362   The case is examined in: Dumberry, *State Succession to International Responsibility*, 141.
363   O'Connell, *State Succession in Municipal Law*, 492; Jacques Barde, *La notion de droit acquis en droit international public* (Paris: Publ. univ. de Paris, 1981), at 179; Dumberry, *State Succession to International Responsibility*, 261.
364   *Lighthouse Arbitration* case, at 196–200.

in place. This tax exemption was alleged by the claimant, a French company, to be in violation of its existing concession rights. France therefore sought reparation from Greece.

247.   The Tribunal indicated that the liability of Greece should not be based on the provisions of the *Lausanne Peace Treaty* of 1923 which dealt with the rights and obligations of Turkey and not Crete. It added that Greece's responsibility 'could result only from a transmission of responsibility in accordance with the rules of customary law or the general principles of law regulating the succession of States in general'.[365] The Arbitral Tribunal concluded that the acts constituted breaches of a *contractual* obligation,[366] which had been committed by the authorities of Crete, described as an 'autonomous island State the population of which had for decades passionately aspired to be united, by force of arms if necessary, with Greece, which was regarded as the mother country'.[367] The Tribunal concluded on this point that:

> [T]he Tribunal can only come to the conclusion that Greece, having adopted the illegal conduct of Crete in its recent past as autonomous State, is bound, as successor State, to take upon its charge the financial consequences of the breach of the concession contract. Otherwise, the avowed violation of a contract committed by one of the two States, linked by a common past and a common destiny, with the assent of the other, would, in the event of their merger, have the thoroughly unjust consequence of cancelling a definite financial responsibility and of sacrificing the undoubted rights of a private firm holding a concession to a so-called general principle of non-transmission of debts in cases of territorial succession, which in reality does not exist as a general and absolute principle.[368]

248.   There is no doubt that Greece was held responsible for its *own* internationally wrongful acts (delict of omission) committed *after* 1913 when Crete was officially ceded to Greece. Greece was thus responsible for maintaining in place the discriminatory practice *after* it had undeniable sovereignty over the island.[369] This is therefore an example of the successor State being held responsible for *continuing* (after the date of succession) a wrongful act.[370] The reasoning of the Tribunal suggests that Greece was *also* held liable for the acts committed *before* the transfer of territory.[371] We have already examined above the question as to whether or not a successor State can be held responsible for the consequences of the portion of a *continuing* wrongful act which took place *before* the date

365   Ibid., at 90.
366   The Tribunal noted that its conclusion would have been the same even if the obligation had been regarded as *delictual* and not contractual. See ibid., at 92.
367   Ibid., at 92.
368   Ibid.
369   See analysis in: Dumberry, *State Succession to International Responsibility*, 136; ILC Special Rapporteur, Second Report, 2018, para. 145.
370   See Article 9(1) and the analysis above.
371   There is a controversy among scholars as to whether or not this is actually the case. See the analysis and the position of writers on the matter in: Dumberry, *State Succession to International Responsibility*, 138–141.

of succession.[372] One reason why the Tribunal held that Greece was responsible is because the acts were committed by the largely autonomous government of Crete before the date of succession.[373]

ARTICLE 12:

Separation of parts of a State

1.   With the exception of the situations referred to in paragraphs 2 to 4 of the present Article, the rights and obligations arising from an internationally wrongful act in relation to which the predecessor State has been either the author or the injured State do not pass to the successor State or States when a part or parts of the territory of a State separate to form one or more States and the predecessor State continues to exist.

2.   The rights arising from an internationally wrongful act committed against the predecessor State pass to the successor State or States if there exists a direct link between the consequences of this act and the territory or the population of the successor State or States.

3.   If particular circumstances so require, the obligations arising from the commission of an internationally wrongful act by the predecessor State pass to the successor State when the author of that act was an organ of a territorial unit of the predecessor State that has later become an organ of the successor State.

4.   If particular circumstances indicated in paragraphs 2 and 3 of this Article so require, the obligations arising from an internationally wrongful act committed before the date of succession of States are assumed by the predecessor and the successor State or States.

5.   In order to determine an equitable apportionment of the rights or obligations of the predecessor and the successor States, criteria that may be taken into consideration include the existence of any special connections with the act giving rise to international responsibility, the size of the territory and of the population, the respective contributions to the gross domestic product of the States concerned at the date of succession of States, the need to avoid unjust enrichment and any other circumstance relevant to the case. The provisions of Article 7 apply *mutatis mutandis*.

---

372   See analysis of Article 9(1) above.
373   See analysis in: Dumberry, *State Succession to International Responsibility*, 140. See also: ILC Special Rapporteur, Second Report, 2018, para. 145 ('there are also other particular circumstances that may justify the transfer of obligations arising from the wrongful acts of the predecessor State (continuing) to the successor State. Here, the award underlines the autonomous status of a territory under the Ottoman Empire').

6. The internationally wrongful act of an insurrectional or other movement which succeeds in establishing a new State on part of the territory of the predecessor State or in a territory under the administration of this latter State shall be considered an act of the new State under international law. Consequently, the predecessor State incurs no responsibility for the acts committed by the insurrectional or other movement.

Commentary

249. This provision deals with the question of succession to rights and obligations arising from the commission of an internationally wrongful act when part (or parts) of the territory of a State separates to form one or more new States. One important feature of this type of succession of States is the fact that the predecessor State continues to exist after the date of succession, although diminished in its population and territory.

250. The most recent case of separation is the creation of the Republic of South Sudan on 9 July 2011, which was admitted as the 193rd Member State of the United Nations.[374] The prior uncontroversial case of separation is that of Montenegro which separated from the State Union of Serbia and Montenegro on 3 June 2006 and became the 192nd Member State of the United Nations.[375] These are cases in which the predecessor State agreed to the separation. It is in fact possible to distinguish between cases of separation on the basis of whether or not any such consent by the dismembered State exists.[376] Cases of separation without consent are sometimes referred to as 'secession', while other situations where such consent exists are known as 'devolution'.[377] In fact, another distinction can be made depending on whether the consent of the predecessor State is given before or after the creation of the new State. Examples of the former are those mentioned before as well as all other cases involving a devolution agreement, such as the case of the separation of Singapore from Malaysia in 1965.[378] An example of secession where the predecessor State later recognised the newly created State is that of Bangladesh, which separated from Pakistan in 1971 and was recognised by the latter in 1974.[379] The Resolution does not distinguish between these different concepts and the term 'separation' is therefore used to cover all situations of separation notwithstanding the question of the timing of the existence of consent by the predecessor State.[380]

---

374 UN GA Resolution 65/308 of 25 August 2011.
375 UN GA Resolution A/60/264 of 12 July 2006.
376 M.G. Kohen, 'Le problème des frontières en cas de dissolution et de séparation d'États: quelles alternatives?', in: O. Corten et al. (eds.), *Démembrement d'États et délimitations territoriales: L'uti possidetis en question(s)* (Brussels: Bruylant, 1999) at 368–369; M.G. Kohen, 'La création d'Etats en droit international contemporain' (2002) 6 *Bancaja Euromediterranean Courses of International Law*, 572; J. Crawford, *The Creation of States in International Law*, 2nd ed. (Oxford: OUP, 2006), 330, 375.
377 O'Connell, *State Succession in Municipal Law*, 88, uses a different dichotomy by distinguishing between cases of 'evolutionary secession' and 'revolutionary secession'. The ILC Special Rapporteur uses a similar terminology (ILC Special Rapporteur, First Report, 2017, para. 25).
378 *Agreement relating to the Separation of Singapore from Malaysia as an Independent and Sovereign State.*
379 Soon after, Bangladesh was admitted to the UN: GA Resolution 3203 (1974), 17 September 1974.
380 The same position is adopted by the ILC Special Rapporteur, Second Report, 2018, para. 79, indicating that 'there are no different meanings given' to the different terms secession and separation and that 'they can be used interchangeably'.

251.   The provision also envisages the possibility that more than one part of a State separates from the predecessor State leading to the creation of *several* new States. These collective cases of separation are legally more complex to grasp than the typical case involving the creation of only one State. The difficult legal question is to differentiate between cases involving a collective separation and those other instances of dissolution. In this context, one crucial point will be whether or not a predecessor State still continues to exist after the date of succession. That very question is, however, sometimes controversial.[381] Examples of such a situation are the break-up of the SFRY and the USSR in 1990 and 1991. The case of the SFRY will be discussed below when analysing Article 15 (dissolution). The terminology employed in the case of the USSR raised some controversy. All States accepted the continuing character of the Russian Federation with regards to the USSR.[382] However, the Minsk Agreement and the Declaration of Alma Ata concluded by constituent Soviet Republics of the USSR referred to it as having 'ceased to exist'.[383] Yet, these statements were merely political. From a legal perspective, the break-up of the USSR should be considered as a case of separation (except for the three Baltic States which are not considered as 'new' States[384]) with Russia being the continuing State.[385]

252.   Article 12(1) sets out the general solution of non-succession which should prevail (discussed in Section 1), while Articles 12(2) and 12(3) deal with two exceptions where there should be a transfer of rights and obligations to the successor State(s) (Section 2). Articles 12(4) and 12(5) envisage the situation where the consequences stemming from an internationally wrongful act may be shared by both the predecessor and the successor State(s) (Section 3). Finally, Article 12(6) deals with the specific situation of acts committed by an insurrectional or national liberation movement (Section 4).

1   Principle: No Transfer of Rights and Obligations to the Successor State

253.   Under Article 12(1), the rights and obligations arising from an internationally wrongful act in relation to which the predecessor State was either the author or the injured State do *not* pass to the successor State when a part (or parts) of the territory of the predecessor State separates to form one (or more) new State(s). Following the general principles set out in Articles 4 and 5 of the Resolution, the criteria of non-succession is adopted in this

---

381   See Article 4, Institut de Droit international, 'State Succession in Matters of Property and Debts'.
382   Letter of Russia to the UN Secretary-General, 24 December 1991, in: UN Doc 1991/RUSSIA, Appendix, 24 December 1991, (1991) 31 ILM 138.
383   The preamble to the Minsk Agreement (*Agreement Establishing the Commonwealth of Independent States*, UN Doc A/46/771, 13 December 1991, in: (1992) 31 ILM 138) clearly states that the USSR 'as a subject of international law and geopolitical reality no longer exists'. *The Alma Ata Declaration*, 21 December 1991, UN Doc A/46/60, 30 December 1991, (1992) 31 ILM 147, also mentions that 'with the establishment of the C.I.S., the USSR ceases to exist'.
384   L. Mälksoo, *Illegal Annexation and State Continuity: The Case of the Incorporation of the Baltic States by the USSR (A Study of the Tension between Normativity and Power in International Law)* (Leiden: Martinus Nijhoff Publ., 2003) at 255–256.
385   The same conclusion is reached in: ILC Special Rapporteur, Second Report, 2018, paras. 84ff.

situation for the simple reason that the predecessor State continues to exist following the separation of part(s) of its territory. That State therefore remains the holder of rights and obligations arising from wrongful acts which took place before the date of succession.

254. This general solution of non-succession for cases of separation is supported by scholars.[386] It is also followed by the ILC Special Rapporteur at Draft Article 7(1).[387] Many municipal law cases, one ICJ case and a number of examples of State practice also support this solution.[388] These examples are briefly examined in the next paragraphs.

255. The principle of non-succession is well established by decisions of municipal courts in the context of the restoration of Poland as an independent State in 1918. Its territory was comprised of territories which previously belonged to Austria-Hungary, Germany and Russia. This principle was adopted by the Supreme Court of Poland regarding acts which were committed by the railway authorities of the Russian Empire before the date of succession.[389] The same Court also concluded that Austria was not a new State in 1917 and that, accordingly, it should be held accountable for the illegal acts committed by Austria-Hungary before that date.[390] The principle of non-succession was also applied by one municipal court of one of the continuing States (Germany) regarding acts committed by Prussia in 1913 when the territory was still part of Germany before the creation of Poland.[391] Yet, it should be noted that these municipal law cases do not involve questions of succession to the consequences of responsibility, as the wrongful acts were committed by the predecessor State not against another State (or a national of another State) but against *its own nationals* (which became nationals of the successor State after the date of succession).[392]

256. A review of State practice shows a clear tendency in support of the principle that whenever the predecessor State continues to exist after the separation of part of its

---

386 See analysis in: Dumberry, *State Succession to International Responsibility*, 142ff, mentioning the position of scholars at 143, including Stern, 'Responsabilité internationale et succession d'États', 335–336; Czapliński, 'State Succession and State Responsibility', 357; Marek, *Identity and Continuity of States,* 11; Volkovitsch, 'Righting Wrongs: Toward a New Theory of State Succession to Responsibility of International Delicts', 2200.

387 ILC Special Rapporteur, First Report, 2017, para. 17; ILC Special Rapporteur, Second Report, 2018, paras. 46, 77, 80. See Draft Article 7(1): 'Subject to the exceptions referred to in paragraphs 2 and 3, the obligations arising from an internationally wrongful act of the predecessor State do not pass to the successor State in case of secession of a part or parts of the territory of a State to form one or more States, if the predecessor State continues to exist'.

388 See analysis in: Dumberry, *State Succession to International Responsibility*, 145ff; See also examples of State practice examined in: ILC Special Rapporteur, Second Report, 2018, paras. 80ff.

389 *Dzierzbicki v. District Electric Association of Czestochowa*, Supreme Court of Poland, First Division, 21 December 1933, in: (1934) OSP no. 288; (1933–1934) *Annual Digest* 89. See analysis in: Dumberry, *State Succession to International Responsibility*, 146–148.

390 *Niemiec and Niemiec v. Bialobrodziec and Polish State Treasury*, decided by the Supreme Court of Poland, Third Division, 20 February 1923, in: 2 *Annual Digest*, case no. 33; *Olpinski v. Polish Treasury (Railway Division)*, Supreme Court of Poland, Third Division, 16 April 1921, OSP I, no. 15; (1919–1922) *Annual Digest* 63. See analysis in: Dumberry, ibid., 146–148

391 *Baron A. v. PrussianTreasury*, Germany, Reichsgericht in Civil Matters, 19 December 1923, in: 107 ERZ 382; (1923–1924) *Annual Digest* 60.

392 On this question, see Dumberry, *State Succession to International Responsibility*, 143, 30.

territory, that State should remain responsible for the commission of *its own* internationally wrongful acts.[393]

257.   Two examples of State practice arose in the context of the break-up of the USSR in 1991. The first example is a treaty entered into by the Russian Federation (as the continuing State) with Germany in 1992 whereby the former continued its responsibility for internationally wrongful acts committed by the USSR during and after the Second World War, namely for the pillage of works of art and cultural property in Germany.[394]

258.   The second example is a treaty signed with France in 1997 whereby the Russian Federation continued the responsibility arising from measures of expropriation of bonds issued in France which were taken by Soviet Russia after the 1917 Revolution.[395] In this agreement, Russia is therefore considered as the continuing State of the Soviet Union, which was itself the 'continuator' of the Russian State existing between 1917 and 1922.[396] The Agreement provides for Russia to compensate France in the amount of US$400 million in exchange for guarantees that France would not exercise diplomatic protection for claims of French nationals and corporations against Russia arising out of the non-payment of bonds expropriated after the 1917 Revolution.[397] The Agreement is construed as a set-off, whereby Russia agreed not to pursue claims for reparation which the USSR had for many years against France. Article 2(al. a) of the Agreement thus makes reference to the claims linked to the Western intervention of 1918–1922 and other military or hostile operations undertaken by Western States (including France) against the new Soviet government during that period.[398] From the information available, it does not appear that France objected to the fact that such claims for reparation were part of the negotiations leading to the Agreement. This is certainly because France considered Russia to be the legal 'continuator' of the USSR and believed that, consequently, it remained entitled to submit a claim for reparation arising from damage which occurred before the break-up of the USSR This is therefore a good illustration of the solution set out at Article 12(1)

---

393   Ibid., 142ff.

394   *Abkommen zwischen der Regierung der Bundesrepublik Deutschland und der Regierung der Russischen Föderation über kulturelle Zusammenarbeit*, 16 December 1992, in: (1993) II BGBl. 1256; see at Article 15. See analysis in: Dumberry, ibid., 153ff; Crawford, *State Responsibility: The General Part*, 453; Jakubowski, *State Succession in Cultural Property*, 195–196, and more generally at 205ff; ILC Special Rapporteur, Second Report, 2018, para. 89.

395   *Accord du 27 mai 1997 entre le Gouvernement de la République française et le Gouvernement de la Fédération de Russie sur le règlement définitif des créances réciproques financières et réelles apparues antérieurement au 9 mai 1945*. The Agreement and the Memorandum of 26 November 1996 for mutual understanding were approved by the French National Assembly on 19 December 1997 (Bill No. 97–1160, in: *JORF*, 15 May 1998). The historical background and a comprehensive analysis of the Agreement can be found in: Sandra Szurek, 'Epilogue d'un contentieux historique. L'accord sur le règlement des créances réciproque entre la France et la Russie' (1998) 44 *AFDI* 144–166; P. Juillard & B. Stern (eds.), *Les emprunts russes et le règlement du contentieux financier franco-russe* (Paris: Cedin Cahiers internationaux n°16, 2002), and, in particular, the article by Eisemann, 'Emprunts russes et problèmes de succession d'Etats', ibid., at 53–78.

396   Crawford, *State Responsibility: The General Part*, 452–453.

397   See Dumberry, *State Succession to International Responsibility*, 323–324; Crawford, *State Responsibility: The General Part*, 452–453; ILC Special Rapporteur, Second Report, 2018, para. 89.

398   Michel Cosnard, 'Les créances au titre de l'intervention occidentale de 1919–1922', in: Juillard & Stern, *Les emprunts russes et le règlement du contentieux financier franco-russe*, 121–149.

of the Resolution whereby both *rights* and *obligations* arising from wrongful acts do not pass to the successor State(s), but remain those of the predecessor State.

259.   This principle of non-succession is also supported by one example concerning the German Democratic Republic (GDR), which considered itself to be a new State different from the German Reich. On the contrary, the FRG was considered to be the continuing State of the German Reich.[399] The official position taken by the GDR was that as a new State, it could not be held responsible for any obligations arising from internationally wrongful acts committed before and during the Second World War.[400] One illustration is the position adopted by the GDR with respect to the claim of Libya for damages arising from the presence of remnants of the Second World War on its territory. The GDR refused to cooperate with Libya on the ground that it could not be held accountable for the acts committed by the Third Reich.

260.   Another older example of State practice supporting the principle of non-succession is the position taken by the 'Allied and Associated Powers' in the context of the break-up of the Austria-Hungary Dual Monarchy in 1918.[401] The legal qualification of this break-up is controversial. It has been debated whether it should be understood as a dissolution of State or instead as a case involving the secession of Poland, Czechoslovakia and Yugoslavia (with both Austria and Hungary being considered as the continuing States). The majority of writers are of the opinion that this is a case of dissolution of a State.[402] This was also the position of Austria.[403] What is relevant for the present purpose is that the 'Allied and Associated Powers' (the British Empire, France, Italy, Japan, United States, etc.) took the view that this was not a case of State dissolution. They believed that post-War Austria and Hungary were in fact *identical* with the now extinct Dual Monarchy.[404] They insisted on both States being considered as continuing States in order to ensure that they would be held responsible for the internationally wrongful acts committed by the Dual Monarchy during the war.[405] They feared that if the break-up of Austria-Hungary were to be interpreted as a case of dissolution, the 'rule' of non-succession would apply. The Peace Treaty of

---

399   The question of the proper status of the GDR is controversial. For an overview of the issue, see: Dumberry, *State Succession to International Responsibility*, 148–149.
400   See ibid., 149. Yet it should be added that there are some other examples which support the opposite position of succession to responsibility. For instance, the GDR actually paid war reparation to the USSR for acts committed during the Second World War. The GDR also made an offer of compensation to Jewish groups for acts committed during the War. These examples are discussed in: ibid., 165–168.
401   See ibid., 145ff. The example is also examined in: ILC Special Rapporteur, Second Report, 2018, paras. 82ff.
402   An overview of the legal arguments advanced by both sides in doctrine is found in: Oskar Lehner, 'The Identity of Austria 1918/19 as a problem of State Succession' (1992) 44 *ÖZöRV* 63–84, at 81.
403   Marek, *Identity and Continuity of States in Public International Law*, 199, 218–219. This claim of non-continuity was approved by the Austrian Constitutional Court in several cases dealing with issues of State succession: *Military Pensions (Austria) Case*, Austrian Constitutional Court, 7 May 1919, case no. 126, in: *Sammlung der Erkenntniss des österreichischen Verfassungsgerichtshofes*, vol. I (1919), no. 9, 17; (1919–1922) *Annual Digest* 66. See also other cases decided by the Austrian Constitutional Court: case no. 253–254, 20 October 1919, in: ibid., no. 18–19, 36–37 (*Annual Digest* 1919–1922, 67); case no. 18, 11 March 1919, in: ibid., no. 2, 5 (*Annual Digest* 1919–1922, 67).
404   See the discussion in: Marek, *Identity and Continuity of States in Public International Law*, 220ff.
405   Verzijl, *International Law in Historical Perspective* (vol. VII), 126.

St. Germain concluded by the Allied Powers with Austria thus contained a clause providing for Austria's responsibility for the loss and damages resulting from the war.[406] The United States also ratified a treaty in 1924 with Hungary and Austria dealing with the determination of the amounts to be paid by these two States as a result of the previous separate treaties it had entered into with them in 1921.[407] The Commission set up under this treaty held that the other States (i.e. Poland, Czechoslovakia and Yugoslavia) should not be held responsible for such damage.[408]

261.   India and Pakistan both became independent States on 15 August 1947 pursuant to the Indian Independence Act (1947) voted by the United Kingdom's House of Commons.[409] India has generally been considered as the *continuing State* of the British Dominion of India,[410] while Pakistan has been viewed as having separated from India in 1947. The relevant legislation dealing with issues of succession is the 1947 Indian Independence (Rights, Property and Liabilities) Order of 14 August 1947.[411] Section 10 of the Order provides for the 'transfer of liabilities for actionable wrong other than breach of contract' from the British Dominion of India to the new independent State of India. Many Indian courts have interpreted this provision to mean that India, the continuing State of the British Dominion, remains responsible for internationally wrongful acts committed before the date of succession.[412]

262.   Finally, there is another more recent example of State practice supporting the principle of non-succession: the separation of Montenegro from the 'State Union of Serbia and Montenegro'. Following a referendum, the National Assembly of Montenegro made a formal declaration of independence in 2006, as envisaged in Article 60 of the Constitutional Chart of the State Union of Serbia and Montenegro.[413] The independence of the new State was soon recognised by several members of the international community (including Serbia)

---

406   *Treaty of Peace between the Allied and Associated Powers and Austria; Protocol, Declaration and Special Declaration*, St. Germain-en-Laye, 10 September 1919, entered into force on 16 July 1920, in: (1919) UKTS No. 11 (Cmd. 400), see Article 177. See also: *Treaty Establishing Friendly Relations between the United States of America and Hungary*, signed in Budapest on 29 August 1921, in: USTS no. 660; (1922) 16 *AJIL*, Suppl., 13–16.

407   *Agreement for the Determination of the Amounts to be paid by Austria and by Hungary in satisfaction of their Obligations under the Treaties concluded by the United States with Austria on August 24, 1921, and with Hungary on August 29, 1921*, Washington, 26 November 1924, 48 LNTS No. 1151, 69; 6 UNRIAA 199.

408   *Administrative Decision no. 1*, 25 May 1927, Tripartite Claims Commission, 6 UNRIAA 203, at 210.

409   Indian Independence Act (1947), 10 and 11 Geo. VI, c. 30; *L.R. Statues* 1947.

410   This is stated in: Indian Independence (International Arrangements) Order, Gazette of India Extraordinary, 14 August 1947. The same opinion was also expressed by the Legal Department of the United Nations: UN Press Release, UN Doc PM/473, 12 August 1947.

411   1947 Indian Independence (Rights, Property and Liabilities) Order, Gazette of India (Extraordinary), 14 August 1947, in: M.M. Whiteman, *Digest of International Law*, vol. II (Washington: Dept. of State, 1973), 873.

412   See Dumberry, *State Succession to International Responsibility*, 173, examining a number of cases.

413   Article 60(1) of Serbia-Montenegro's Constitution mentions the right for each entity to 'secede from' the Union and paragraph 4 of the same provision expressly envisaged the 'secession of the state of Montenegro from the State Union of Serbia and Montenegro'. See also Article 60(5). See also the Decision on Proclamation of Independence of the Republic of Montenegro, Article 1.

and on 28 June 2006 Montenegro was admitted to the United Nations.[414] The accession of Montenegro to independence must be considered in legal terms as a case of separation. Following Montenegro's declaration of independence, the National Assembly of Serbia declared that Serbia was the 'successor (*sic*) State' to Serbia-Montenegro.[415] In the context of this declaration, the word 'succession' was clearly meant to proclaim Serbia as the 'continuator' of the Union as shown by a letter sent to the UN Secretary-General in June 2006.[416]

263.   The independence of Montenegro had some important consequences in the context of the then on-going *Genocide Convention Case* brought by Bosnia and Herzegovina against Serbia-Montenegro before the ICJ.[417] Bosnia and Herzegovina argued that Serbia *and* Montenegro should both remain respondents in this case.[418] Montenegro rejected this position.[419] Serbia simply took the view that this question should be decided by the Court.[420] In its final judgment, the Court first noted that 'the facts and events on which the final submissions of Bosnia and Herzegovina are based occurred at a period of time when Serbia and Montenegro constituted a single State'.[421] The Court also noted Serbia's position of continuity and its commitment to be bound by international treaties concluded by Serbia and Montenegro.[422] For the Court, 'the Republic of Montenegro does not continue the legal personality of Serbia and Montenegro; it cannot therefore have acquired, on that basis, the status of Respondent in the present case'.[423] Since Montenegro had not given its consent to the jurisdiction of the Court over this case,[424] the Court concluded that the Republic of Serbia would remain the only respondent in this case.[425] The Court also recalled that

---

414   UN GA Resolution A/60/264 (12 July 2006).
415   Decision on Obligations of Public Authorities of the Republic of Serbia in Assuming Powers of the Republic of Serbia as Successor State to the State Union of Serbia and Montenegro, 12 June 2006.
416   Letter of 3 June 2006 from the President of the Republic of Serbia to the UN Secretary-General, referred to in *Application of the Convention on the Prevention and Punishment of the Crime of Genocide (Bosnia and Herzegovina v. Serbia and Montenegro)*, Judgment, 26 February 2007, ICJ Rep. 2007, 43, at para. 67.
417   By letters dated 19 July 2006, the Court Registrar requested the Agent of Bosnia and Herzegovina, the Agent of Serbia and Montenegro and the Foreign Minister of Montenegro to communicate to the Court the views of their governments on the consequences to be attached to the developments in the context of the case.
418   Bosnia first acknowledged that Serbia's position as the continuator of Serbia-Montenegro had been accepted by both Montenegro and the international community. It nevertheless added that 'at the time when genocide was committed and at the time of the initiation of this case, Serbia and Montenegro constituted a single state' and that therefore both States 'jointly and severally, are responsible for the unlawful conduct that constitute the cause of action in this case'. (Letter to the Registrar dated 16 October 2006 by the Agent of Bosnia and Herzegovina, referred to in *Application of the Convention on the Prevention and Punishment of the Crime of Genocide (Bosnia and Herzegovina v. Serbia and Montenegro)*, Judgment, 26 February 2007, ICJ Rep. 2007, 43, at para. 71).
419   Letter dated 29 November 2006 by the Chief State Prosecutor of Montenegro, referred to in: ibid., at para. 72.
420   Ibid., para. 73.
421   Ibid., para. 74.
422   Ibid., para. 75. In a letter of 26 July 2006 (referred to in: ibid., at para. 70), the 'Agent of Serbia and Montenegro' took the view that 'there [was] continuity between Serbia and Montenegro and the Republic of Serbia'.
423   Ibid., para. 76.
424   Ibid., para. 76.
425   Ibid., para. 77.

Montenegro, like any other State party to the Genocide Convention, has undertaken the obligations flowing from it, and in particular the obligation to cooperate in order to punish the perpetrators of genocide.[426] The Court did not address the possibility of joint and several responsibility by Serbia and of Montenegro, let alone any kind of obligation incumbent on Montenegro for the internationally wrongful act committed by the predecessor State. Yet, as noted in the Final Report, 'what is beyond doubt in the Court's reasoning is that the continuator State has to assume the obligations of internationally wrongful acts committed before the date of State succession as a result of the separation of part of its population and territory in order to constitute a new State'.[427] The same conclusion about the continuing responsibility of Serbia was (at least implicitly) reached by the arbitral tribunal in the case of *Mytilineos Holdings SA v. The State Union of Serbia & Montenegro and Republic of Serbia* involving a Greek claimant starting arbitration proceedings in 2004 under the 1997 Greece–FRY bilateral investment treaty.[428]

2   Exception: Situations Calling for the Transfer of Rights and Obligations to the Successor State

264.   To the general principle of non-succession set out at Article 12(1), the second and third paragraphs of this provision provide for two exceptions. There is support for this solution among scholars.[429] The position is also followed by the ILC Special Rapporteur.[430] While the first exception (Article 12(2)) deals with the question of succession to *rights* arising from the commission of a wrongful act (Section 2.1), the second one (Article 12(3)) concerns succession to *obligations* (Section 2.2). It should be recalled the subsidiary character of the solutions mentioned at Articles 12(2) and (3). Thus, they should prevail only insofar as the parties 'concerned' have not themselves specifically agreed to a different solution.

2.1   EXISTENCE OF A 'DIRECT LINK' BETWEEN THE CONSEQUENCES OF A WRONGFUL ACT AND THE TERRITORY/POPULATION OF THE SUCCESSOR STATE

265.   The first exception to the principle of non-succession is mentioned at Article 12(2). It concerns the specific situation of the existence of a 'direct link' between the consequences

---

426   Ibid., paras. 71–77. The Court, nevertheless, indicated that 'it has to be borne in mind that any responsibility for past events determined in the present Judgment involved at the relevant time the State of Serbia and Montenegro' (ibid., para. 78).

427   Final Report, para. 79, in: (2015) 76 *Annuaire de l'Institut de Droit international*, 541. See ILC Special Rapporteur, Second Report, 2018, para. 91 (endorsing this position).

428   *Mytilineos Holdings SA v. State Union of Serbia & Montenegro and Republic of Serbia*, UNCITRAL, Partial Award on Jurisdiction, 8 Sept. 2006, where the Tribunal noted that since the claim had been filed, 'Montenegro, a constituent unit of the State Union of Serbia and Montenegro, declared its independence', and adding that 'while the Tribunal has not been requested to rule on any ensuing State succession issues, it takes note that it appears uncontroversial that the Republic of Serbia will continue the legal identity of the State Union of Serbia and Montenegro on the international level' (para. 158). This case is examined in: Dumberry, *A Guide to State Succession in International Investment Law*, 159.

429   Dumberry, *State Succession to International Responsibility*, 207ff.

430   ILC Special Rapporteur, Second Report, 2018, para. 92. See also: ILC, Working-Group Recommendations, 401.

of an internationally wrongful act committed *against* the predecessor State before the date of succession and the territory or the population of the successor State(s). When such a link exists, the *rights* arising from a wrongful act pass to the successor State(s). In other words, after the date of succession the successor State(s) becomes the holder of any right arising from the consequences of the commission of a wrongful act which has directly affected its territory or its population. Article 12(2) is a concrete illustration, in the specific context of separation, of the general principle set out at Article 5(2).

266.   The ILC Special Rapporteur has generally followed the solution adopted at Article 12(2).[431] It should be noted, however, that ILC Draft Article 7(3) indicates that the existence of such a 'direct link' would result in the transfer of obligations only 'if particular circumstances so require'.[432] The provision also does not refer to 'population', but only to the link with the territory of the successor State. Another distinction made under this provision is discussed below.

267.   The meaning and the nature of any such 'direct link' between a wrongful act and the territory/population of the successor State have already been examined above.[433] The comments made earlier in the context of transfer of territory also apply to cases of separation. Suffice to recall here that such a link would exist, for instance, if a wrongful act had destroyed property or infrastructures situated in the territory over which the new State was now sovereign. The same solution should prevail if the act damaged the environment or natural resources in that territory. Under this scenario, while the acts were undoubtedly committed against the predecessor State, it remains that, after the date of succession, the real and lasting consequences of the act are clearly suffered by the new State, and not by the continuing State. The Final Report also made the following comment regarding the possibility of a 'direct link' between a wrongful act and the population of the successor State:

> [t]he same reasoning applies to the existence of a direct link between the consequences of the wrongful act and the population concerned. Putting aside the fact that territorial rights are in general for the benefit of a given population, even though the legal holder may be the State concerned, it may occur that the wrongful act has a specific population as a direct victim. This is particularly relevant in cases of violations of human or minority rights. If the population directly concerned by the wrongful act becomes the population of the successor State, the situation also deserves to constitute an exception to the non-succession rule in cases in which the predecessor State continues to exist.[434]

---

431   ILC Special Rapporteur, Second Report, 2018, paras. 98ff. See Article 7(3): 'If particular circumstances so require, the obligations arising from an internationally wrongful act of the predecessor State, where there is a direct link between the act or its consequences and the territory of the successor State or States, are assumed by the predecessor and the successor State or States'.
432   Ibid.; see also at para. 103: 'To sum up, the successor State is not automatically responsible for obligations arising from internationally wrongful acts committed by the predecessor State before the date of succession solely based on the fact that such acts took place on what is now its territory. The linkage of the acts to the territory is only one relevant element that needs to be taken into account'.
433   See analysis of Articles 5(2) and 11(2) above.
434   Final Report, para. 62, in: (2015) 76 *Annuaire de l'Institut de Droit international*, 536. As mentioned above, Draft Article 7(3) proposed by ILC Special Rapporteur, Second Report, 2018, does not refer to 'population'.

268.   Two examples of State practice can be mentioned where the successor States were allowed to claim reparation for internationally wrongful acts committed against the predecessor State before the date of succession.[435] In both cases, the different parties accepted the transfer of the right to claim reparation to the new State since that State was considered to have been injured by the wrongful act.

269.   The first example concerns an agreement which was reached after the Second World War for the establishment of an Inter-Allied Reparation Agency for the equitable distribution among several States of the total assets declared to be available as war reparation from Germany.[436] The Dominion of India was a party to the Treaty, i.e. before it formally became an independent State (in August 1947).[437] After Pakistan seceded from India in 1947, both States reached an agreement on 22 January 1948 under which they agreed on the division of the share of war reparation allocated to India under the 1946 Agreement. This agreement between India and Pakistan led to the conclusion of an Additional Protocol to the 1946 Agreement, which was entered into on 15 March 1948.[438] The Protocol provided that Pakistan would receive some war reparation, even if it did not exist as an independent State when the wrongful acts were committed by Germany. One of the reasons why the parties may have agreed to such a succession to rights is presumably because of the existence of a 'direct link' between the consequences of the wrongful acts and the territory and population of Pakistan (particularly the latter). Otherwise, India (the continuing State) should have logically been the only State receiving war reparation from Germany

270.   The second example also deals with events that took place after the Second World War. The victory of the Soviet Red Army in 1945 was followed by the taking of some 2.5 million works of art and cultural property, which were transferred from Germany to the Soviet Union.[439] A Protocol was entered into by the USSR and the GDR in 1958 for the restitution of some of 1.9 million art treasures, books and archives which had been taken away by the Red Army from the territory of Germany.[440] Again, the parties agreed to such a succession to rights arising from the commission of wrongful acts presumably because of the existence of a 'direct link' between the consequences of these acts and the territory and population of East Germany.

271.   It should be mentioned that Article 12(2) only concerns the existence of a 'direct link' between the consequences of an internationally wrongful act committed *against* the predecessor State before the date of succession and the territory or the population of the successor State(s). It does not address the reverse situation of a wrongful act committed

---

435   Dumberry, *State Succession to International Responsibility*, 324ff.
436   *Agreement on Reparation from Germany, on the Establishment of an Inter-Allied Reparation Agency and on the Restitution of Monetary Gold*, signed in Paris on 14 January 1946, entered into force on 24 January 1946, in: 555 UNTS 69.
437   Indian Independence Act (1947), 10 and 11 Geo. VI, c. 30; *LR Statutes* 1947.
438   *Additional Protocol to the Agreement on Reparation from Germany, on the Establishment of an Inter-Allied Reparation Agency, and on the Restitution of Monetary Gold of 14 January 1946*, signed in Brussels on 15 March 1948, entered into force on 15 March 1948, in: 555 UNTS 104.
439   Dumberry, *State Succession to International Responsibility*, 325.
440   The Protocol was signed on 8 September 1958 and the Final Protocol on 29 July 1960. See the analysis in: Jakubowski, *State Succession in Cultural Property*, 108ff.

by the predecessor State.[441] The reason for making such a distinction is the same as for the identical solution proposed under Article 11(2) regarding transfer of territory.[442] Thus, since the author of the wrongful act, the predecessor State, continues to exist, it should bear responsibility for that act.

272.   Nevertheless, as already mentioned above in the context of transfer of territory,[443] it may be argued that in some situations the consequences of the commission of an internationally wrongful act *by* the predecessor State may be directly linked to the territory or the population of the successor State. In fact, in his proposed Draft Article 7(3), the ILC Special Rapporteur specifically refers to the existence of such a linkage as one situation where the succession solution should prevail not only in the context of rights but also in the context of the *obligation* to repair.[444]

273.   As discussed below, the Resolution adopts a more cautious approach. This is in fact a situation where Article 12(4) of the Resolution could find application. The provision (further examined below) indicates that if 'particular circumstances indicated in paragraphs 2 and 3 so require' the obligations arising from a wrongful act can be assumed by both the predecessor State and the successor State. The provision recognises that the author of the wrongful act (the predecessor State) continues to exist in the context of a separation and should, consequently, bear responsibility for the consequences of any wrongful act. Yet, there may be circumstances where the succession State should take over such consequences of responsibility together with the predecessor State.[445] One such situation would be the existence of a linkage between the wrongful act and the territory and population of the new State. In fact, the Final Report indicates that joint responsibility could be envisaged whenever the consequences of a wrongful act are directly linked to the territories and populations of both the predecessor and the successor State(s).[446]

274.   The following example of State practice provides an illustration of the existence of a direct territorial link between a wrongful act committed *by* the predecessor and the new State.[447] Belgium became an independent State in 1830. Several years later, it had to pay

---

441   As further discussed in the following paragraphs, a different approach has been adopted in: ILC Special Rapporteur, Second Report, 2018, para. 103. See Draft Article 7(3). The other question regarding succession to the right to claim reparation will be examined in the Special Rapporteur's Third Report (see para. 21) (not yet published at the time of writing).
442   See the analysis above dealing with Article 11(2).
443   Ibid.
444   ILC Special Rapporteur, Second Report, 2018, para. 103. See Draft Article 7(3): 'If particular circumstances so require, the obligations arising from an internationally wrongful act of the predecessor State, where there is a direct link between the act or its consequences and the territory of the successor State or States, are assumed by the predecessor and the successor State or States'.
445   The following comment made by the ILC Special Rapporteur, Second Report, 2018, para. 100, is therefore incorrect: 'while Dumberry refers to the transfer of *obligations* arising from an internationally wrongful act of the predecessor State specifically linked to the territory in question, the Institute of International Law in its resolution refers to this situation in the context of secession only – with respect to the transfer of *rights* (art. 12, para. 2)' (emphasis in the original).
446   Final Report, para. 80, in: (2015) 76 *Annuaire de l'Institut de Droit international*, 541.
447   The example is mentioned in: Dumberry, *State Succession to International Responsibility*, 161ff, 257–258; ILC Special Rapporteur, Second Report, 2018, para. 101.

compensation for acts which were committed against foreigners by the predecessor State (the Netherlands) before its independence. During the armed revolt which eventually led to independence, the city of Antwerp (situated in the Belgian provinces) was bombarded in October 1830 by the Dutch forces. During the bombardment, a public warehouse was destroyed in which were stored the goods of several foreigners. Some years later, Austria, Brazil, France, Great Britain, Prussia and the United States submitted claims for compensation for the damage suffered by their nationals.[448] France, Great Britain, Prussia and the United States made a joint application to Belgium requesting compensation for the damage 'solely [based] upon the ground that the obligation to indemnify for such losses rested upon the country within which the injury was inflicted'.[449] One of the legal grounds invoked by the United States for Belgium to be held responsible for the action concerned was indeed the territorial link between the internationally wrongful act and the tortfeasor.[450] In other words, since the acts took place in the territory of what would later become Belgium, the United States took the view that the new State should therefore be held responsible for it. Belgium agreed to pay compensation to the owners.[451]

275.   Finally, as mentioned above, Article 12(1) envisages the possibility that more than one State is created by separation. Whenever this is the case, it may be that the consequences of a wrongful act will be felt in the territory (and by the population) of two (or more) new States. This is a situation where there exists a plurality of successor States. Article 7 explains that in these circumstances, all successor States will enjoy the right to reparation in an equitable manner.[452]

2.2   THE AUTHOR OF THE WRONGFUL ACT WAS AN ORGAN OF THE PREDECESSOR STATE THAT LATER BECAME AN ORGAN OF THE SUCCESSOR STATE

276.   Article 12(3) contains a second exception to the principle of non-succession. Importantly, the Final Report considers that this is a 'possible' exception which can apply only if 'particular circumstances so require'.[453] This exception concerns the specific situation where the author of a wrongful act was an 'organ of the territorial unit of the predecessor State that has later become an organ of the successor State'.[454] When this is the case, the *obligations* arising from such an act may pass to the successor State. The rationale and the nature of this exception have already been explained above when examining Article

448   John Bassett Moore, *Digest of International Law*, vol. VI (Washington: GPO, 1906), 942.
449   Ibid., 929.
450   Letter of US Secretary of State Mr. Marcy to French Minister Count Sartiges concerning the claims of French subjects as a result of the US bombardment of Greytown in 1854, 26 February 1857, in: MS. Notes to French Leg. VI. 301; S. Ex. Doc. 9, 35 Cong. 1 sess. 3, in: Moore, ibid., 929–930
451   Verzijl, *International Law in Historical Perspective* (vol. VII), 226–227. See Dumberry, *State Succession to International Responsibility*, 287.
452   The question of the 'equitable apportionment' of rights between the successor States has already been examined above when analysing Article 7(2).
453   Final Report, para. 63, in: (2015) 76 *Annuaire de l'Institut de Droit international*, 536. The same language is used by ILC Special Rapporteur, Second Report, 2018, in Draft Article 7(2).
454   On this question, see analysis in: Dumberry, *State Succession to International Responsibility*, 136.

11(3). The comments made earlier in the context of transfer of territory also apply to cases of separation. The solution adopted at Article 12(3) has been followed by the ILC Special Rapporteur.[455]

277.　One recent example where the solution set out at Article 12(3) was applied is the case of *Bijelic v. Montenegro* decided by the European Court of Human Rights. The case involved three Serb nationals who started proceedings in 2005–2006 against Serbia-Montenegro.[456] After Montenegro became a new State (June 2006), the Court asked the question: 'Which State, Montenegro or Serbia, could be held responsible for the impugned inaction of the authorities between 2 March 2004 and 5 June 2006?'[457] Serbia took the position that it could not be held responsible for the acts since they took place in the territory of Montenegro, which was at the time an autonomous entity having an obligation to protect human rights in its own territory:

> The Serbian Government firstly noted that each constituent republic of the State Union of Serbia and Montenegro had the obligation to protect human rights in its own territory (see paragraph 37, Article 9 above). Secondly, the impugned enforcement proceedings were themselves solely conducted by the competent Montenegrin authorities. Thirdly, although the sole successor of the State Union of Serbia and Montenegro (see paragraph 37, Article 60 above), Serbia cannot be deemed responsible for any violations of the Convention which might have occurred in Montenegro prior to its declaration of independence. Lastly, Serbia could not, within the meaning of Article 46 of the Convention, realistically be expected to implement any individual and/ or general measures in the territory of another State. In view of the above, the Serbian Government concluded that the application as regards Serbia was incompatible ratione personae and maintained that, to hold otherwise, would be contrary to the universal principles of international law.[458]

278.　In response to a question asked by the Court, Montenegro made the following statement: '[it] "support[ed] the remarks presented to the Court" by the Serbian Government "relating to the issue of … [succession as regards] … the enforcement of the judgment … [in question]'.[459] Montenegro also mentioned Article 5 of the Constitutional Law on the Implementation of the Constitution of Montenegro that provided that 'Provisions of international treaties on human rights and freedoms, to which Montenegro acceded before 3 June 2006, shall be applied to legal relations which have arisen after their signature'.[460] Montenegro accepted succession to human rights treaties to which the State Union of

---

455　ILC Special Rapporteur, Second Report, 2018, paras. 94ff. See Draft Article 7(2): 'If particular circumstances so require, the obligations arising from an internationally wrongful act of the predecessor State will transfer to the successor State when the act was carried out by an organ of a territorial unit of the predecessor that has later become an organ of the successor State'.
456　*Bijelic v. Montenegro and Serbia,* 11 June 2009, Application no. 11890/05.
457　Ibid., para. 61.
458　Ibid., para. 62.
459　Ibid., para. 63.
460　Ibid., para. 42.

Serbia and Montenegro were parties with retroactive effect. It therefore consented to being held responsible for acts which took place on its territory before it became an independent State. The Court held that Montenegro was indeed responsible for violations of the Convention.[461]

279.   This decision has been considered by some as the recognition of the principle of automatic succession to the Convention.[462] The Court did mention that 'fundamental rights protected by international human rights treaties should indeed belong to individuals living in the territory of the State party concerned, notwithstanding its subsequent dissolution or succession.'[463] This statement refers to the existence of rights of individuals that do not cease because of the emergence of a situation of State succession. Yet, the statement does not per se explain which of the predecessor or the successor State must be the holder of the obligation to repair the breach of those rights. In any event, what is clear is that this example does not undermine the soundness of the general rule of non-succession set out at Article 12(1) whenever the predecessor State continues to exist. It does not support in any way the proposition that a new State should generally be responsible for wrongful acts committed before the date of succession. In fact, as argued by Serbia and agreed by Montenegro, the present case deals with the particular situation of acts committed by the Montenegrin authorities before the date of succession.

280.   One writer has pointed out that this is 'the first decision of the ECHR to confirm the importance of attributing the impugned situations to a (previously) sub-national authority that shares an identity with a successor respondent state'.[464] This was indeed a case where the author of the wrongful act was an 'organ of the territorial unit of the predecessor State that has later become an organ of the successor State'.[465] The ILC

---

461   Ibid., paras. 70, 85, 92–99.
462   Benjamin E. Brockman-Hawe, 'Succession, the Obligation to Repair and Human Rights; The European Court of Human Rights Judgment in the Case of Bijelic v. Montenegro and Serbia' (2010) 59(3) *ICLQ* 853–854. See also the comments made in: ILC Special Rapporteur, Second Report, 2018, paras. 120–121.
463   *Bijelic v. Montenegro,* para. 69.
464   Brockman-Hawe, 'Succession, the Obligation to Repair and Human Rights', 864. See also: Marko Milanovic, 'The Spatial Dimension: Treaties and Territory', in: C.J. Tams, A. Tzanakopoulos & A. Zimmermann (eds.), *Research Handbook on the Law of Treaties* (Cheltenham: Edward Elgar, 2014) 220 ('[the Court] applied a functional approach whereby it allocated responsibility to that (new) State which organically continued the part of the old joint State whose conduct was the object of the case. Thus, if it were Montenegrin courts that were alleged to have breached the applicant's right to a fair trial before Montenegro's independence, it would be the State of Montenegro and not Serbia that would be responsible for that act post-independence'); Marcel Szabó, 'State Succession and the Jurisprudence of the European Court of Human Rights', in: Christina Binder & Konrad Lachmayer (eds.), *The European Court of Human Rights and Public International Law Fragmentation or Unity?* (Baden-Baden: Nomos, 2014) 143 ('the responsibility of Montenegro was based on the fact that even at the time of the federation, issues related to execution belonged in the exclusive competence of Montenegrin authorities, therefore, Serbia was relieved of any responsibility in this respect').
465   This is indeed the position put forward by the European Commission for Democracy through Law (Venice Commission) in its amicus brief, 20 Oct. 2008, opinion no. 495/2008, CDL-AD(2008)021, paras. 38ff, 43: 'it is undoubtedly reasonable to hold the newly-independent state of Montenegro responsible for all the alleged breaches of the ECHR which occurred in Montenegro between 3 March

Special Rapporteur examined this example as an illustration of that proposition,[466] as well as from the angle of a new State being responsible for having continued the wrongful act.[467]

3   Situations of Shared Responsibility between the Predecessor and the Successor State

281.   Article 12(4) indicates that if 'particular circumstances indicated in paragraphs 2 and 3 so require' the obligations arising from a wrongful act can be assumed by both the predecessor State and the successor State. In other words, this is a situation where both the direct link between the consequences of the wrongful act with the territory and population concerned, as well as the organ having committed that act can be taken into consideration. The Final Report mentions the example of a wrongful act committed by both the central organ of the predecessor State and one local organ which later becomes the organ of the successor State. Another example mentioned in the Final Report is the situation where the consequences of the wrongful act benefited both the predecessor and the successor State. Finally, as mentioned above,[468] joint responsibility could also be envisaged whenever the consequences were directly linked to the territories and populations of both the predecessor and the successor State(s).[469]

282.   Article 12(5) may apply to any of the hypotheses envisaged in paragraphs (2) to (4). It mentions the criteria which may be taken into account to determine an 'equitable apportionment of the rights or obligations' between the predecessor and the successor State(s). These criteria have already been mentioned when analysing Article 7 and the comments made earlier apply here.[470]

2004 and 6 June 2006. Conversely, it would be unreasonable to hold Serbia, as the "continuing state" of the former State Union, responsible for these alleged breaches. As already explained (paragraph 9 above), the relevant public services within Montenegro were under the full control of the Montenegrin authorities. There is full continuity between these authorities and the authorities of the present state of Montenegro. If, in different factual circumstances, the European Court of Human Rights were to be satisfied beyond reasonable doubt that an alleged *specific* breach of the ECHR in Montenegrin territory was wholly due to the action, or inaction, of the *Union* authorities, the Court would be justified in holding that this responsibility would not *wholly* devolve to the Montenegrin authorities' (emphasis in the original).

466   ILC Special Rapporteur, Second Report, 2018, para. 121. He also adds that 'following the Bijelić case, the European Court of Human Rights accepted as a rule that, in case of a wrongful act committed by organs of Montenegro in time of the State Union of Serbia and Montenegro, responsibility is succeeded by Montenegro' (referring to the following cases: *O. Lakićević and Others v. Montenegro and Serbia*, Nos. 27458/06 and 3 others, 13 December 2011; *Milić v. Montenegro and Serbia*, No. 28359/05, 11 December 2012; *Mandić v. Montenegro*, Serbia and Bosnia and Herzegovina, No. 32557/05, Decision (Fourth Section) of 12 June 2012).

467   ILC Special Rapporteur, Second Report, 2018, para. 62.

468   See section 2.1 above.

469   Final Report, para. 80, in: (2015) 76 *Annuaire de l'Institut de Droit international*, 541.

470   See the analysis above regarding Article 7.

4 Acts Committed by Insurrectional or Other Movements Before the Date of Succession

283. Article 12(6) deals with another situation related to State responsibility in cases of separation that deserves particular consideration. This is when a wrongful act is committed before the date of succession not by the predecessor State, but by an 'insurrectional or other movement' which succeeds in establishing *a new State*. Whenever a new State is created as a result of the action of such a movement, the act shall be considered as that of the new State under international law. The provision further adds that after the date of succession, the predecessor State incurs no responsibility for the acts committed by the insurrectional movement.

284. The following sections first examine the origin of this provision which is based on Article 10(1) of the ILC Articles on State Responsibility (Section 4.1). This analysis will be followed by a survey of State practice applying the solution adopted at Article 12(6) (Section 4.2).

4.1 THE ORIGIN OF ARTICLE 12(6): ARTICLE 10(1) OF THE ILC ARTICLES ON STATE RESPONSIBILITY

285. This special situation was addressed by Article 10(1) of the ILC Articles on State Responsibility, which followed what was considered to be the traditional approach on the matter.[471] Under that provision, whenever a 'movement, insurrectional or other' succeeds in establishing a new State, its pre-succession conduct and its wrongful acts committed against a third State 'shall be considered an act of the new State under international law' once it comes into power.[472] The ILC has explained why this should be so:

> The structure of the organisation of the insurrectional movement then becomes those of the organisation of the new State. In such a case, the affirmation of the responsibility of the newly-formed State for any wrongful acts committed by the organs of the insurrectional movement which preceded it would be justified by virtue of the continuity which would exist between the personality of the insurrectional movement and that of the State to which it has given birth... [A]n existing subject of international law would merely change category: from a mere embryo State it would become a State proper, without any interruption in its international personality resulting from the change.[473]

---

471 See, however, the analysis below at Section 4.2 on the question as to whether Article 10(1) indeed reflects State practice.
472 Article 10(2), Articles on State Responsibility. In doctrine: see H. Atlam 'National Liberation Movements and International Responsibility', in: M Spinedi & B Simma (eds.), *United Nations Codification of State Responsibility* (New York: Oceana, 1987), 35–56.
473 ILC, 'Fourth Report on State Responsibility of the Special Rapporteur', Mr Roberto Ago, 24th session of the ILC, 1972, UN Doc. A/CN.4/264 and Add.1, ILC Report, A/8710/Rev.1 (A/27/10), 1972, chp. IV(B), paras. 72–73, in: (1972) II *Yearbook ILC* 71, at 150, paras. 159, 194.

286.   Thus, according to the ILC, it is the 'structural' continuity between the organisation of the insurrectional movement and that of the new State which explains why responsibility should be transferred to the latter for internationally wrongful acts committed by the former.[474] Thus, 'the same entity which previously had the characteristics of an insurrectional or other movement has become the government of the State it was struggling to establish'.[475] This is indeed the position supported by many writers.[476] This conception has been rejected, however, by Judge Kreca in his separate opinion in the *Croatia Genocide Convention* case for the following reasons:

> Or, in the elaborated concept of 'shared identity', which is, in fact, the negation of legal identity and continuity as usually understood, the crucial role is given to the notion of 'organic substitution', according to which, even in the case where succession took place, 'organic forces' or 'constitutive elements' of the predecessor State (its territory and its population) survive its disintegration, being only affected, but not extinguished (P. Dumberry, *State Succession to International Responsibility*, 2007, pp. 49–50). The concept implies that the successor State is equipped with an identity similar to that held by the predecessor State. Precisely 'shared identity' justifies the transfer of any responsibility that existed at the time of the succession.
>
> It appears that the concept of 'organic substitution' fails to take into account the element of legal identity and continuity as the very substance of international personality in the frame of territorial changes. It reduces the State to its physical attributes (territory, population), which are also possessed by territorial non-State entities devoid of the quality of subjects in terms of international law.
>
> 'Shared identity' as the product of the concept of 'organic substitution' portrays new States as a specific mix of the successor State and the continuator State expressed in percentage share, because each of them possesses a part of the territory and population of the predecessor State. It contains an element of legal absurdity, which is, perhaps, best illustrated in the case when, after separation of any part(s) of its territory, the predecessor State continues to exist, both States, the predecessor State and the newly emerged successor State possess identity ¾ the successor State with its predecessor State, whereas the predecessor State, retains its own.[477]

287.   One important point to mention is that this continuity of responsibility is solely based on the mechanisms of State responsibility, and *not on any rules of State*

474   ILC, 'Report of the International Law Commission on the work of its Fifty-third session', Official Records of the General Assembly, Fifty-sixth session, Supplement No. 10, UN doc. A/56/10, ch. IV.E.2, 2001, 114, para. 6.
475   Ibid.
476   Crawford, *State Responsibility: The General Part*, 178–9; Dumberry, 'New State Responsibility for Internationally Wrongful Acts by an Insurrectional Movement', 611ff; G. Cahin, 'Attribution of Conduct to a State: Insurrectional Movements', in: Crawford, J., Pellet, A. & Olleson, S. (eds.), *The Law of International Responsibility* (Cambridge: CUP, 2010), 249.
477   *Application of the Convention on the Prevention and Punishment of the Crime of Genocide (Croatia v. Serbia)*, Judgment of 3 February 2015, Separate Opinion of Judge Kreca, paras. 65.3, 65.4.

succession.[478] Yet, as noted by the Final Report, 'the question falls within the realm of the matter under consideration here, since the problem would be one of determining whether the predecessor or the successor State bears responsibility for such conduct'.[479] In this particular case, the question is not one of a new State's succession to obligations arising from internationally wrongful acts committed before the date of succession. It is rather that of its *responsibility* for acts committed by the insurrectional or other movement in the context of its struggle for the creation of the new State.[480] Thus, the principle established at Article 10(2) of the ILC Articles on State responsibility seems to be perfectly applicable to cases of separation.[481] The same position has been adopted by the ILC Special Rapporteur.[482]

288.   For this reason, the Resolution adopted the position of the ILC and included at Article 12(6) the same type of provision as Article 10(2) of the ILC Articles on State Responsibility. Draft Article 7(4) proposed by the ILC Special Rapporteur is to the same effect.[483]

289.   The text of Article 12(6) of the Resolution specifically mentions the acts of 'an insurrectional or other movement'. Insurrectional movements typically involve situations of civil armed strife. However, this is not the only case that is envisaged at Article 12(6). The provision also covers other situations where a separation results from the actions of peaceful political movements or even local organs of the predecessor State. This explains why the expression 'other movement' is used at Article 12(6). The goal is to include other potential authors of wrongful acts occurring before the date of succession.

290.   Finally, it should be added that the ILC Articles on State Responsibility did not specifically address the different question of the responsibility of the predecessor State for its *own acts* accomplished in the situation envisaged at Article 10(2) of the ILC Articles on State Responsibility. Yet, in its work on State responsibility, the ILC makes it clear that in this situation the predecessor State remains responsible for its own wrongful acts.[484] This is also the position supported by scholars[485] and the solution which has prevailed in a number

---

478   ILC, 'Report of the International Law Commission on the Work of its Twenty-Seventh Session', 5 May to 25 July 1975, Draft Articles on State Responsibility, UN Doc. A/10010/Rev.1, in: (1975) II *Yearbook ILC*, 47, at 101, para. 8. See also in: ILC, 'Fourth Report on State Responsibility' (1972) II *Yearbook ILC* at 131, para. 159.

479   Final Report, para. 82, in: (2015) 76 *Annuaire de l'Institut de Droit international*, 542.

480   The same position is adopted in: ILC Special Rapporteur, Second Report, 2018, paras. 109ff.

481   Dumberry, 'New State Responsibility for Internationally Wrongful Acts by an Insurrectional Movement', 617ff.

482   ILC Special Rapporteur, Second Report, 2018, para. 108.

483   Ibid., paras. 107ff. See Draft Article 7(4): 'The conduct of a movement, insurrectional or other, which succeeds in establishing a new State in part of the territory of a predecessor State or in a territory under its administration shall be considered an act of the new State under international law'.

484   ILC, 'Report of the International Law Commission on the Work of its Twenty-Seventh Session', 5 May to 25 July 1975, Draft Articles on State Responsibility, UN Doc. A/10010/Rev.1, in: (1972) II *Yearbook ILC*, 47, at 101, at para. 6: '[T]he acts of the organs of the pre-existing State are in no way attributable to the new State, which has separated from the pre-existing State by secession or decolonization. These are and remain exclusively the acts of the pre-existing State, which as a general rule, moreover, will continue to exist after the constitution of the new State by the insurrectional movement'.

485   See analysis in Dumberry, *State Succession to International Responsibility*, 251.

of cases.[486] In any event, the question of the predecessor State's responsibility for its *own acts* accomplished in the context of a conflict involving an insurrectional movement is ultimately one that is governed by the rules of State responsibility. This is the reason why Article 12(6) of the Resolution does not deal specifically with this issue. Moreover, the matter is covered by Article 4(2) indicating that whenever the predecessor State continues to exist after the date of succession it will remain responsible for any acts committed before that date. Other provisions of the Resolution dealing with succession may also find application if specific circumstances so require.

4.2   EXAMPLES OF STATE PRACTICE SUPPORTING THE PRINCIPLE

291.   While the principle expressed at Article 10(2) of the ILC Articles on State responsibility is certainly necessary and justified in contemporary international law, it remains that an analysis of State practice shows that it does not rest on grounds as solid as it is often believed in doctrine.[487] Thus, the Final Report mentions that 'the relevant case law only referred to situations of an insurrectional movement becoming the government of the State or cases of State succession in which the person concerned had acquired the nationality of the same State having caused the injury, not cases of secession or decolonisation'.[488] The same assessment was made by Judge Kreca in his separate opinion in the 2015 *Croatia Genocide Convention* case, noting that 'more recent decisions and practice do not, on the whole, give any reason to doubt [that] the propositions contained in Article 10' are a characterisation which 'is, in terms of law, wishful thinking rather than a respectable argument'.[489]

292.   In the *Croatia Genocide Convention* case, Article 10(2) of the ILC Articles on State Responsibility was expressly invoked by Croatia.[490] It should be noted that the example is one involving an alleged case of dissolution of State rather than a case of separation. The Court described the argument as follows:

> According to Croatia, that provision is part of customary international law. Croatia maintains that, although the FRY was not proclaimed as a State until

---

486 See the review of State practice in: Dumberry, *State Succession to International Responsibility*, 252–258; Dumberry, 'New State Responsibility for Internationally Wrongful Acts by an Insurrectional Movement', 617ff. Yet, reference is also made in this work to other examples where, on the contrary, a new State was held responsible for wrongful acts committed by the predecessor State against foreigners during an armed struggle for independence (see at 257–258).

487 See analysis in: Dumberry, 'New State Responsibility for Internationally Wrongful Acts by an Insurrectional Movement', 612ff. Some examples are referred to in: Crawford, *State Responsibility: The General Part*, 176–177.

488 Final Report, para. 82, in: (2015) 76 *Annuaire de l'Institut de Droit international*, 542, referring to examples cited in: ILC, 'Commentaries to the Draft Articles on Responsibility of States for Internationally Wrongful Acts Adopted by the International Law Commission at its Fifty-Third Session (2001)', analysing Article 10, at 116–118, paras. 12–14. The question is also examined in: Crawford, *The Creation of States in International Law*, 658–664.

489 *Application of the Convention on the Prevention and Punishment of the Crime of Genocide (Croatia v. Serbia)*, Judgment of 3 February 2015, ICJ Rep. 2015, Separate Opinion of Judge Kreca, paras. 66.2, 67ff (referring to the work of Dumberry, *State Succession to International Responsibility*).

490 Ibid., paras. 82, 102. The example is examined in: ILC Special Rapporteur, Second Report, 2018, para. 119.

27 April 1992, that proclamation merely formalized a situation that was already established in fact. During the course of 1991, according to Croatia, the leadership of the republic of Serbia and other supporters of what Croatia describes as a 'Greater Serbia' movement took control of the JNA and other institutions of the SFRY, while also controlling their own territorial armed forces and various militias and paramilitary groups. This movement was eventually successful in creating a separate State, the FRY. Croatia contends that its claim in relation to events prior to 27 April 1992 is based upon acts by the JNA and those other armed forces and groups, as well as the Serb political authorities, which were attributable to that movement and thus, by operation of the principle stated in Article 10 (2), to the FRY.[491]

293.   Serbia's position in response was summarised as follows by the Court:

Serbia counters that Article 10 (2) represents progressive development of the law and did not form part of customary international law in 1991–1992. It is therefore inapplicable to the present case. Furthermore, even if Article 10 (2) had become part of customary law at that time, it is not applicable to the facts of the present case, since there was no "movement" that succeeded in creating a new State. Serbia also denies that the acts on which Croatia's claim is based were attributable to an entity that might be regarded as a Serbian State *in statu nascendi* during the period before 27 April 1992. Finally, Serbia contends that even if Article 10 (2) were applicable, it would not suffice to bring within the scope of Article IX that part of Croatia's claim which concerns events said to have occurred before 27 April 1992. According to Serbia, Article 10 (2) of the ILC Articles is no more than a principle of attribution; it has no bearing on the question of what obligations bind the new State or the earlier "movement", nor does it make treaty obligations accepted by the new State after its emergence retroactively applicable to acts of the pre-State "movement", even if it treats those acts as attributable to the new State. On that basis, Serbia argues that any "movement" which might have existed before 27 April 1992 was not a party to the Genocide Convention and could, therefore, only have been bound by the customary international law prohibition of genocide.[492]

294.   In its 2008 preliminary objections judgment in the same case, the Court used the following expression: 'In so far as Article 10, paragraph 2, of the ILC Articles on State Responsibility reflects customary international law on the subject (…)'.[493] In its 2015 decision on the merits, the Court 'consider[ed] that, even if Article 10(2) of the Articles on State Responsibility could be regarded as declaratory of customary international law at the relevant time, that Article is concerned only with the attribution of acts to a new State; it does not create obligations binding upon either the new State or the movement that succeeded in

---

491   Ibid., para. 102.
492   Ibid., para. 103.
493   *Application of the Convention on the Prevention and Punishment of the Crime of Genocide (Croatia v. Serbia)*, Preliminary Objections, ICJ Rep. 2008, 459, paras. 126–127.

establishing that new State'.[494] This is precisely the reason why the Court did not have to take a stance on the customary nature of Article 10(2) invoked by Croatia.[495]

295.   The Court explained that 'the FRY was not bound by the obligations contained in the Genocide Convention until it became party to that Convention', i.e. on 27 April 1992 (the date of the notification of succession by FRY and the date when the new State came into existence).[496] Hence, the Court concluded that even if any acts alleged by Croatia which took place before that date could be attributable to a 'movement', 'they cannot have involved a violation of the provisions of the Genocide Convention but, at most, only of the customary international law prohibition of genocide'.[497] Having rejected Croatia's principal argument regarding the application of Article 10(2), the Court then examined its alternative argument based on succession to international responsibility.[498] Finally, it should be added that while Judge Tomka rejected the Court's jurisdiction over events taking place before 27 April 1992, he nevertheless recognised that nothing should prevent the Court from considering these acts, adding that 'there was undoubtedly a certain factual continuation and identity between those who were actors in the period of armed conflict which raged in Croatia both before and after 27 April 1992'.[499] The same conclusion was also reached by Judge Cançado Trindade in his dissenting opinion.[500]

ARTICLE 13:

Merger of States

When two or more States unite and form a new successor State, and no predecessor State continues to exist, the rights or obligations arising from an internationally wrongful act of which a predecessor State has been either the author or the injured State pass to the successor State.

Commentary

296.   Article 13 deals with the merger (or 'unification') of two (or more) States to form a new State. In such a case, there is an extinction of two (or more) predecessor States resulting in the creation of one *new* State. International practice draws a clear distinction between 'unification' of States and the different situation of the 'incorporation' of one State into another *already existing* State. In the case of merger, all predecessor States cease to exist, whereas in the case of incorporation only the incorporated State ceases to exist and the enlarged (successor) State continues its prior legal personality. For this reason, the

---

494 *Application of the Convention on the Prevention and Punishment of the Crime of Genocide (Croatia v. Serbia)*, Judgment of 3 February 2015, ICJ Rep. 2015, 52, para. 104. According to the ILC Special Rapporteur, Second Report, 2018, para. 119, this passage 'implies that the rule under article 10, paragraph 2, will have its full effect in cases where the breached obligation continues to be binding on a new State'.

495 *Application*, ibid., para. 104.

496 Ibid., paras. 104–105.

497 Ibid., para. 105.

498 See analysis below when examining Article 15 on dissolution.

499 *Application of the Convention on the Prevention and Punishment of the Crime of Genocide (Croatia v. Serbia)*, Judgment of 3 February 2015, ICJ Rep. 2015, Separate Opinion of Judge Tomka, para. 26.

500 Ibid., dissenting opinion Judge Cançado Trindade, paras. 24–25.

Resolution deals with these two cases separately.[501] Cases of incorporation are dealt with in Article 14. The most recent case of unification is that of Yemen in 1990.[502]

297.   The first section examines the principle of succession adopted at Article 13 (Section 1). Examples of State practice supporting the principle will be analysed in the following section (Section 2).

1   The Principle of Succession to Rights and Obligations

298.   Under Article 13, since the predecessor States cease to exist as a consequence of the unification, it follows that the rights and obligations arising from an internationally wrongful act regarding which one of the predecessor States was either the author or the victim pass to the successor State. This solution is supported by scholars[503] and was followed by Mohammed Bedjaoui, the first ILC Special Rapporteur on succession of States on matters other than treaties.[504] The ILC Special Rapporteur adopted the same solution at Draft Article 10(1).[505]

299.   This provision is an illustration of one of the fundamental goals guiding the Resolution: to prevent 'situations of State succession from leading to an avoidance of the consequences of internationally wrongful acts, particularly in the form of the extinction or disappearance of the obligation to repair, by virtue of the mere fact of the State succession'.[506] Thus, any other solution than the transfer of the obligation to repair in the context of merger would lead to the unfair consequence that the internationally wrongful act committed before the date of succession would remain unpunished and the injured State victim of such an act would be left (after the date of succession) with no debtor against whom it could file a claim for reparation.[507] The same general approach has been adopted

---

501   The same approach is adopted by ILC Special Rapporteur, Second Report, 2018, paras. 149–151, distinguishing the two different categories under the common umbrella term 'Uniting of States' (Draft Article 10).

502   The Yemen Arab Republic (North Yemen) and the People's Democratic Republic of Yemen (South Yemen) merged on 22 May 1990 to form a unified Republic of Yemen. Article 1 of the *Agreement on the Establishment of the Republic of Yemen and the Organisation of the Thirty-Month Interim Period*, 22 April 1990, entered into force on 21 May 1990, in: (1990) 30 ILM 820.

503   See analysis in: Dumberry, *State Succession to International Responsibility*, 93–94, referring to many writers, including Verzijl, *International Law in Historical Perspective* (vol. VII), 219–220; Crawford, *Brownlie's Principles of Public International Law*, 424; Volkovitsch, 'Righting Wrongs: Toward a New Theory of State Succession to Responsibility of International Delicts', 2200; Peterschmitt, *La succession d'États et la responsabilité internationale pour fait illicite*, 67–69.

504   ILC, 'First Report on Succession of States in Respect of Rights and Duties Resulting from Sources other than Treaties', by Mr Mohammed Bedjaoui, Special Rapporteur, 20th session of the ILC, 1968, UN Doc. A/CN.4/204, ILC Report, A/7209/Rev.1 (A/23/9), 1968, chp. III(C)(a), paras. 45–50, in: (1968) II *Yearbook ILC*, 94, at 101, para. 47.

505   ILC Special Rapporteur, Second Report, 2018, paras. 149ff. See Draft Article 10(1): 'When two or more States unite and form a new successor State, the obligations arising from an internationally wrongful act of any predecessor State pass to the successor State.'

506   Final Report, para. 53, in: (2015) 76 *Annuaire de l'Institut de Droit international*, 534.

507   Dumberry, *State Succession to International Responsibility*, 95.

by the ILC Special Rapporteur.[508] It should be added that the Report considers this principle as a 'presumption' finding application 'unless the States concerned (which include an injured State) otherwise agreed'.[509]

2   Examples of State Practice Supporting the Principle

300. The solution of succession adopted at Article 13 is supported by State practice. There are three examples in the context of the unification of Egypt and Syria into a single State in 1958 (the 'United Arab Republic', which lasted only three years). The United Arab Republic (the successor State) took over the responsibility for obligations arising from internationally wrongful acts committed by the predecessor States and provided compensation to injured third States.[510] All examples (examined in the next paragraphs) involved actions taken by Egypt (the predecessor State) against Western properties in the context of the nationalisation of the Suez Canal in 1956 and the 'Egyptianisation' of foreign-owned properties.

301. One example is the agreement concluded between the United Kingdom and the United Arab Republic in 1959.[511] The preamble to the agreement expressly provided that it was entered into by the United Arab Republic 'as successor of the Government of the Republic of Egypt, and acting so far only as concerns the territory of the Republic of Egypt'. Under this agreement, the United Arab Republic undertook to terminate all sequestration measures taken against British property and also provided for a lump sum of UK£27.5 million to be paid as compensation 'in full and final settlement' of British claims. While neither side expressly admitted 'liability in respect of any of these claims', it is evident that they did not reject it either.[512] Another similar agreement was concluded by the United Arab Republic with France in 1958.[513] These are two illustrations of the principle of succession to *obligations* arising from the commission of a wrongful act in the context of a merger of States.

---

508 ILC Special Rapporteur, Second Report, 2018, para. 147: 'Unlike the categories of succession analysed so far, where the general rule of non-succession implies the responsibility of the predecessor State, this scenario presents a different issue. The wrongdoing State does not exist any longer, but the consequences of its international wrongful acts continue. The application of the general rule of non-succession to such cases would mean that no State incurs obligations arising from internationally wrongful acts. Such a solution would be hardly compatible with the objectives of international law, which include equitable and reasonable settlement of disputes.'
509 Ibid., para. 164.
510 See analysis in: Dumberry, *State Succession to International Responsibility*, 95ff. See also: ILC Special Rapporteur, First Report, 2017, para. 42; ILC Special Rapporteur, Second Report, 2018, para. 153. More generally on the question, see: Eugene Cotran, 'Some Legal Aspects of the Formation of the United Arab Republic and the United Arab States' (1959) 8 *ICLQ* 367.
511 *Agreement between the Government of the United Kingdom of Great Britain and Northern Ireland and the Government of the United Arab Republic Concerning Financial and Commercial Relations and British Property in Egypt*, 343 UNTS, no. 4925, 159.
512 Final Report, para. 86, in: (2015) 76 *Annuaire de l'Institut de Droit international*, 543.
513 *Accord général entre le gouvernement de la République française et le gouvernement de la République arabe unie*, in: La documentation française, 18 October 1958, no. 2473; (1958) *RGDIP* 738ff. See analysis in: Dumberry, *State Succession to International Responsibility*, 96.

302.   Finally, a third example in the context of the creation of the United Arab Republic supports the solution of succession to *rights*. The new State submitted claims requesting 'adequate compensation' (UK£78 million) to the United Kingdom and France for acts committed during the 1956 Suez Canal crisis against Egypt (one of the two predecessor States).[514] In an exchange of notes which led to the conclusion of the agreement in 1959 and mentioned in the previous paragraph, the United Kingdom refused to admit any responsibility and rejected having to pay any compensation to the United Arab Republic.[515] Ultimately, the United Arab Republic waived all its claims for war damage against the United Kingdom in return for the latter waiving its own claims for compensation arising out of Egypt's seizure of the Suez Canal. What matters for the present purpose is the fact that the United Kingdom did not seem to have objected, as a matter of principle, to the right of the new State (the United Arab Republic) to seek reparation for internationally wrongful acts which had been committed against one of the predecessor States (Egypt) before the date of succession.[516]

303.   In his Second Report, the ILC Special Rapporteur refers to another relevant example in the context of the merger of South and North Vietnam to create a new State in 1976.[517] In 1995, Vietnam and the United States concluded a lump-sum agreement under which the former would provide compensation to US nationals whose property had been expropriated at the end of the war in return for the United States releasing US$240 million-worth of assets belonging to South Vietnam held in US banks.[518]

ARTICLE 14:

Incorporation of a State into another existing State

> When a State is incorporated into another existing State and ceases to exist, the rights or obligations arising from an internationally wrongful act of which the predecessor State has been the author or the injured State pass to the successor State.

Commentary

304.   Article 14 deals with the case of the incorporation of a State into another existing State. This type of succession differs from a transfer of territory, which only concerns *part of a territory* of a State which is integrated into another State. Incorporation involves the *whole territory and population* of the State which is integrated into another State. Another difference between these two types is that in the context of transfer of territory, the predecessor State is not extinguished as a result of the loss of part of its territory.[519] On the

---

514   See analysis in: Dumberry, ibid., 316ff.
515   The text of the exchange of notes is found in: (1960) 54 *AJIL* 511–519; M.M. Whiteman, *Digest of International Law*, vol. II (Washington: Dept. of State, 1973), 875.
516   Dumberry, *State Succession to International Responsibility*, 318.
517   ILC Special Rapporteur, Second Report, 2018, paras. 154ff.
518   *Agreement between the Government of the United States of America and the Government of the Socialist Republic of Vietnam concerning the settlement of certain property claims*, signed in Hanoi, 28 January 1995, 2420 UNTS No. 43661.
519   See Dumberry, *State Succession to International Responsibility*, 18, 21.

contrary, in the context of incorporation, the predecessor State ceases to exist. Importantly, the extinction of the predecessor State does not result in the creation of a *new* State but simply in the enlargement of the territory and population of an existing State. The most recent case of the incorporation of a State into another existing one is that of the GDR into the FRG on 3 October 1990.

305.   The first section examines the principle of succession adopted at Article 14 (Section 1). Examples of State practice supporting the principle will be analysed in the following section (Section 2).

1   The Principle of Succession to Rights and Obligations

306.   Under Article 14, the rights and obligations arising from an internationally wrongful act regarding which the predecessor State was the author or the victim pass to the successor State. Again, this solution is coherent with the general aim of the Resolution. Given the fact that the predecessor State ceases to exist as a consequence of its incorporation into another existing State, any other solution than succession would result in an internationally wrongful act committed before the date of succession remaining unpunished and the injured State (or international law subject) victim of such an act being left with no debtor against whom to file a claim for reparation. The application of the principle of succession in the context of incorporation prevents such an unjust result.[520] This solution of succession is also supported by scholars.[521] The ILC Special Rapporteur adopted the same solution at Draft Article 10(2).[522] It should be added that the Report considers this principle as a 'presumption' finding application 'unless the States concerned (which include an injured State) otherwise agreed'.[523]

2   Examples of State Practice Supporting the Principle

307.   There are several examples of State practice in the context of the incorporation of the GDR into the FRG whereby the successor State took over the obligations arising from internationally wrongful acts committed by the former (the predecessor State) before the date of succession.[524] *The Treaty on the Establishment of German Unity* between the FRG and the GDR of 31 August 1990 offers an example.[525] As mentioned above,[526] Article 24(1)

---

520   Ibid., 84.
521   See ibid., referring to the position of a number of writers.
522   ILC Special Rapporteur, Second Report, 2018, paras. 147, 157ff. See Draft Article 10(2): 'When a State is incorporated into another existing State and ceases to exist, the obligations from an internationally wrongful act of the predecessor State pass to the successor State'.
523   ILC Special Rapporteur, Second Report, 2018, para. 164.
524   See analysis in: Dumberry, *State Succession to International Responsibility*, 84ff; ILC Special Rapporteur, Second Report, 2018, paras. 157ff.
525   *Treaty on the Establishment of German Unity*, 31 August 1990, in: (1991) 30 ILM 457, (1991) 51 ZaöRV 494.
526   The question is examined at Section 1.1.1 of the Article 6 Commentary above, analysing devolution agreements.

is considered as a recognition of the succession of the FRG to the claims and liabilities of the GDR.[527] Another example concerns different laws adopted by Germany regarding the restitution and compensation for property which had been expropriated in the GDR before the date of succession.[528] The question of State succession for acts of expropriation committed by East Germany was addressed in a decision of 1 July 1999 by the Federal Administrative Court.[529] The Court rejected, as a matter of principle, the responsibility of the FRG for obligations arising from internationally wrongful acts (expropriation of real property) committed by the former GDR against a Dutch national. However, the Court also stated that because the expropriated property was now part of 'unified' Germany, the unfulfilled obligations of the GDR to pay compensation to the injured individual had now passed to the successor State.[530] Also, under an agreement for the settlement of property claims signed in 1992 between the FRG and the United States, Germany provided compensation to US nationals for expropriated property which had been located in the territory of the former GDR.[531]

308. In his Second Report, the ILC Special Rapporteur refers to another example in the context of the incorporation of Singapore into the Federation of Malaya, which became Malaysia.[532]

309. It should be noted that there are also other, older examples, involving *annexation* of territories, which have, on the contrary, followed the opposite solution and where the successor State was *not* considered responsible for obligations arising from internationally wrongful acts which had been committed by the predecessor State.[533] The following paragraphs will briefly examine these examples and explain why they are, in fact, not relevant for the interpretation of Article 14.

---

527 See analysis in: Dumberry, *State Succession to International Responsibility*, 86; ILC Special Rapporteur, Second Report, 2018, paras. 158–159.

528 See analysis in: Dumberry, ibid., 87ff. See also: Crawford, *State Responsibility: The General Part*, 449–450.

529 German Federal Administrative Court, Decision of 1 July 1999, *BVerwG* 7 B 2.99, reprinted in: (1999) 52 *NJW* 3354. The case is examined in: Dumberry, ibid., 90ff. See also: Crawford, ibid., 450; ILC Special Rapporteur, Second Report, 2018, para. 160.

530 The Court stated that the successor State's obligation would be limited to the payment of compensation and not extend to the restitution of property. It should be noted that the claim was ultimately dismissed by the Court on the ground that the injured Dutch national had already received some sort of compensation for his lost property from the GDR. To the extent that the victim had no valid claim for expropriation against the GDR *before the date of succession*, the Court simply decided that no such valid claim existed against the FRG after the date of succession.

531 *Agreement between the Government of the Federal Republic of Germany and the Government of the United States of America Concerning the Settlement of Certain Property Claims*, 13 May 1992, in: TIAS no. 11959; 1911 UNTS 27. See analysis in: Dumberry, *State Succession to International Responsibility*, 91ff; Crawford, *State Responsibility: The General Part*, 449–450; ILC Special Rapporteur, Second Report, 2018, para. 161.

532 ILC Special Rapporteur, Second Report, 2018, para. 162, referring to Article 76 of Annex A of an Agreement, the 'Malaysia Bill', providing as follows: 'All rights, liabilities and obligations relating to any matter which was immediately before Malaysia Day the responsibility of the government of a Borneo State or of Singapore, but which on that day becomes the responsibility of the Federal Government, shall on that day devolve upon the Federation, unless otherwise agreed between the Federal Government and the government of the State'.

533 Dumberry, *State Succession to International Responsibility*, 63ff.

310. The practice of non-succession was adopted by States in the context of the unification of Italy (1860–1861), the annexation of Burma by Great Britain (in 1886), the
annexation of Madagascar by France (in 1896) and the annexation of the Boer Republic of
South Africa by Great Britain (in 1902).[534] It was also adopted by municipal courts, such as
English courts, in the context of the latter annexation.[535]

311. The position of non-succession was also adopted on two occasions by a U.S./Great
Britain Arbitral Commission. One such case is the *R.E. Brown* case (1923) involving a
claim by the United States on behalf of one national against Great Britain for acts taken
by the Boer Republic of South Africa (the predecessor State) before it was annexed by
Great Britain in 1902.[536] The Arbitral Commission made statements which constitute the
very first *dictum* of an international tribunal in support of the doctrine of non-succession
to obligations arising from the commission of internationally wrongful acts.[537] It indicated
that it could not endorse a doctrine based on 'an assertion that a succeeding state acquiring
a territory by conquest without any undertaking to assume such liabilities is bound to take
affirmative steps to right the wrong by the former state'.[538]

312. Another relevant case decided by the same arbitral commission is the *Redward* case
(better known as the *Hawaiian Claims* case, 1925) involving a group of British nationals
who had been illegally detained and expelled from Hawaii by the 'Republic of Hawaii'
(the predecessor State) in 1895 before these islands were formally annexed by the United
States in 1898.[539] The Arbitral Commission rejected the argument in favour of succession
put forward by Great Britain:

> In the first place it assumes a general principle of succession to liability for
> delicts, to which the case of succession of one State to another through con-
> quest would be an exception. We think there is no such principle. It was denied
> in the Brown case and has never been contended for to any such extent (...)
> nor do we see any valid reason for distinguishing termination of a legal unit
> of international law through conquest from termination by any other mode of
> merging in, or swallowing up by, some other legal unit. In either case the legal
> unit which did the wrong no longer exists, and legal liability for the wrong
> has been extinguished with it.[540]

313. These old examples of State practice involving annexation of States were influenced
by the idea that responsibility is an *intuitu personae* phenomenon, i.e. that it is intrinsically
linked to the personality of the State, and that, consequently, there cannot be any succession
in this field. As explained above, the Resolution does not deal with the question of

534 See the detailed analysis of all cases in: ibid., 65ff.
535 *West Rand Central Gold Mining Company Ldt. v. The King*, decision of 1 June 1905, in: (1905) LR 2
      K.B., 391; *British International Law Cases*, vol. II (London: Stevens, 1965) 283.
536 *R.E. Brown* (United States v. Great Britain), Award of 23 November 1923, 6 UNRIAA 130. See the
      analysis of this case in: Dumberry, *State Succession to International Responsibility*, 73–77.
537 Ibid.
538 Ibid.
539 *Hawaiian Claims* case (Great Britain v. United States), Award of 10 November 1925, 6 UNRIAA 158.
      See the analysis of this case in: Dumberry, *State Succession to International Responsibility*, 78ff.
540 *Hawaiian Claims* case, 158.

succession to responsibility, but rather with the issue of succession to rights and obligations arising as a consequence of responsibility.[541] Another reason for discarding the relevance of the *Brown* and *Hawaiian* cases is mentioned in the *USA Restatement*: 'These cases date from the age of colonialism when colonial powers resisted any rule that would make them responsible for delicts of states which they regarded as uncivilized. The authority of those cases a century later is doubtful.'[542]

ARTICLE 15:

Dissolution of a State

1.   When a State dissolves and ceases to exist and the parts of its territory form two or more successor States, the rights or obligations arising from an internationally wrongful act in relation to which the predecessor State has been the author or the injured State pass, bearing in mind the duty to negotiate and according to the circumstances referred to in paragraphs 2 and 3 of the present Article, to one, several or all the successor States.

2.   In order to determine which of the successor States becomes bearer of the rights described in the preceding paragraph, a relevant factor will in particular be the existence of a direct link between the consequences of the internationally wrongful act committed against the predecessor State and the territory or the population of the successor State or States.

3.   In order to determine which of the successor States becomes bearer of the obligations described in paragraph 1, a relevant factor will in particular be, in addition to that mentioned in paragraph 2, the fact that the author of the internationally wrongful act was an organ of the predecessor State that later became an organ of the successor State.

Commentary

314.   This provision deals with the question of succession to rights and obligations arising from the commission of an internationally wrongful act in the context of a dissolution of a State. This is the situation where the predecessor State is dissolved and ceases to exist and parts of its territory form two or more new successor States. The provision is also applicable in the rarer case where a State ceases to exist and its territory and population become part of other existing States.[543] The latter situation is different from that of transfer of territory regulated by Article 11, since the predecessor State ceases to exist. The situation

---

541   See the analysis above examining Article 2(1).
542   Restatement (Third) of the Foreign Relations Law of the United States, § 209; Reporters' Note 7 (1987), adding that 'At least in some cases, it would be unfair to deny the claim of an injured party because the state that committed the wrong was absorbed by another state'.
543   This was the case in the context of the extinction of Poland in 1775. The former territory of Poland was divided among Austria, Prussia and Russia.

can be assimilated to that of the incorporation of a State into another existing one under Article 14. However, the difference with incorporation is that the rarer case of dissolution examined here leads to the emergence of several successor States, not just one.

315. The break-up of the Czech and Slovak Federal Republic in 1990 was an uncontroversial case of dissolution. While the question of the legal qualification of the break-up of the SFRY raised controversy for years, it was ultimately settled with the acceptance by the then FRY (Serbia and Montenegro) of its status as a successor State rather than as the continuing State.[544] Some elements of State practice relating to these cases are discussed below.

316. While Article 15(1) sets out the general principle of succession (discussed in Section 1), paragraphs (2) and (3) refer to two factors that are relevant to determine which of the different successor States should be the holder of rights or obligations arising from the commission of a wrongful act (Section 2). One important point to mention is that these provisions can be of assistance in the context of the negotiations between successor States and are without prejudice to any agreement between them leading to other solutions in specific cases. As mentioned in Article 3, the guiding principles proposed in the Resolution only have a subsidiary character. One example of such an agreement between the successor States is the *Agreement on Succession Issues* of 29 June 2001 entered into by the successor States to the former Yugoslavia.[545] The preamble indicates that the Agreement was reached after discussions and negotiations 'with a view to identifying and determining the equitable distribution among themselves of rights, obligations, assets and liabilities of the former Socialist Federal Republic of Yugoslavia'. Article 7 mentions that this Agreement 'finally settles the mutual rights and obligations of the successor States in respect of succession issues covered by this Agreement'. Article 2 of Annex F of the Agreement (entitled 'Other rights, interests and liabilities') specifically deals with the issue of internationally wrongful acts committed by the SFRY against third States before the date of succession. It reads as follows:

> All *claims against the SFRY* which are not otherwise covered by this Agreement shall be considered by the Standing Joint Committee established under Article 4 of this Agreement. The successor States shall inform one another of all such claims against the SFRY.[546]

317. The fact that '[a]ll claims against the SFRY' will be 'considered' by the Standing Joint Committee clearly shows that the obligations of the predecessor State towards

544 The FRY was officially admitted (as a new State) to the United Nations on 1 November 2000: UN GA Res. 55/12.
545 *Agreement on Succession Issues*, 29 June 2001. For an analysis of this Agreement in doctrine, see: Castren Stahn, 'The Agreement on Succession Issues of the Former Socialist Federal Republic of Yugoslavia' (2002) 96(2) *AJIL* 379–397; Jenny Stavridi & Alexandros Kolliopoulos, 'L'Accord du 29 juin 2001 portant sur des questions de succession entre les Etats issus de la dissolution de l'ex-Yougoslavie' (2002) *AFDI* 163–184; Ryszard Piotrowicz, 'Status of Yugoslavia: Agreement at Last' (2001) 77 *ALJ* 95–99; Dumberry, *State Succession to International Responsibility*, 119–122.
546 Ibid. (emphasis added).

injured States do not simply disappear as a result of the dissolution of the SFRY.[547] This is indeed the position which was adopted by Serbia in its pleadings in the *Croatia Genocide Convention* case:

> [B]oth Croatia and Serbia are parties to the 2001 'Agreement on Succession Issue' which in Article 2 of its Annex F provides that (…) 'All claims against the SFRY which are not otherwise covered by this Agreement shall be considered by the Standing Joint Committee established under Article 4 of this Agreement.'. This provision, according to the former Special Negotiator, the late Sir Arthur Watts, *governs claims arising out of succession to international responsibility directed against the SFRY.* It precludes the submission of the claim in the current proceedings, or, at the very least, presupposes that prior to bringing the matter before the Court, Croatia ought to have seised the Committee set up by the Agreement. Yet, Croatia has so far never done so.[548]

318.   Yet, as noted in the Final Report, in the specific context of dissolution, the 'successor State(s) will assume the rights and obligations stemming from an internationally wrongful act suffered or committed by the predecessor State, no matter whether an agreement between them so provides'.[549] On this last point, the ILC Special Rapporteur mentioned in his Second Report that no reference is made to agreements under Article 15(1) of the Resolution. In his Report he takes what he calls 'a slightly more cautious approach':[550] 'While accepting the presumption of the transfer of obligations from the predecessor State to the successor State or States, [the ILC Special Rapporteur] underlines the role of agreements.'[551]

319.   The absence of any reference to agreements at Article 15(1) is simply due to the fact that the Resolution has already established that the parties to the State succession relationship cannot solely decide on their own about which of them will bear the obligation to repair.[552] The victim must be allowed to take position on the matter. The injured State will therefore need to approve any outcome of allocation of obligations decided by other States.

1   The Principle of Succession to Rights and Obligations

320.   Article 15(1) establishes the solution of succession, i.e. that the rights and obligations stemming from the commission of an internationally wrongful act regarding which the

---

547 Dumberry, *State Succession to International Responsibility*, 119–122; Crawford, *State Responsibility: The General Part*, 452; Šturma, 'State Succession in Respect of International Responsibility', 665; ILC Special Rapporteur, First Report, 2017, para. 109; ILC Special Rapporteur, Second Report, 2018, para. 178.
548 *Application of the Convention on the Prevention and Punishment of the Crime of Genocide (Croatia v. Serbia)*, Verbatim Record, Andreas Zimmermann (Serbia), Mar. 27, 2014, paras. 52–53 (emphasis added).
549 Final Report, para. 49, in: (2015) 76 *Annuaire de l'Institut de Droit international*, 532.
550 ILC Special Rapporteur, Second Report, 2018, para. 187.
551 Ibid. Later, he added that he 'wishes to make it clear that a transfer of obligations may take place according to or in the absence of an agreement' (para. 189).
552 See analysis of Articles 3, 6 and 8, above.

predecessor State was the author or the victim pass to the successor State(s). This provision is in accordance with one of the most fundamental principles guiding the Resolution: the need to prevent the consequences of internationally wrongful acts simply disappearing as a result of the extinction of the predecessor State. The application of the principle of non-succession in the context of dissolution would indeed result in the injured State being left with no debtor to provide compensation for the damage it suffered.[553] The same general approach has been adopted by the ILC Special Rapporteur.[554] The Resolution adopted by the Institute ensures that whenever the predecessor State ceases to exist, the rights and obligations arising from the commission of a wrongful act will pass to the successor State(s).[555] The Resolution indeed adopts the same principle for cases of merger (Article 13) and incorporation of a State (Article 14).

321.   Similarly to the situation examined above in the context of incorporation of a State (Article 14), a number of old examples of State practice and municipal courts cases in the context of dissolution have followed the doctrine of non-succession.[556] For instance, Austria argued that it was a *new* State in 1918 and that the break-up of the Austria-Hungary Dual Monarchy after the First World War was a case of dissolution. Austria took that position precisely in order to avoid having to assume any obligations arising out of the War.[557] Its position was based on the assumption that the doctrine of non-succession would apply in the context of dissolution. This claim of non-continuity and non-succession was endorsed by the Austrian Constitutional Court in several cases dealing with issues of State succession. In these cases, it was decided that Austria was not responsible for the obligations of Austria-Hungary, with the exception of those for which the new State had expressly indicated its willingness to succeed.[558] It should be added that other older examples of State practice have, however, followed the principle of succession. One illustration is in the context of the dissolution of the Union of Colombia (taking place between 1829 and 1831).[559]

322.   In several recent examples of State practice, the successor States have agreed to take over the obligations arising from internationally wrongful acts committed by the

---

553   Dumberry, *State Succession to International Responsibility*, 104.
554   ILC Special Rapporteur, Second Report, 2018, paras. 147, 167, 185. See Draft Article 11(1): 'When a State dissolves and ceases to exist and the parts of its territory form two or more successor States, the obligations arising from the commission of an internationally wrongful act of the predecessor State pass, subject to an agreement, to one, several or all the successor States'. Importantly, as mentioned above, that provision adds the expression 'subject to an agreement'.
555   Final Report, paras. 54–55, in: (2015) 76 *Annuaire de l'Institut de Droit international*, 534; Dumberry, *State Succession to International Responsibility*, 104–105.
556   See a number of examples analysed in: Dumberry, *State Succession to International Responsibility*, 98ff; ILC Special Rapporteur, Second Report, 2018, para. 167.
557   Marek, *Identity and Continuity of States in Public International Law*, 199, see also at 218–219. The example is examined in: Dumberry, ibid., 99.
558   *Military Pensions (Austria) Case*, Austrian Constitutional Court, 7 May 1919, case no. 126, in: *Sammlung der Erkenntnisse des österreichischen Verfassungsgerichtshofes*, vol. I (1919), no. 9, 17; (1919–1922) *Annual Digest* 66. Other cases are mentioned in: Dumberry, ibid., 102.
559   This case is examined in: Dumberry, ibid., 106; ILC Special Rapporteur, Second Report, 2018, paras. 168–169.

predecessor State.[560] For the ILC Special Rapporteur, 'modern State practice, though not very frequently occurring (some agreements and cases), allows for a rejection of a strict and automatic application of the principle of non-succession'.[561] An example already mentioned is the 2001 *Agreement on Succession Issues* entered into among all successor States to the former SFRY.[562] This agreement is also an example where successor States have accepted the validity of the principle of succession to the right to claim reparation.[563] Thus, Article 1 of Annex F to the Agreement deals with the outcome of internationally wrongful acts committed by third States against the SFRY before its dissolution. Under this provision, claims of the SFRY for reparation against other States before its dissolution are considered as 'rights and interests which belonged to the SFRY' and, as such, they should be 'shared' among the successor States.

323.   The succession rule is also supported by scholars.[564] The unfairness which would result from the application of the principle of non-succession in cases of dissolution was acknowledged by the Arbitral Tribunal in the 1956 *Lighthouse Arbitration* case.[565] There is also support among scholars for the principle of succession to the right to reparation arising from the commission of a wrongful act.[566]

324.   Given the firm principle of succession set out at Article 15(1), the relevant question in the context of dissolution is which of the different successor States should be the holder of the rights and obligations after the date of succession.[567] Article 15(1) indicates that such rights and obligations will pass to 'one, several or all the successor States' depending on the circumstances referred to at Articles 15(2) and (3). These circumstances are examined in the next sections.[568]

---

560   A number of examples are analysed in: Dumberry, ibid., 103ff.
561   ILC Special Rapporteur, Second Report, 2018, para. 167.
562   *Agreement on Succession Issues* of 29 June 2001. This case is examined in: Dumberry, *State Succession to International Responsibility*, 119ff.
563   Ibid., 318, 322; ILC Special Rapporteur, Second Report, 2018, para. 178.
564   See Dumberry, ibid., 104–105, referring to the position of several writers. See inter alia: Verzijl, *International Law in Historical Perspective* (vol. VII), 219–220; Georg Schwarzenberger, *International Law as Applied by International Courts and Tribunals* 3rd ed., vol. I (London: Steven & Sons, 1957), 175–176; Crawford, *Brownlie's Principles of Public International Law*, 424.
565   *Lighthouse Arbitration* case, at 93: 'What justice, or even what juridical logic, would there be, for example, in the hypothesis of an international wrong committed against another Power by a State which subsequently splits up into two new independent States, in regarding the latter as being free from an international obligation to make compensation which would without any doubt have lain on the former, predecessor, State which had committed the wrong?'
566   Dumberry, *State Succession to International Responsibility*, 318–319, referring to the position of several writers.
567   See also ILC Special Rapporteur, Second Report, 2018, para. 185: 'in cases of dissolution of State, obligations arising from the internationally wrongful act do not disappear and usually pass to one or more successor States. It is less clear, however, to which of the successor States they pass and to what extent those States would be bound by such obligations.'
568   Again, the subsidiary character of the solutions mentioned at Article 15(2) and (3) should be highlighted. Thus, these solutions should prevail only insofar as the successor States have not themselves specifically agreed to a different solution (Article 3).

2   Circumstances Determining which of the Successor State(s) Should Be the Holder of Rights and Obligations

325. Paragraphs (2) and (3) of Article 15 deal with two different situations depending on whether the predecessor State was the author or the victim of a wrongful act. Thus, while Article 15(2) deals with the issue of succession to *rights* (discussed in Section 2.1), Article 15(3) concerns the question of succession to *obligations* (Section 2.2). The next sections examine the following two circumstances[569]:

-    Existence of a 'direct link' between the consequences of a wrongful act and the territory or population of one successor State (Section 2.1);

-    The author of the wrongful act was an organ of the predecessor State that later became an organ of the successor State (Section 2.2).

2.1   EXISTENCE OF A 'DIRECT LINK' BETWEEN THE CONSEQUENCES OF A WRONGFUL ACT AND THE TERRITORY/POPULATION OF ONE SUCCESSOR STATE

326. Article 15(2) concerns the situation of an internationally wrongful act committed *against* the predecessor State. The question is which of the successor States should be considered as the holder of the right to reparation after the date of succession. The existence of a 'direct link' between the consequences of the internationally wrongful act committed against the predecessor State and the territory or the population of the successor State(s) is a 'relevant factor'. Thus, the existence of such a link militates in favour of transferring this right to reparation to that specific successor State. The meaning and the nature of such 'direct link' have already been discussed above.[570] However, a distinction regarding the drafting of Articles 12(2) and 15(2) should be highlighted. On the one hand, Article 12(2) affirms the passing of rights to the successor State in cases of separation if that direct link exists. On the other hand, under Article 15(2) the existence of such a link is only considered as a relevant factor for the determination of whether or not rights should pass to a particular successor State. The reason for this distinction is that in the case of separation the question concerns the relationship between the predecessor and a single successor State, while in the case of dissolution there is a plurality of successor States. Article 15(2) thus leaves open the possibility that other relevant factors

569 For ILC Special Rapporteur, Second Report, 2018, para. 189, these two circumstances 'are certainly relevant but not the only possible factors. In cases where no territorial link exists, the distribution of the obligation of reparation (in particular, compensation) may follow the equitable proportion used for distribution of State property and debts. In addition, other factors should be taken into account, such as the nature and form of reparation. It may include the situations where, due to the nature of restitution, only a given successor State is in a position to make such restitution, etc. At this stage, it seems impossible to determine with a sufficient clarity all the relevant factors. They can be better addressed at a later stage, in the context of the plurality of States and their shared responsibility'. The matter is addressed in the Resolution at Article 7 (Plurality of successor States).

570 See analysis of Articles 5(2), 11(2) and 12(2) above.

may be taken into consideration at the moment of the distribution of the rights belonging to the predecessor State among the successor States.[571]

327.   The 'direct link' approach adopted by the Resolution in the context of dissolution has since then been endorsed by writers.[572] Article 15(2) is a concrete illustration in the specific context of dissolution of the general principle set out at Article 5(2).

328.   At Draft Article 11(2), the ILC Special Rapporteur does refer to the importance of this 'direct link' in the following manner: 'Successor States should negotiate in good faith with the injured State and among themselves in order to settle the consequences of the internationally wrongful act of the predecessor State'. The provision further adds that in this context, 'they should take into consideration a territorial link, an equitable proportion and other relevant factors'.[573] This proposal partially integrates what the Resolution refers to in Article 7, dealing with cases of plurality of successor States.

329.   In the *Gabčíkovo/Nagymaros Project* case, the principle of succession to *rights and obligations* was recognised (at least implicitly) in the Special Agreement entered into between Slovakia and Hungary to refer a dispute to the ICJ.[574] Thus, the parties explicitly stipulated that 'the Slovak Republic is one of the two successor States of the Czech and Slovak Federal Republic and the sole successor State in respect of rights and obligations relating to the Gabčíkovo-Nagymaros Project'.[575] The reason why both parties agreed that Slovakia (and not the Czech Republic, the other successor State to the former Czechoslovakia) should be the holder of such rights and obligations is because of the existence of a 'direct link' between the alleged wrongful acts and the territory and the population of that successor State.[576] On the Czechoslovakian side, the project was indeed located in the territory of Slovakia. It should be added, however, that in their pleadings both Hungary and Slovakia denied the existence of any general principle of succession to responsibility.[577] The Court did not directly address this specific point. The Court simply noted that:

> [a]ccording to the Preamble of the Special Agreement, the Parties agreed that Slovakia is the sole successor State to Czechoslovakia in respect of rights and obligations relating to the Gabcikovo-Nagymaros Project. Slovakia thus may be liable to pay compensation not only for its own wrongful conduct

---

571   See also: ILC Special Rapporteur, Second Report, 2018, para. 189,
572   Jakubowski, *State Succession in Cultural Property*, 269–271.
573   It should be noted that this provision does not refer to 'population', but only to the territorial link.
574   This is the position adopted by a number of writers: Dumberry, *State Succession to International Responsibility*, 103; Mikulka, 'Succession of States in Respect of Rights of an Injured State', 966; Mikulka, 'State Succession and Responsibility', 295–296.
575   *Gabčíkovo-Nagymaros Project case*, 11, para. 2.
576   Dumberry, *State Succession to International Responsibility*, 289–290. See also: ILC Special Rapporteur, Second Report, 2018, para. 175, indicating that 'the close link between the internationally wrongful act or its consequences and the territory is another important factor' which explain the decision of the Court. See also at para. 188.
577   *Reply of the Republic of Hungary*, vol. I, 20 June 1995, at para. 3.163; *Counter-Memorial of the Slovak Republic*, vol. I, 5 December 1994, at paras. 3.59, 3.60. See the analysis in: Dumberry, *State Succession to International Responsibility*, 115–116, 290, 319–321.

but also for that of Czechoslovakia, and it is entitled to be compensated for the damage sustained by Czechoslovakia as well as by itself as a result of the wrongful conduct of Hungary.[578]

330. This was the manner by which the Court decided to refer to the succession rule without taking a stance about its customary law character. Given that the parties concerned recognised the existence of the rule, there was indeed no need for the Court to take position on the matter. Nevertheless, it can be argued that the Court did not reject the validity of the possibility of the succession to rights and obligations from the predecessor State to the successor States.[579] The ILC Special Rapporteur has taken the position that in this case the Court has *endorsed* the principle of succession.[580] For him, this case may be the 'most important judicial decision in favour of the transfer of responsibility'[581]:

> Notwithstanding its reference to the special agreement (compromis) between Hungary and Slovakia, the Court thus seems to recognize the succession in respect of secondary (responsibility) obligations and secondary rights resulting from wrongful acts. Indeed, the present report does not deny the role of the Special Agreement. However, it was not a perfect agreement on all issues of succession and responsibility, which remained the object of dispute... It means that the Court had to decide the issue of responsibility in spite of the contradictory pronouncements of the parties to this dispute. It seems therefore that the role of the presumed consent (in the Special Agreement) should not be overestimated. However important was this Agreement, there are nevertheless also other relevant circumstances. They include the fact that the 1977 treaty established a territorial regime, an argument maintained by Slovakia, denied by Hungary and ultimately upheld by the International Court of Justice. Indeed, the close link between the internationally wrongful act or its consequences and the territory is another important factor. Last but not least, the case also bears on the acts of the authorities of one of the republics of the Czechoslovak federation, committed in 1992, i.e. before the date of succession, which devolved in the independent and sovereign Slovak Republic.[582]

---

578   *Gabčíkovo-Nagymaros Project case,* 81, para. 151.
579   Dumberry, *State Succession to International Responsibility*, 103, 113ff. See also: Stern, 'Responsabilité internationale et succession d'États', 346–347; Jakubowski, *State Succession in Cultural Property*, 190–191; Crawford, *State Responsibility: The General Part*, 446.
580   ILC Special Rapporteur, First Report, 2017, para. 50 ('Notwithstanding the special agreement between Hungary and Slovakia, the Court thus seems to recognize the succession in respect of secondary (responsibility) obligations and secondary rights resulting from wrongful acts'); ILC Special Rapporteur, Second Report, 2018, para. 59 ('Slovakia did not incur responsibility on the basis of continuing the breach of Czechoslovakia after the date of succession (1 January 1993). Its responsibility, held by the International Court of Justice, thus can only be explained as a matter of succession to certain obligations arising from the wrongful act committed by Czechoslovakia'). See also at para. 102. He has adopted the same position elsewhere: Šturma, 'State Succession in Respect of International Responsibility', 664 ('The ICJ thus recognized succession with respect to secondary responsibility obligations and secondary rights resulting from wrongful acts').
581   ILC Special Rapporteur, Second Report, 2018, para. 172.
582   Ibid., paras. 173, 175.

331.   Importantly, under Article 15(3), further examined in the next section, the existence of a 'direct link' between the consequences of an internationally wrongful act committed *by* the predecessor State and the territory or the population of one successor State is also relevant regarding the different question of succession to *obligations*. Thus, under Article 15(3), the existence of such a direct link is a relevant factor 'in order to determine which of the successor States becomes bearer of the obligations' to repair.

332.   One example supporting the principle of succession to obligations because of the existence of a direct link between the commission of a wrongful act and the territory of one successor State arose in the context of the dissolution of the United Arab Republic in 1961.[583] After the dissolution, Egypt (as one of the two successor States) entered into several agreements with other States whereby it provided compensation to foreign nationals whose property had been nationalised by the United Arab Republic (the predecessor State) before the date of succession (i.e. during the period 1958–1961).[584] Egypt's decision to provide compensation to these injured States is most likely based on the ground that the acts of nationalisation were actually committed *in the territory of Egypt itself* and not in Syria.[585] In other words, the parties to these agreements have considered that there was a 'direct link' between the consequences of the internationally wrongful act committed by the United Arab Republic and the territory of Egypt.

2.2   THE AUTHOR OF THE WRONGFUL ACT WAS AN ORGAN OF THE PREDECESSOR STATE THAT LATER BECAME AN ORGAN OF THE SUCCESSOR STATE

333.   Article 15(3) concerns the situation of an internationally wrongful act committed before the date of the succession *by* the predecessor State against another State or subject of international law. The question is which of the successor States should be considered as the holder of the obligation to repair after the date of succession. Two factors are considered relevant under this paragraph. The first one is the existence of a 'direct link' between the consequences of an internationally wrongful act committed by the predecessor State and the territory or the population of one of the successor States.[586] This factor was examined in the previous section above. The second relevant factor is when the author of

---

583   This example is examined in: Dumberry, *State Succession to International Responsibility*, 107ff; ILC Special Rapporteur, Second Report, 2018, para. 170.

584   See, inter alia: *Agreement Between Italy and the United Arab Republic Relative to the Indemnisation of Italian Interests in Egypt with Protocol for the Application of the Exchange of Notes*, 23 March 1965, entered into force on 5 September 1966, in: *Gaz. Off.*, No. 215, 1 April 1966; in: (1966) 7 *Diritto Internazionale*, Pt. II, at 231; *Agreement between the Government of the United Kingdom of Great Britain and Northern Ireland and the Government of the Arab Republic of Egypt Regarding Compensation for British Property, Rights and Interests Affected by Arab Republic of Egypt Measures of Nationalisation and other Matters Concerning British Property in the Arab Republic of Egypt*, entered into force on 28 March 1972, in: (1972) UKTS no. 62 (Cmd. 4995); 858 UNTS 3. A number of other treaties are referred to in: Dumberry, *State Succession to International Responsibility*, 108.

585   ILC Special Rapporteur, Second Report, 2018, para. 170 ('it seems to be undisputed that the parties to those agreements, albeit implicitly, referred to a "territorial limitation" clause, in order to confine responsibility to assets located within the territory of the signatory State, namely Egypt').

586   This is clear from the used of the words 'in addition to that mentioned in paragraph 2' at Article 15(3).

the internationally wrongful act was an organ of the predecessor State that later became an organ of the successor State. Yet, succession is not automatic under Article 15(3); these are just 'relevant factors' to be considered for the distribution of obligations among the successor States. The meaning and the nature of this special circumstance involving the organ of the predecessor State has been discussed above.[587]

334.   At Draft Article 11(2), the ILC Special Rapporteur does not refer specifically to this 'organ' factor. He does however mention this factor in his Second Report in the context of dissolution.[588] As mentioned above, under that provision the successor States 'should take into consideration' in the context of their negotiation regarding the allocation of responsibility between them, 'a territorial link, an equitable proportion and other relevant factors'. The 'organ' factor is certainly one of those 'other relevant factors' which would have to be taken into account.

335.   In the *Croatia Genocide Convention* case, Croatia invoked the argument of acts committed by organs of the SFRY that later became organs of the Respondent, although in terms of succession to responsibility. Thus, if the acts allegedly occurring *prior* to 27 April 1992 (the date of succession) were attributable to the SFRY, Serbia (as a new State) should be considered as having succeeded to such responsibility.[589] The argument was that 'one of the entities that emerged as a successor – the FRY – largely controlled the armed forces of the SFRY during the last year of the latter's formal existence, justify[ing] the succession of the FRY to the responsibility incurred by the SFRY for the acts of armed forces that subsequently became organs of the FRY'.[590] Croatia thus argued that there was a 'structural and organic continuity between the Serbian military and political leadership and the FRY'.[591] Serbia contended that 'there is no principle of succession to responsibility in general international law'.[592]

336.   Examining its jurisdiction on the basis of Article IX of the Genocide Convention, the Court noted that 'Article IX speaks generally of the responsibility of a State and contains no limitation regarding the manner in which that responsibility might be engaged'.[593] Consequently, it considered that it had jurisdiction to deal with facts occurring before the date of succession.[594] While this conclusion was endorsed by the majority,[595] it was

---

587   See discussion when analysing Articles 11(3) and 12(3).
588   See, for instance, ILC Special Rapporteur, Second Report, 2018, para. 188.
589   *Application of the Convention on the Prevention and Punishment of the Crime of Genocide (Croatia v. Serbia),* Judgment of 3 February 2015, ICJ Rep. 2015, para. 106. The issue is discussed in: Verbatim Record, 21 March 2014, pleadings of Croatia, 24ff.
590   Ibid., para. 107.
591   Ibid., Verbatim Record, 21 March 2014, pleadings of Croatia, 28.
592   Ibid., Judgment of 3 February 2015, para. 108.
593   Ibid., para. 114.
594   Ibid., para. 117.
595   Ibid., dissenting opinion of Judge Cançado Trindade, paras. 12ff, stating that it is 'generally accepted that certain types of treaties – such as human rights treaties – remain in force by reason of their special nature' and that the Genocide Convention applied to events taking place before 27 April 1992: 'I am of the view that there is automatic State succession to universal human rights treaties, and that Serbia has succeeded to the Genocide Convention (under customary law), without the need for any formal confirmation of adherence as the successor State. In light of the declaratory character of the Convention

rejected by some judges.[596] Yet, for the Court, the question whether there was succession to responsibility 'would require a decision only if the Court finds that the acts relied upon by Croatia were contrary to the Convention and were attributable to the SFRY at the time of their commission'.[597] Since the Court did not find those acts to be contrary to the Convention, the question of succession to the obligations stemming from the alleged breaches occurring before 27 April 1992 did not arise. The Court therefore did not take a position on the argument developed by Croatia that a new State should be responsible for wrongful acts committed by an organ of the predecessor State that later becomes an organ of the successor State. It should be highlighted that a number of judges took the view that the Court had actually based its analysis on a 'presumption' that any such succession to responsibility was indeed possible. This was the position adopted by Judge Xue.[598] On the other hand, following the traditional approach, Judge Skotnikov was very critical of the position adopted by the Court and rejected the possibility of any such succession to responsibility.[599]

337.   In his Second Report, the ILC Special Rapporteur cites the *Gabčíkovo-Nagymaros Project* case (mentioned above) as supporting the 'organ' exception under Article 15(3).[600] For him, this case 'bears on the acts of the authorities of one of the republics of the Czechoslovak federation, committed in 1992, i.e. before the date of succession, which devolved in the independent and sovereign Slovak Republic'.[601]

338.   In sum, both State practice and logical necessity require in the context of dissolution the application of the solution of succession to rights and obligations arising from internationally wrongful acts committed before the date of succession.

ARTICLE 16:

Newly independent States

> 1.   When the successor State is a newly independent State, the obligations arising from an internationally wrongful act committed by the predecessor State shall not pass to the successor State.

and the need to secure the effective protection of the rights enshrined therein, the *de facto* organs of the nascent Serbia were bound by the Genocide Convention before 27.04.1992' (para. 33).

596 Ibid., Separate Opinion of Judge Tomka, paras. 7ff; Separate Opinion of Judge Owada, paras. 17ff.
597 Ibid., para. 114.
598 Ibid., Declaration of Judge Xue, para. 22: 'When the Court sets out to determine whether the alleged acts of genocide relied on by Croatia against Serbia were attributable to the SFRY and thus engaged its responsibility, its consideration, regardless of the ultimate finding, is necessarily based on the presumption in favour of succession to responsibility and the presumption that Serbia may succeed to the responsibility of the SFRY for the latter's violation of the obligations under the Convention. Thus, the Convention is actually applied retroactively to Serbia'. See also: Separate Opinion of Judge Owada, para. 17.
599 Ibid., Separate Opinion of Judge Skotnikov, para. 5. His position has been discussed above (see discussion regarding the Preamble of the Resolution). Thus, he refers to the three questions asked by the Court (Judgment, para. 112) and concluded that 'the fact that the Court limits itself to answering only the first question does not render this "three-step solution" any more tenable.'
600 Dumberry, *State Succession to International Responsibility*, 262 also refers to this example as relevant in the context of acts committed by an autonomous government.
601 ILC Special Rapporteur, Second Report, 2018, para. 175. See also at para. 188.

2.   When the successor State is a newly independent State, the rights arising from an internationally wrongful act committed against the predecessor State pass to the successor State if that act has a direct link with the territory or the population of the newly independent State.

3.   The conduct, prior to the date of succession of States, of a national liberation movement which succeeds in establishing a newly independent State shall be considered the act of the new State under international law.

4.   The rights arising from an internationally wrongful act committed before the date of the succession of States by the pre-decessor State or any other State against a people entitled to self-determination shall pass after that date to the newly independent State created by that people.

Commentary

339.   This provision deals with the question of succession to rights and obligations arising from the commission of an internationally wrongful act in the context of the creation of a newly independent State. In the following paragraphs, the specific characteristics of newly independent States as a unique type of succession of States will be first examined (Section 1). This will be followed by an analysis of Article 16(1) setting out the general solution which should prevail (Section 2). Finally, we will analyse Articles 16(2), (3) and (4) dealing with specific situations (Section 3).

1   The Specific Characteristics of Newly Independent States

340.   This type of succession of States involves the predecessor State continuing to exist after the date of succession. Newly independent States share this feature with the category of separation dealt with at Article 12 of the Resolution. Yet, it is a fundamentally different type of State succession because of the unique context of decolonisation. Thus, the territory of a colony is not considered as part of the territory of the colonial State that administers it.[602] In that sense, a newly independent State is a new State which cannot be said to have 'separated' or 'seceded' from the colonial power to the extent that its territory was not part of it.

341.   The Resolution followed the definition of 'newly independent State' adopted by the 1978 and 1983 Vienna Conventions on succession of States:

---

602 Declaration of Principles of International Law Concerning Friendly Relations and Co-Operation Among States in Accordance with the Charter of the United Nations, GA Res 2625 (XXV), UNGAOR, 25th Sess, Supp No, UN Doc A/8082, (1970) 121: 'The territory of a colony or other Non-Self-Governing Territory has, under the Charter, a status separate and distinct from the territory of the State administering it; and such separate and distinct status under the Charter shall exist until the people of the colony or Non-Self-Governing Territory have exercised their right of self-determination in accordance with the Charter, and particularly its purposes and principles'.

'Newly independent State' means a successor State the territory of which immediately before the date of the succession of States was a dependent territory for the international relations of which the predecessor State was responsible.[603]

342.   The crucial element of this definition is the dependent character of the territory concerned. In other words, only States having emerged from territories under the former League of Nations' Mandates regime, trust territories referred to under Chapter XII of the UN Charter, and Non-Self-Governing Territories governed by Chapter XI of the Charter and General Assembly Resolution 1514(XV) can be candidates for this category.[604]

343.   As mentioned in the Final Report, some members of the Commission cast doubts about the relevance of continuing to refer to newly independent States as a distinct category in a post-decolonisation world.[605] The fact that the ILC Articles on Nationality of Natural Persons in Relation to the Succession of States does not refer to this category was also mentioned. In contrast to the outcome of the work of the Institute on State Succession in Matters of Property and Debts,[606] the Final Report put forward three reasons why it was considered 'indispensable' to include newly independent States as a specific category of State succession on its own:

First, as some cases mentioned at the beginning of this report show, there can still be cases of emergence of new States that could fall within the realm of the category of newly independent States, as defined in the 1978 and 1983 Conventions. Second, as a recent judicial decision in the United Kingdom demonstrates, problems relating to the commission of internationally wrongful acts during colonial times and the question of responsibility of the predecessor or the successor States may emerge even long after the acts have occurred. Hence, cases of State succession giving rise to the emergence of a newly independent State that occurred in the past may have still kept open situations concerning international responsibility. Third, as for treaties, archives, debts and property, the subject matter of the consequences of internationally wrongful acts committed before the date of State succession also appeals for a specific treatment of succession with regards to States having been dependent territories before coming into existence. Given the particular territorial status prior to independence, the cases of newly independent States cannot be assimilated to those of the separation of a State, whether by agreement or not.[607]

603   Article 1(e) of the Resolution. See Article 2(f), *Vienna Convention on Succession of States in Respect of Treaties*, and Article 2(e), *Vienna Convention on Succession of States in Respect of State Property, Archives and Debts*.
604   See ILC Special Rapporteur, Second Report, 2018, paras. 127ff, discussing whether international protectorates should be considered as included in the category of newly independent States.
605   Final Report, para. 17, in: (2015) 76 *Annuaire de l'Institut de Droit international*, 520.
606   Institut de Droit international, 'State Succession in Matters of Property and Debts', 121.
607   Final Report, para. 18, in: (2015) 76 *Annuaire de l'Institut de Droit international*, 520.

344. The same approach has been adopted by the ILC Special Rapporteur which includes Draft Article 8 dealing specifically with this category of succession.[608] The following sections examine the scope and content of Article 16.

2   Principle: No Transfer of Obligations to the Newly Independent State

345. Under Article 16(1), the obligations arising from an internationally wrongful act committed by the (colonial) predecessor State do not pass to the newly independent State. The principle of non-succession is adopted in this situation not only for the reason that the predecessor State continues to exist following the creation of the newly independent State, but also because of the dependent nature of the relationship between the predecessor and the successor State. The predecessor State always remains the holder of obligations arising from wrongful acts which took place before the date of succession. This solution is an illustration of the basic principle applicable under Articles 4 and 5 to cases where the predecessor State continues to exists after the date of succession. Moreover, the reasons mentioned above for including this category of State succession as a separate one, commands, as a logical necessity, the conclusion that there is no succession to obligations arising from an internationally wrongful act committed by the predecessor State.[609] Writers largely support the principle of non-succession in the context of the creation of newly independent States whereby it should be for the colonial power to provide reparation to an injured State.[610] The ILC Special Rapporteur has adopted the same position.[611]

346. One important distinction between newly independent States and cases of separation needs to be highlighted here. As mentioned above, the Resolution envisages some exceptions to the non-succession rule with respect to the obligation to repair in the context of separation.[612] There exists no such exception for newly independent States. The above-mentioned unique characteristics of this type of succession require such a solution. The ILC Special Rapporteur has adopted a different position on the matter. Thus, Draft Article 8(2) provides for an exception to the non-succession principle (set out at Article 8(1)) whereby two 'particular circumstances' 'may be taken into consideration': the existence of a 'direct link between the act or its consequences' and the territory of the new State, and 'where the former dependent territory had substantive autonomy'.[613] The language actually

---

608   ILC Special Rapporteur, Second Report, 2018, paras. 124ff.
609   Final Report, para. 97, in: (2015) 76 *Annuaire de l'Institut de Droit international*, 546.
610   Dumberry, *State Succession to International Responsibility*, 169–170, referring to a long list of writers. See also: ILC, Working-Group Recommendations, 401.
611   ILC Special Rapporteur, Second Report, 2018, paras. 124, 130. See Draft Article 8(1): 'Subject to the exceptions referred to in paragraph 2, the obligations arising from an internationally wrongful act of the predecessor State do not pass to the successor State in case of establishment of a newly independent State'.
612   See Articles 12(3) and (4) of the Resolution.
613   ILC Special Rapporteur, Second Report, 2018. See Draft Article 8(2): 'If the newly independent States agrees, the obligations arising from an internationally wrongful act of the predecessor State may transfer to the successor State. The particular circumstances may be taken into consideration where there is a direct link between the act or its consequences and the territory of the successor State and where the former dependent territory had substantive autonomy'.

used under this provision (and the words 'may be taken into consideration') suggest that these two 'particular circumstances' are in fact envisaged only as potential exceptions to the non-succession principle.[614] However, the inclusion of the substantive autonomy of the dependent territory as a possible exception to the non-succession principle may undermine the very reason for distinguishing between newly independent States and cases of separation. Even if the newly independent State could be considered as having enjoyed some substantial autonomy in some areas, it remains that what characterises this category is the *dependent* nature of its relationship with the predecessor State.

347.   Several examples of State practice and decisions of municipal courts support this principle of non-succession.[615] These examples will be briefly examined in the next paragraphs.

348.   One example is the former French colony of Algeria which became an independent State in 1962 after a national liberation war which lasted for eight years.[616] The scope and meaning of Article 18 of the Déclaration de principes relative à la cooperation économique et financière (dated 19 March 1962), which is part of the Evian Accords that ended the war, gave rise to divergent interpretations by the parties.[617] France decided to compensate *French nationals* who had suffered damage during the national liberation war.[618] One important limitation to the new French policy was that *it excluded foreigners* (as well as companies) from receiving any compensation for damage suffered during the war. This is an important point that somewhat limits the relevance of this example. Thus, it is not at all surprising that France decided to provide compensation to individuals who were its nationals at the time the events took place and who had remained so after the independence of Algeria and were now living in France.[619] It should be added, however, that France also recognised its responsibility regarding acts committed against a Swiss national by the *Organisation armée secrète*, a para-military organisation of French nationals in Algeria opposed to independence.[620] In 1963, the Ministry of Foreign Affairs of France submitted to the Conseil d'Etat an official interpretation of Article 18 of the Déclaration, stating that Algeria should not be responsible for the acts and measures taken by France that were specifically directed against the rebellion of the National Liberation Front and that France

---

614   It should be added that the Second Report does not explain specifically why these two exceptions should apply in the specific context of newly independent States. In the section dealing with separation, the Second Report mentions that 'It remains to be examined, however, whether the same rules and exceptions [i.e. the direct link and organs exceptions mentioned at Draft Articles 7 (2) (3)] are relevant, *mutatis mutandis*, to the situation of newly independent States' (at para. 122). The Report also mentions that 'A more complicated question may arise regarding other possible exceptions to the general rule of non-succession'. Yet, the Report does not further examine the matter.

615   Dumberry, *State Succession to International Responsibility*, 172ff; ILC Special Rapporteur, Second Report, 2018, para. 130.

616   Dumberry, ibid., 177; ILC Special Rapporteur, ibid., paras. 131 (fn 212), 116–117.

617   Article 18 reads as follows: 'Algeria shall assume the obligations and enjoy the rights contracted on behalf of itself or of Algerian public establishments by the competent French authorities'. The text of the Agreement is found in: *JORF*, 20 March 1962, 3019–3032.

618   The position taken by France is explained by the French Minister of Foreign Affairs in response to a question asked at the National Assembly: *JORF, Assemblée nationale*, no. 9458, 7 March 1970, at 540, quoted in: Jean Charpentier, 'Pratique française du droit international' (1970) *AFDI* 942–943.

619   Dumberry, *State Succession to International Responsibility*, 178.

620   P. Guggenheim, 'La pratique suisse 1965' (1966) 23 *ASDI*, 87. See also: Dumberry, ibid., 181, 256.

should remain responsible for the consequences of such measures.[621] This principle of non-succession was consistently applied by French municipal courts.[622] The position adopted by the government and its domestic courts is in accordance with the principle that whenever damage is inflicted by the *actions of the predecessor State* (i.e. the French colonial authorities) in fighting secessionist 'rebels' (which later become an independent State), the consequences of these internationally wrongful acts should not be supported by the new State upon its independence.[623] In such a case, the continuing State should remain responsible for the acts *it committed* before the date of succession.

349.   The principle of non-succession was also adopted by Belgian courts in the context of the independence of the Congo.[624] For instance, in *Crépet v. Etat belge et Société des forces hydro-électriques de la colonie*, decided without the appearance of the Congo, the Civil Tribunal of Brussels refused to hold the new State (Congo) responsible for obligations arising from internationally wrongful acts on the ground that, as a matter of principle, these acts do not pass automatically to the new State without any specific agreement to that effect between the predecessor State and the successor State.[625] This principle of non-succession has also been applied by the French Conseil d'Etat in the context of the independence of Vanuatu,[626] and by Indian courts in the context of the partition of India.[627]

350.   In one recent case, the United Kingdom High Court rejected the position taken by the UK Foreign Office according to which the British Government was not responsible for acts of torture committed by the Colonial Government in Kenya during the Mau-Mau rebellion in the 1950s and that therefore Kenya should be liable for those acts which occurred before its independence in 1963.[628] The position of the UK Foreign Office was summarised as follows by Justice McCombre:

> The FCO [Foreign and Commonwealth Office] has brought applications to strike out the claims and for summary judgment in its favour, in advance of a full trial, on the grounds that the claims disclose no cause of action in law and have no real prospect of success against the UK Government. The

---

621   Position of the Ministry of Foreign Affairs of France, 'Conclusions de M. le Commissaire du Gouvernement Fournier', extract of which can be found in an analysis by R. Pinto, in: (1967) 2 *JDI* 387. This position was delivered to the Conseil d'Etat in letters dated 13 February 1963 and 30 July 1963 in the *Union régionale d'Algérie de la C.F.T.C.* case, decided by the Conseil d'Etat, 5 March 1965 (in: Ch. Rousseau, 'Jurisprudence française en matière de droit international public' (1965) *RGDIP* 846–847; 44 ILR 43).
622   See several cases examined in: Dumberry, *State Succession to International Responsibility*, 253ff.
623   Ibid., 250ff.
624   See the analysis in: ibid., 173–177. One case examined is: *Pittacos c. Etat belge,* Brussels Court of Appeal (2nd Chamber), 1 December 1964, (1965) *Journal des tribunaux*, 9; and Cour de cassation, 26 May 1966, (1966) *Pasicrisie belge*, Part I, 1221, also in: 48 ILR 22.
625   *Crépet c. Etat belge et Société des forces hydro-électriques de la colonie* (Civil Tribunal of Brussels, 30 January 1962, (1962) *Journal des tribunaux*, 242.
626   *Russet,* Conseil d'Etat, 5 October 1984, case no. 51543, in: *Recueil Lebon.* See the analysis in: Dumberry, *State Succession to International Responsibility,* 181.
627   See the analysis in: Dumberry, ibid., 172–173.
628   See the judgment of the High Court of Justice (Justice McCombe): *Mutua et al. v. The Foreign and Commonwealth Office,* 21 July 2011, [2011] EWHC 1913 (QB) and of 5 October 2012, [2012] EWHC 2678 (QB).

FCO's case (in very broad outline) is that any claim that the claimants might have had could only have been brought against the direct perpetrators of the alleged assaults and/or their employer at the time, the Colonial Government in Kenya, and not against the British government.[629]

351.   The claimants' arguments were summarised as follows:

The claimants have argued in contrast that the British government are at least arguably liable to them for their injuries on five different legal bases. First, they say that the liabilities of the old Colonial Government (which ceased to exist in 1963) devolved upon the UK Government on independence, under the common law incorporating general principles of public international law. Secondly and thirdly, it is said that the UK Government was and is directly liable to the claimants for having instigated and procured, through (a) the Army and (b) the Colonial Office, a system of torture and ill-treatment of detainees as part of a common design shared with the Colonial Government in Kenya. Fourthly, the claimants argue that in July 1957 the British government expressly instructed, authorised or approved a policy of mistreatment of detainees, as shown by a series of exchanges between the Governor of the colony and the Colonial Office in London. (Copies of the most important documents on this issue, as presently available, are annexed to the judgment.) Fifthly, it is said that the UK Government, as paramount colonial power, owed a duty of care in law to the claimants to prevent abuses, which it knew were being committed and which it had the power to prevent; it is alleged that the UK Government is liable to the claimants for breach of that duty.[630]

352.   Regarding the more specific question of State succession to responsibility, the claimants argued (referring to French cases mentioned above in the context of the independence of Algeria) that 'in the context of decolonialization it has been accepted by predecessor states that liabilities for tortious acts of their colonial administrations in respect of the suppression of an insurrectional movement should be opposable to the predecessor state upon independence'.[631] Justice McCombre was not persuaded by that position: 'I agree with the defendant, however, that the claimants have not been able to establish with any clarity a sufficiently "extensive and virtually uniform" rule of customary international law to constitute it as the basis of a claim under the common law of England'.[632] The High Court considered that it was for Kenya, as an independent State, to decide whether or not it was willing to assume the liabilities of the British Colonial Administration. The Court noted that Kenya had decided not to do so.[633] The High Court was therefore hesitant to recognise the principle which had been adopted by France in the context of the independence of Algeria whereby a new State should not be held responsible for the actions of the

629   Ibid., Summary of Judgment, para. 3.
630   Ibid., Summary of Judgment, para. 5.
631   Ibid., Judgment, para. 90.
632   Ibid., para. 95.
633   Ibid., paras. 83ff.

predecessor State (i.e. the colonial authorities) in fighting secessionist 'rebels' which later establish an independent State. A first judgment then opened the way for an examination of the responsibility of the British Government for the alleged acts at the merits stage. A settlement was eventually reached between the claimants and the United Kingdom in 2013 for the 'payment of a settlement sum in respect of 5,228 claimants, as well as a gross costs sum, to the total value of £19.9 million.'[634] In his declaration to the House of Commons, Foreign Secretary Hague stated that while the United Kingdom 'continue to deny liability (…) for the actions of the colonial administration in respect of the claims' and that 'the courts have made no finding of liability against the Government in this case', it nevertheless 'recognises that Kenyans were subject to torture and other forms of ill treatment at the hands of the colonial administration' and 'sincerely regrets that these abuses took place, and that they marred Kenya's progress towards independence'.[635]

353.   State practice and municipal court decisions also show cases where the successor State took over the obligations arising from internationally wrongful acts committed before the date of succession.[636] One illustration (mentioned above[637]) is the Constitution of Namibia, which indicates that (as a matter of principle) the new State is responsible for the obligations arising from internationally wrongful acts committed by South Africa (but also that Namibia may repudiate such acts).[638] The principle of succession to the obligation to repair was applied by the Supreme Court of Namibia in the case of *Minister of Defence, Namibia v. Mwandinghi*.[639] While the finding of the Court is controversial on many grounds,[640] it rightly interpreted the Constitution. This is all the more so since Namibia had the opportunity to repudiate the internationally wrongful acts by an Act of Parliament and it failed to do so. This example does not challenge the soundness of the general applicable rule of non-succession set out at Article 16(1). It simply shows that a newly independent State, like any other State, can decide on its own to take the burden

634   'Statement to Parliament on settlement of Mau Mau claims', Foreign & Commonwealth Office and The Rt Hon William Hague, 6 June 2013, www.gov.uk/government/news/statement-to-parliament-on-settlement-of-mau-mau-claims.

635   Ibid.

636   Dumberry, *State Succession to International Responsibility*, 184ff, examining (at 186), inter alia, Dutch courts' decisions which held that the new State of Indonesia took over the obligations arising from internationally wrongful acts committed by the Netherlands during the Second World War: *Poldermans v. State of the Netherlands*, Netherlands, Court of Appeal of The Hague (First Chamber), 8 December 1955, in: (1959) *NJ* no. 7 (with an analysis by Boltjes), reported in: (1957) ILR 69; *Poldermans v. State of the Netherlands*, Netherlands, Supreme Court, 15 June 1956, in: ibid.; *Van der Have v. State of the Netherlands*, District Court of The Hague, 12 January 1953, in: (1953) *NJ* no. 133, in: (1953) ILR 80. It should be noted that these municipal law cases do not involve questions of succession to international responsibility, as the wrongful acts were committed by the predecessor State not against another State (or a national of another State) but against its own nationals.

637   See analysis of unilateral acts by successor States under Article 6(3).

638   Article 140(3), Constitution of Namibia, adopted by the Constituent Assembly of Namibia on 9 February 1990, entered into force on 21 March 1991, UN Doc. S/20967/Add.2. See the analysis in: Dumberry, *State Succession to International Responsibility*, 192ff; ILC Special Rapporteur, Second Report, 2018, paras. 133–136.

639   *Minister of Defence, Namibia v. Mwandinghi*, 25 October 1991, in: 1992 (2) *SA* 355 (NmS), in: 91 ILR 358. See: Dumberry, ibid., 194ff.

640   See the analysis in: Dumberry, ibid.

of reparation of internationally wrongful acts committed by the predecessor State.[641] The same position has been followed by the ILC Special Rapporteur; he has included a provision specifically dealing with this situation where a newly independent State agrees to such transfer of obligations.[642] In any event, the regime prevailing under the Constitution was no doubt influenced by the political context in which Namibia became an independent State, after the end of the apartheid regime in South Africa and the accession to power of the ANC, a national liberation movement that had always supported the struggle for independence of the Namibian liberation national movement.

3   Exceptions: Specific Situations Deserving Different Solutions

354.   Article 16(2) deals with a situation involving the succession to rights arising from the commission of a wrongful act. The solution is different from that of non-succession to obligations prevailing under Article 16(1). Here, the possibility of succession does exist. It concerns the existence of a 'direct link' between the consequences of a wrongful act and the territory/population of the newly independent State (see Section 3.1).

355.   As mentioned above, contemporary international law recognises legal subjectivity to peoples who are holders of the right to self-determination. These peoples and their representatives may be involved in internationally wrongful acts, either as injured subjects or as perpetrators.[643] While this question is not strictly speaking one of State succession, it is nevertheless fundamentally correlated to the situation under analysis. The Resolution addresses both situations:

-    The conduct of a national liberation movement representing a people entitled to self-determination committing an internationally wrongful act against another State (Article 16(3), Section 3.2); and

-    The conduct of the predecessor or any other State committing an internationally wrongful act against the people concerned or the individuals composing it (Article 16(4), Section 3.3).

3.1   EXISTENCE OF A 'DIRECT LINK' BETWEEN THE CONSEQUENCES OF A WRONGFUL ACT AND THE TERRITORY/POPULATION OF THE NEWLY INDEPENDENT STATE

356.   Article 16(2) concerns the specific situation of the existence of a 'direct link' between the consequences of an internationally wrongful act committed *against* the predecessor State before the date of succession and the territory or the population of what becomes later

---

641   See analysis above of unilateral acts by successor States under Article 6(3).
642   ILC Special Rapporteur, Second Report, 2018, para. 136. See Draft Article 8(2): 'If the newly independent States agrees, the obligations arising from an internationally wrongful act of the predecessor State may transfer to the successor State'.
643   Final Report, para. 102, in: (2015) 76 *Annuaire de l'Institut de Droit international*, 548.

the newly independent State. Whenever such a link exists, the *rights* arising from the act pass to the new State. In other words, after the date of succession the new State becomes the holder of any right arising from the consequences of the commission of a wrongful act which had directly affected its territory or its population. This solution is in line with what the 1983 Vienna Convention established with regards to property and archives.[644] Article 16(2) is a concrete illustration in the specific context of newly independent States of the general principle set out at Article 5(2). The meaning and the nature of any such 'direct link' between a wrongful act and the territory/population of the successor State has been discussed above.[645]

357. It can be added here that, given the particular nature of the relationship between the administering power (the predecessor State) and the dependent territory, if the internationally wrongful act committed concerned that territory or its population, the party truly injured is not the administering power but the people of the territory. The position adopted by Portugal while instituting proceedings against Australia for the agreement concluded by the Australian government with Indonesia affecting the continental shelf of East Timor is telling in this respect. Portugal dissociated its own rights as the administering power of East Timor and those rights of the people of East Timor. Specifically, it considered that Australia's negotiation, conclusion and performance of the 1989 Treaty with Indonesia:

(a)   has infringed and is infringing the right of the people of East Timor to self-determination, to territorial integrity and unity and its permanent sovereignty over its natural wealth and resources, and is in breach of the obligation not to disregard but to respect that right, that integrity and that sovereignty;

(b)   has infringed and is infringing the powers of Portugal as the administering Power of the Territory of East Timor, is impeding the fulfilment of its duties to the people of East Timor and to the international community, is infringing the right of Portugal to fulfil its responsibilities and is in breach of the obligation not to disregard but to respect those powers and duties and that right.[646]

358. Other examples of State practice support the solution adopted under Article 16(2). They include treaties concluded after the Second World War under which the defeated States agreed to pay compensation for acts that occurred during that war and whose victims were peoples that only constituted independent States later on. As mentioned above, the FRG concluded in 1952 a reparation agreement with the State of Israel concerning the treatment of Jews before and during the Second World War.[647] This is an example where the parties concerned considered the existence of a direct link between the population which has suffered during that period and the new State. Another example involves Japan, which

---

644   See Articles 15 and 28, *Vienna Convention on Succession of States in Respect of State Property, Archives and Debts.*
645   See analysis of Articles 5(2), 11(2) and 12(2) above.
646   *East Timor (Portugal v. Australia)*, Judgment, ICJ Rep. 1995, 94, para. 10.
647   *Agreement between the State of Israel and the Federal Republic of Germany on Compensation of 10 September 1952*, 162 UNTS no. 2137, 205.

entered into peace agreements after the Second World War with Indonesia,[648] Malaysia[649] and Singapore.[650] Importantly, these States did not exist when the internationally wrongful acts were committed by Japan during the War. This did not prevent Japan from making reparation to these new States.[651] Thus, it was clear that the territory and the population of these newly independent States had been injured as a result of the wrongful acts committed by Japan.

3.2   CONDUCT OF A NATIONAL LIBERATION MOVEMENT AGAINST ANOTHER STATE OR SUBJECT

359.   The scope and content of Article 16(3) is similar to that of Article 12(6) in the context of separation. Article 12(6) deals with the situation where a wrongful act was committed before the date of succession by an 'insurrectional or other movement' which later succeeds in establishing a new State. Whenever this is the case, the act committed before the date of succession shall be considered as that of the new State under international law.[652] Article 16(3) provides for the same principle but in the specific context of a newly Independent State, that is to say, for the conduct of a movement representing a people entitled to self-determination struggling for independence. Thus, under Article 16(3) the conduct of a national liberation movement which succeeds in establishing a newly independent State will be considered as an act of that State under international law. The solution is supported by scholars.[653] The same position has also been adopted by the ILC Special Rapporteur under Draft Article 8(3).[654]

360.   This is in line with the traditional position taken with regards to belligerents who succeed in becoming the government of an existing State or in creating a new one. As mentioned above, this situation is contemplated in the ILC Articles on State Responsibility. The wording used at Article 10(2) of the ILC Articles on State Responsibility clearly indicates that it applies to newly Independent States.[655] Thus, the provision uses the expression 'or in a territory under its administration', which is a specific reference to the situation of a dependant colony not having yet attained independent statehood.[656] This is also

---

648   *Treaty of Peace between Japan and the Republic of Indonesia*, entered into force on 15 April 1958, in: 324 UNTS 227; (1959) 3 *Jap. Ann. Int'l L.* 158.

649   *Treaty of Peace between Japan and Malaysia*, signed on 11 September 1967, entered into force on 7 May 1968, in: (1969) 13 *Jap. Ann. Int'l L.* 209.

650   *Treaty of Peace between Japan and Singapore*, signed on 21 September 1967, entered into force on 7 May 1968, in: Ibid., 244.

651   See analysis in: Dumberry, *State Succession to International Responsibility*, 327.

652   Article 12(6) further adds that after the date of succession, the predecessor State incurs no responsibility for the acts committed by the insurrectional or other movement.

653   Dumberry, *State Succession to International Responsibility*, 171–172, 247, referring to a long list of writers.

654   ILC Special Rapporteur, Second Report, 2018, para. 131. See Draft Article 8(3): 'The conduct of a national liberation or other movement which succeeds in establishing a newly independent State shall be considered an act of the new State under international law'.

655   See also: ILC Special Rapporteur, Second Report, 2018, paras. 108, 131.

656   See the analysis in: Dumberry, *State Succession to International Responsibility*, 247–248.

clear from the use of the words 'movement, insurrectional or other' at Article 10(2), which includes national liberation movements struggling for independence in the particular context of decolonisation.

361. One already mentioned example where the principle set out at Article 16(3) was applied is in the context of the armed struggle leading to the independence of Algeria in 1962.[657] French municipal courts applied Article 18 of the Déclaration de principes relative à la coopération économique et financière by holding that France should remain responsible for the internationally wrongful acts committed by France before the independence of Algeria. However, they took a different position regarding acts committed by the FLN, the national liberation movement. French courts have consistently held that the new State of Algeria should in principle provide compensation to French nationals who were victims of internationally wrongful acts committed by the FLN in its war efforts to achieve independence.[658] However, since Algeria was not a party to any of these proceedings, the court decisions did not formally hold Algeria responsible for the obligations arising from such acts committed by the FLN.[659]

3.3 WRONGFUL ACTS COMMITTED AGAINST A PEOPLE ENTITLED TO SELF-DETERMINATION

362. Article 16(4) deals with the reverse situation where an internationally wrongful act is committed before the date of succession against a people entitled to self-determination. The act can be committed by the administering (predecessor) State itself or by another State. Under this provision, the rights arising from such an internationally wrongful act pass to the newly independent State after the date of succession. This solution adopted by the Resolution has since then been endorsed by writers.[660] During the discussion at the IDI's Tallinn session one member stated that this provision should not only cover acts committed by the predecessor State against a people entitled to self-determination, but also those committed by a non-State actor subject of international law.[661] The Rapporteur agreed to this solution, but it was finally decided not to formally amend the text of the provision by replacing the term 'or any other State' by the expression 'any other subject of international law'.[662]

---

657 On this question, see: ibid., 188ff; Dumberry, 'New State Responsibility for Internationally Wrongful Acts by an Insurrectional Movement', 613ff.

658 See cases examined in: Dumberry, 'New State Responsibility for Internationally Wrongful Acts by an Insurrectional Movement', 614ff, referring to, inter alia, *Perriquet*, Conseil d'Etat, case no. 119737, 15 March 1995, in: *Recueil Lebon*; *Hespel*, Conseil d'Etat, 2/6 SSR, case no. 11092, 5 December 1980, in: *Tables du Recueil Lebon*; and *Grillo*, Conseil d'Etat, case no. 178498, 28 July 1999, in: *Tables du Recueil Lebon*. These cases are also mentioned in: ILC Special Rapporteur, Second Report, 2018, para. 117.

659 Dumberry, *State Succession to International Responsibility*, 190.

660 Jakubowski, *State Succession in Cultural Property*, 267–268.

661 Institut de Droit international, Session de Tallinn – 2015, PVPL plénière n° 7, 6ièm séance plénière, 14ème Commission, 20–21, 24–26, in: (2015) 76 *Annuaire de l'Institut de Droit international*, 675–677.

662 Ibid., 24–25, 28–29, in: (2015) 76 *Annuaire de l'Institut de Droit international*, 678, 681–683.

363. The *Certain Phosphate Lands in Nauru* case before the ICJ offers an example of the concrete application of Article 16(4).[663] In its application against Australia, Nauru invoked alleged internationally wrongful acts committed by Australia as the administering power at the time Nauru was a UN Trust Territory. In its Memorial, Nauru submitted that '[t]he emergence of a new State from the status of a trust territory in accordance with the principle of self-determination embodied in the trusteeship arrangements is not the emergence *ab initio* of an entirely new legal entity, but the emergence from a state of dependence of a people whose rights and status are already distinctly recognised, and to which the predecessor State is in principle accountable'.[664] Australia challenged the jurisdiction of the Court, but not on the ground that Nauru was not in a position to advance claims for the conduct of the Administering Power before Nauru's existence as an independent State. On the contrary, Australia invoked the fact that the Nauruan authorities had allegedly waived all claims relating to the rehabilitation of the phosphate lands even before independence.[665] The Court considered that it had jurisdiction over the case and that the application was admissible. The case did not go to the merits stage, however, because the parties reached an agreement by which Australia made an *ex gratia* payment and the parties asked the Court to discontinue the proceedings.[666]

364. Finally, before the independence of Namibia in 1990, the United Nations explicitly recognised its right, upon its independence, to claim reparation for damage against South Africa as a result of its illegal occupation. Thus, the UN General Assembly recognised the right for Namibia to claim reparation against South Africa for the illegal occupation and other human rights violations.[667] The United Nations also recognised such a right for Namibia against other States, individuals and corporations.[668]

663   Dumberry, *State Succession to International Responsibility*, 328.
664   *Certain Phosphate Lands in Nauru*, Memorial of Nauru, vol. I, 169, para. 467.
665   *Certain Phosphate Lands in Nauru (Nauru v. Australia)*, Preliminary Objections, Judgment, ICJ Rep. 1992, 247, para. 12.
666   Agreement between Australia and Nauru of 10 August 1993, 32 ILM 1471–1479. See: *Certain Phosphate Lands in Nauru (Nauru v. Australia)*, Order of 13 September 1993, ICJ Rep. 1993, 322.
667   UN GA Res. 36/121 of 10 December 1981, at para. 25, demanding 'that South Africa account for all 'disappeared' Namibians and release any who are still alive and declares that South Africa shall be liable for damages to compensate the victims, their families *and the future lawful Government of an independent Namibia for the losses sustained*' (emphasis added). The same content is also found in UN GA Res. 38/36 of 2 December 1983, at para. 42.
668   Decree on the Natural Resources of Namibia, Addendum to the Report of the United Nations Council for Namibia, 29 UN GAOR Supp. 24A, at 27–28, UN Doc. A/9624/add 1(1975). See also: UN GA Res. 40/52 of 2 December 1985, para. 14; UN GA Res. 38/36 of 2 December 1983, para. 42. The question is examined in: Dumberry, *State Succession to International Responsibility*, 334–335.

INSTITUTE OF INTERNATIONAL LAW, RESOLUTION ON STATE SUCCESSION AND STATE RESPONSIBILITY
(ENGLISH AND FRENCH TEXTS)

JUSTITIA ET PACE
INSTITUT DE DROIT INTERNATIONAL
Session de Tallinn – 2015

14th Commission

28 August 2015

FOURTEENTH COMMISSION

State Succession in Matters of State Responsibility

Rapporteur: M. Kohen

RESOLUTION
(FINAL TEXT)

The *Institute of International Law*,

Noting that the work of codification and progressive development carried out in the field of succession of States has not covered matters relating to international responsibility of States, and that work in the latter field has set aside matters relating to succession of States,

Convinced of the need for the codification and progressive development of the rules relating to succession of States in matters of international responsibility of States, as a means to ensure greater legal security in international relations,

Bearing in mind that cases of succession of States should not constitute a reason for not implementing the consequences arising from an internationally wrongful act,

Taking into account that different categories of succession of States and their particular circumstances may lead to different solutions,

Considering that law and equity require the identification of the States or other subjects of international law to which, after the date of succession of States, pertain the rights and obligations arising from internationally wrongful acts committed by the predecessor State or injuring it,

Noting that the principles of free consent, good faith, equity and *pacta sunt servanda* are universally recognized,

Recalling the principles of international law embodied in the Charter of the United Nations, such as the principles of the equal rights and self-determination of peoples, of the sovereign equality and independence of all States, of non-interference in the domestic affairs of States, of the prohibition of the threat or use of force, and of universal respect for, and observance of, human rights and fundamental freedoms for all,

Noting that respect for the territorial integrity and political independence of any State is required by the Charter of the United Nations,

Adopts the following Resolution:

CHAPTER I:
GENERAL PROVISIONS

ARTICLE I:
Use of terms

For the purposes of this Resolution:

a)   "Succession of States" means the replacement of one State by another in the responsibility for the international relations of territory.

b)   "Predecessor State" means the State which has been replaced by another State on the occurrence of a succession of States.

c)   "Successor State" means the State which has replaced another State on the occurrence of a succession of States.

d)   "Date of the succession of States" means the date upon which the successor State replaced the predecessor State in the responsibility for the international relations of the territory to which the succession of States relates.

e)   "Newly independent State" means a successor State the territory of which immediately before the date of the succession of States was a dependent territory for the international relations of which the predecessor State was responsible.

f)   "Devolution agreement" means an agreement, concluded by the predecessor State and the successor State or a national liberation, insurrectional or other movement, or an entity or organ that later becomes the organ of the successor State, providing that rights and/or obligations of the predecessor State shall devolve upon the successor State.

g)   "Internationally wrongful act" means conduct consisting of an action or omission which: (i) is attributable to the State or another subject under international law; and (ii) constitutes a breach of an international obligation of the State or the other subject. The characterization of an act as internationally wrongful is governed by international law.

h)   "international responsibility" refers to the legal consequences of an internationally wrongful act.

Scope of the present Resolution

1.   The present Resolution applies to the effects of a succession of States in respect of the rights and obligations arising out of an internationally wrongful act that the predecessor State committed against another State or another subject of international law prior to the date of succession, or that a State or another subject of international law committed against the predecessor State prior to the date of succession.

2.   The present Resolution applies only to the effects of a succession of States occurring in conformity with international law and, in particular, the principles of international law embodied in the Charter of the United Nations.

3.   The present Articles do not govern the situations resulting from political changes within a State, including changes in the regime or name of the State.

CHAPTER II:
COMMON RULES

ARTICLE 3:

Subsidiary character of the guiding principles

The guiding principles mentioned below apply in the absence of any different solution agreed upon by the parties concerned by a situation of succession of States, including the State or other subject of international law injured by the internationally wrongful act.

ARTICLE 4:

Invocation of responsibility for an internationally wrongful act committed by the predecessor State before the date of succession of States

1.   International responsibility arising from an internationally wrongful act committed before the date of succession of States by a predecessor State falls on this State.

2.   If the predecessor State continues to exist, the injured State or subject of international law may, even after the date of succession,

invoke the international responsibility of the predecessor State for an internationally wrongful act committed by that State before the date of succession of States and request from it reparation for the injury caused by that internationally wrongful act.

3.   In conformity with the following Articles, the injured State or subject of international law may also or solely request reparation from a successor State for the injury caused by an internationally wrongful act of the predecessor State.

ARTICLE 5:

Invocation of responsibility for an internationally wrongful act committed against the predecessor State before the date of succession of States

1.   The predecessor State which after the date of succession of States continues to exist may invoke the international responsibility of another State or subject of international law for an internationally wrongful act committed against it before that date by that State or subject and may request reparation for the injury caused by this act.

2.   If the injury caused by an internationally wrongful act committed before the date of succession of States against a predecessor State affected the territory or persons which, after this date, are under the jurisdiction of a successor State, the successor State may request reparation for the injury caused by such act, as provided in the following Articles, unless reparation was already obtained in full before the date of succession of States.

ARTICLE 6:

Devolution agreements and unilateral acts

1.   Devolution agreements concluded before the date of succession of States between the predecessor State and an entity or national liberation movement representing a people entitled to self-determination, as well as agreements concluded by the States concerned after the date of succession of States, are subject to the rules relating to the consent of the parties and to the validity of treaties, as reflected in the Vienna Convention on the Law of Treaties. The same principle applies to devolution agreements concluded between the predecessor State and an autonomous entity thereof that later becomes a successor State.

2.   The obligations of a predecessor State arising from an internationally wrongful act committed by it against another State or another subject of international law before the date of succession of States do not become the obligations of the successor State towards the injured State or subject only by reason of the fact that the predecessor State and the successor State have concluded an agreement, providing that such obligations shall devolve upon the successor State.

3.   The obligations of a predecessor State in respect of an internationally wrongful act committed by it against another State or another subject of international law before the date of succession of States do not become the obligations of the successor State towards the injured State or subject only by reason of the fact that the successor State has accepted that such obligations shall devolve upon it.

4.   Where the injured State or subject of international law does not accept the solution envisaged by the devolution agreement or unilateral act, good faith negotiations must be pursued by the States or subjects concerned. If these negotiations do not succeed within a reasonable period of time, the solution envisaged by the relevant Article of Chapter III of the present Resolution is applicable.

ARTICLE 7:
Plurality of successor States

1.   In case of succession in which it is not possible to determine a single successor State, all the successor States will enjoy the rights or assume the obligations arising from the commission of an internationally wrongful act in an equitable manner, unless otherwise agreed by the States or subjects of international law concerned.

2.   In order to determine an equitable apportionment of the rights or obligations of the successor States, criteria that may be taken into consideration include the existence of any special connections with the act giving rise to international responsibility, the size of the territory and of the population, the respective contributions to the gross domestic product of the States concerned at the date of succession, the need to avoid unjust enrichment and any other circumstance relevant to the case.

3.   Negotiations in good faith must be pursued by the successor States, with the goal of reaching a solution within a reasonable time.

ARTICLE 8:
States or subjects of international law concerned

For the purposes of Articles 6 and 7, "States or subjects of international law concerned" are:

a)   in the case of an internationally wrongful act committed by the predecessor State, the injured State or subject of international law and all the successor States;

b)   in the case of an internationally wrongful act committed against the predecessor State, all the successor States.

ARTICLE 9:

Internationally wrongful acts having a continuing or composite character performed or completed after the date of succession of States

1.   When a successor State continues the breach of an international obligation constituted by an act of the predecessor State having a continuing character, the international responsibility of the successor State for the breach extends over the entire period during which the act continues and remains not in conformity with the international obligation.

2.   When a successor State completes a series of actions or omissions initiated by the predecessor State defined in the aggregate as a breach of an international obligation, the international responsibility of the successor State for the breach extends over the entire period starting with the first of the actions or omissions of the series and lasts for as long as these actions or omissions are repeated and remain not in conformity with the international obligation.

3.   The provisions of the present Article are without prejudice to any responsibility incurred by the predecessor State if it continues to exist.

ARTICLE 10:

Diplomatic protection

1.   A successor State may exercise diplomatic protection in respect of a person or a corporation that is its national at the date of the official presentation of the claim but was not a national at the date of injury, provided that the person or the corporation had the nationality of the predecessor State or lost his or her previous nationality and acquired, for a reason unrelated to the bringing of the claim, the nationality of the successor State in a manner not inconsistent with international law.

2.   A claim in exercise of diplomatic protection initiated by the predecessor State may be continued after the date of succession of States by the successor State under the same conditions set out in paragraph 1 of this Article.

3.   A claim in exercise of diplomatic protection initiated by a State against the predecessor State may be continued against the successor State if the predecessor State has ceased to exist. In the case of a plurality of successor States, the claim shall be addressed to the successor State having the most direct connection with the act giving rise to the exercise of diplomatic protection. When it is not possible to determine a single successor State having such a direct connection, the claim may be continued against all the successor States. The provisions of Article 7 apply *mutatis mutandis*.

4. Where the predecessor State continues to exist and the individual or corporation possesses the nationality of both the predecessor and the successor States, or the nationality of a third State, the question is governed by the rules of diplomatic protection concerning dual or multiple nationality.

CHAPTER III:
PROVISIONS CONCERNING SPECIFIC CATEGORIES OF SUCCESSION OF STATES

ARTICLE II:
Transfer of part of the territory of a State

1. With the exception of the situations referred to in the following paragraphs, the rights and obligations arising from an internationally wrongful act in relation to which the predecessor State has been either the author or the injured State do not pass to the successor State when part of the territory of the predecessor State, or any territory for the international relations of which this State is responsible, becomes part of the territory of the successor State.

2. The rights arising from an internationally wrongful act committed against the predecessor State pass to the successor State if there exists a direct link between the consequences of this act and the territory transferred and/or its population.

3. If particular circumstances so require, the obligations arising from an internationally wrongful act pass to the successor State when the author of this act was an organ of the territorial unit of the predecessor State that has later become an organ of the successor State.

ARTICLE 12:
Separation of parts of a State

1. With the exception of the situations referred to in paragraphs 2 to 4 of the present Article, the rights and obligations arising from an internationally wrongful act in relation to which the predecessor State has been either the author or the injured State do not pass to the successor State or States when a part or parts of the territory of a State separate to form one or more States and the predecessor State continues to exist.

2. The rights arising from an internationally wrongful act committed against the predecessor State pass to the successor State or States if there exists a direct link between the consequences of this act and the territory or the population of the successor State or States.

3.   If particular circumstances so require, the obligations arising from the commission of an internationally wrongful act by the predecessor State pass to the successor State when the author of that act was an organ of a territorial unit of the predecessor State that has later become an organ of the successor State.

4.   If particular circumstances indicated in paragraphs 2 and 3 of this Article so require, the obligations arising from an internationally wrongful act committed before the date of succession of States are assumed by the predecessor and the successor State or States.

5.   In order to determine an equitable apportionment of the rights or obligations of the predecessor and the successor States, criteria that may be taken into consideration include the existence of any special connections with the act giving rise to international responsibility, the size of the territory and of the population, the respective contributions to the gross domestic product of the States concerned at the date of succession of States, the need to avoid unjust enrichment and any other circumstance relevant to the case. The provisions of Article 7 apply *mutatis mutandis*.

6.   The internationally wrongful act of an insurrectional or other movement which succeeds in establishing a new State on part of the territory of the predecessor State or in a territory under the administration of this latter State shall be considered an act of the new State under international law. Consequently, the predecessor State incurs no responsibility for the acts committed by the insurrectional or other movement.

ARTICLE 13:
Merger of States

When two or more States unite and form a new successor State, and no predecessor State continues to exist, the rights or obligations arising from an internationally wrongful act of which a predecessor State has been either the author or the injured State pass to the successor State.

ARTICLE 14:
Incorporation of a State into another existing State

When a State is incorporated into another existing State and ceases to exist, the rights or obligations arising from an internationally wrongful act of which the predecessor State has been the author or the injured State pass to the successor State.

ARTICLE 15:

Dissolution of a State

1.   When a State dissolves and ceases to exist and the parts of its territory form two or more successor States, the rights or obligations arising from an internationally wrongful act in relation to which the predecessor State has been the author or the injured State pass, bearing in mind the duty to negotiate and according to the circumstances referred to in paragraphs 2 and 3 of the present Article, to one, several or all the successor States.

2.   In order to determine which of the successor States becomes bearer of the rights described in the preceding paragraph, a relevant factor will in particular be the existence of a direct link between the consequences of the internationally wrongful act committed against the predecessor State and the territory or the population of the successor State or States.

3.   In order to determine which of the successor States becomes bearer of the obligations described in paragraph 1, a relevant factor will in particular be, in addition to that mentioned in paragraph 2, the fact that the author of the internationally wrongful act was an organ of the predecessor State that later became an organ of the successor State.

ARTICLE 16:

Newly independent States

1.   When the successor State is a newly independent State, the obligations arising from an internationally wrongful act committed by the predecessor State shall not pass to the successor State.

2.   When the successor State is a newly independent State, the rights arising from an internationally wrongful act committed against the predecessor State pass to the successor State if that act has a direct link with the territory or the population of the newly independent State.

3.   The conduct, prior to the date of succession of States, of a national liberation movement which succeeds in establishing a newly independent State shall be considered the act of the new State under international law.

4.   The rights arising from an internationally wrongful act committed before the date of the succession of States by the predecessor State or any other State against a people entitled to self-determination shall pass after that date to the newly independent State created by that people.

JUSTITIA ET PACE   14ème Commission
INSTITUT DE DROIT INTERNATIONAL
Session de Tallinn – 2015   28 août 2015

14ème COMMISSION

La succession d'Etats en matière de responsabilité internationale

Rapporteur: M. Kohen

RESOLUTION
(TEXTE FINAL)

L'*Institut de droit international*,

Constatant que le travail de codification et de développement progressif réalisé dans le domaine de la succession d'Etats n'a pas couvert les questions relatives à la responsabilité de l'Etat, et que celui réalisé dans le domaine de la responsabilité de l'Etat n'a pas examiné les questions relatives à la succession d'Etats,

Convaincu de la nécessité de codifier et développer progressivement les règles relatives à la succession d'Etats en matière de responsabilité internationale de l'Etat, afin de garantir une plus grande sécurité juridique dans les relations internationales,

Ayant présent à l'esprit que les cas de succession d'Etats ne doivent pas constituer une raison pour ne pas mettre en œuvre les conséquences qui découlent d'un fait internationalement illicite,

Compte tenu du fait que les différentes catégories de succession d'Etats ainsi que leurs circonstances particulières peuvent conduire à des solutions différentes,

Considérant que, le droit et l'équité imposent que soient déterminés, après la date de succession d'Etats, à quels Etats ou d'autres sujets de droit international incomberont les droits et les obligations qui découlent des faits internationalement illicites commis ou subis par l'Etat prédécesseur,

Attendu que les principes du libre consentement, de la bonne foi, de l'équité et *pacta sunt servanda* sont universellement reconnus,

Rappelant les principes de droit international incorporés dans la Charte des Nations Unies, tels que les principes concernant l'égalité des droits des peuples et leur droit à disposer d'eux-mêmes, l'égalité souveraine et l'indépendance de tous les Etats, la non-ingérence dans les affaires intérieures des Etats, l'interdiction de la menace ou de l'emploi de la force et le respect universel et effectif des droits de l'homme et des libertés fondamentales pour tous,

Attendu que le respect de l'intégrité territoriale et de l'indépendance politique de tout Etat est exigé par la Charte des Nations Unies,

Adopte la résolution suivante:

CHAPITRE I:
DISPOSITIONS GÉNÉRALES

ARTICLE I:
Expressions employées

Aux fins de la présente résolution:

a)   L'expression « succession d'Etats » s'entend de la substitution d'un Etat à un autre dans la responsabilité des relations internationales d'un territoire.

b)   L'expression « Etat prédécesseur » s'entend de l'Etat auquel un autre Etat s'est substitué à l'occasion d'une succession d'Etats.

c)   L'expression « Etat successeur » s'entend de l'Etat qui s'est substitué à un autre Etat à l'occasion d'une succession d'Etats.

d)   L'expression « date de la succession d'Etats » s'entend de la date à laquelle l'Etat successeur s'est substitué à l'Etat prédécesseur dans la responsabilité des relations internationales du territoire auquel se rapporte la succession d'Etats.

e)   L'expression « Etat nouvellement indépendant » s'entend d'un Etat successeur dont le territoire, immédiatement avant la date de la succession d'Etats, était un territoire dépendant dont l'Etat prédécesseur avait la responsabilité des relations internationales.

f)   L'expression «accord de dévolution» s'entend d'un accord conclu entre l'Etat prédécesseur et l'Etat successeur ou un mouvement de libération nationale, insurrectionnel ou autre, ou une entité ou un organe qui devient ultérieurement l'organe de l'Etat successeur, stipulant que les droits et/ou obligations de l'Etat prédécesseur sont dévolus à l'Etat successeur.

g)   L'expression «fait internationalement illicite» s'entend d'un comportement consistant en une action ou une omission: (i) attribuable à l'Etat ou à un autre sujet en vertu du droit international; et (ii) constituant une violation d'une obligation internationale de l'Etat ou de l'autre sujet. La qualification du fait comme internationalement illicite relève du droit international.

h)   L'expression «responsabilité internationale» s'entend des conséquences juridiques d'un fait internationalement illicite.

ARTICLE 2:

Portée de la présente résolution

1.   La présente résolution s'applique aux effets d'une succession d'Etats relatifs aux droits et obligations qui découlent d'un fait internationalement illicite commis par l'Etat prédécesseur contre un autre Etat ou un autre sujet de droit international avant la date de la succession d'Etats, ou commis par un Etat ou un autre sujet de droit international contre l'Etat prédécesseur avant cette date.

2.   La présente résolution s'applique uniquement aux effets d'une succession d'Etats se produisant conformément au droit international, et plus particulièrement aux principes du droit international incorporés dans la Charte des Nations Unies.

3.   Les présents articles ne régissent pas les situations résultant de changements politiques internes à l'Etat, y compris les changements de régime ou de nom de l'Etat.

CHAPITRE II:
RÈGLES COMMUNES

ARTICLE 3:

Caractère subsidiaire des principes directeurs

Les principes directeurs mentionnés ci-après sont d'application en l'absence de toute autre solution convenue entre les parties concernées par la situation de succession d'Etats, y compris l'Etat ou le sujet lésé par le fait internationalement illicite.

ARTICLE 4:

Invocation de la responsabilité pour un fait internationalement illicite commis par l'Etat prédécesseur avant la date de la succession d'Etats

1.   La responsabilité internationale découlant d'un fait internationalement illicite commis avant la date d'une succession d'Etats par un Etat prédécesseur incombe à cet Etat.

2.   Si l'Etat prédécesseur continue d'exister, l'Etat ou le sujet lésé peut, même après la date de la succession, invoquer la responsabilité internationale de l'Etat prédécesseur pour le fait internationalement illicite qu'il a commis avant la date de la succession et lui demander réparation pour le préjudice causé par ce fait internationalement illicite.

3.   Conformément aux articles suivants, l'Etat ou le sujet lésé peut demander réparation également ou uniquement à l'Etat ou Etats

successeurs pour le préjudice causé par le fait internationalement illicite commis par l'Etat prédécesseur.

Invocation de la responsabilité pour un fait internationalement illicite commis contre l'Etat prédécesseur avant la date de la succession d'Etats

1.   L'Etat prédécesseur qui continue d'exister après la date de la succession d'Etats peut invoquer la responsabilité internationale pour le fait internationalement illicite commis à son égard avant cette date par un autre Etat ou sujet de droit international et peut demander réparation pour le préjudice causé par ce fait.

2.   Si le préjudice causé par un fait internationalement illicite commis avant la date de la succession d'Etats contre l'Etat prédécesseur affecte le territoire ou des personnes qui, après cette date, sont sous la juridiction d'un Etat successeur, l'Etat successeur peut demander une réparation pour le préjudice causé par ce fait, conformément aux articles suivants, à moins que la réparation n'ait été intégralement obtenue avant la date de la succession d'Etats.

ARTICLE 6:

Accords de dévolution et actes unilatéraux

1.   Les accords de dévolution conclus avant la date de succession d'Etats entre l'Etat prédécesseur et une entité ou mouvement de libération nationale qui représente un peuple ayant le droit de disposer de lui-même, de même que les accords conclus par les Etats intéressés après la date de succession d'Etats, sont soumis aux règles relatives au consentement des parties et à la validité des traités, telles qu'énoncées par la Convention de Vienne sur le droit des traités. Le même principe s'applique aux accords de dévolution conclus entre l'Etat prédécesseur et une de ses entités autonomes qui deviendrait plus tard un Etat successeur.

2.   Les obligations d'un Etat prédécesseur découlant d'un fait internationalement illicite qu'il a commis à l'égard d'un autre Etat ou d'un autre sujet de droit international avant la date de la succession d'Etats ne deviennent pas les obligations de l'Etat successeur vis-à-vis de l'Etat ou du sujet lésé du seul fait que l'Etat prédécesseur et l'Etat successeur ont conclu un accord stipulant que lesdites obligations sont dévolues à l'Etat successeur.

3.   Les obligations d'un Etat prédécesseur découlant d'un fait internationalement illicite qu'il a commis à l'égard d'un autre Etat ou d'un autre sujet de droit international avant la date de la succession

d'Etats ne deviennent pas les obligations de l'Etat successeur vis-à-vis de l'Etat ou du sujet lésé du seul fait que l'Etat successeur ait accepté que lesdites obligations lui soient dévolues.

4.   Lorsque l'Etat lésé ou le sujet de droit international lésé n'accepte pas la solution envisagée par l'accord de dévolution ou par l'acte unilatéral, des négociations doivent être poursuivies de bonne foi par les Etats ou sujets intéressés. Si ces négociations n'aboutissent pas dans un délai raisonnable, la solution envisagée par l'article pertinent du chapitre III de la présente résolution est applicable.

ARTICLE 7:

Pluralité d'Etats successeurs

1.   Dans les cas de succession où il n'est pas possible d'identifier un Etat successeur unique, tous les Etats successeurs seront bénéficiaires de droits ou assumeront les obligations découlant de la commission d'un fait internationalement illicite d'une manière équitable, à moins qu'il n'en soit convenu autrement par les Etats ou sujets intéressés.

2.   Pour établir une répartition équitable des droits ou obligations entre les Etats successeurs, pourront être pris en considération des critères tels que l'existence de liens spéciaux avec l'acte qui engage la responsabilité internationale, l'étendue du territoire et la taille de la population, les participations respectives dans le produit national brut des Etats concernés à la date de la succession, la nécessité d'éviter toute situation d'enrichissement sans cause et toute autre circonstance pertinente.

3.   Des négociations doivent être poursuivies de bonne foi par les Etats successeurs en vue d'aboutir à une solution dans un délai raisonnable.

ARTICLE 8:

Etats ou sujets de droit international intéressés

Aux fins des articles 6 et 7, les « Etats ou sujets de droit international intéressés » sont:

a)   dans le cas d'un fait internationalement illicite commis par l'Etat prédécesseur, l'Etat lésé ou le sujet de droit international lésé et tous les Etats successeurs;

b)   dans le cas d'un fait internationalement illicite subi par l'Etat prédécesseur, tous les Etats successeurs.

ARTICLE 9:

Faits internationalement illicites à caractère continu ou composite s'étant produits ou achevés après la date de la succession d'Etats

1.   Quand un Etat successeur poursuit la violation d'une obligation internationale par un fait à caractère continu de l'Etat prédécesseur, la responsabilité internationale de l'Etat successeur pour la violation s'étend sur toute la période durant laquelle le fait se poursuit et reste non conforme à l'obligation internationale.

2.   Quand l'Etat successeur complète une série d'actions ou omissions initiées par l'Etat prédécesseur définies dans leur ensemble comme illicites, la responsabilité internationale de l'Etat successeur pour la violation s'étend sur toute la période débutant avec la première des actions ou omissions de la série et dure aussi longtemps que ces actions ou omissions se répètent et restent non conformes à ladite obligation internationale.

3.   Les dispositions du présent article sont sans préjudice de toute responsabilité qui incombe à l'Etat prédécesseur s'il continue d'exister.

ARTICLE 10:

Protection diplomatique

1.   Un Etat successeur est en droit d'exercer la protection diplomatique à l'égard d'une personne ou d'une société qui a sa nationalité à la date de la présentation officielle de la réclamation mais qui n'avait pas cette nationalité à la date du préjudice, à condition que la personne ou société ait eu la nationalité de l'État prédécesseur ou qu'elle ait perdu sa première nationalité et acquis, pour une raison sans rapport avec la présentation de la réclamation, la nationalité de l'État successeur d'une manière non contraire au droit international.

2.   Une réclamation présentée par l'Etat prédécesseur dans l'exercice de la protection diplomatique peut être poursuivie après la date de la succession d'Etats par l'Etat successeur dans les mêmes conditions énoncées au paragraphe premier du présent article.

3.   Une réclamation présentée par un Etat dans l'exercice de la protection diplomatique contre l'Etat prédécesseur peut être poursuivie contre l'Etat successeur si l'Etat prédécesseur a cessé d'exister. Dans le cas d'une pluralité d'Etats successeurs, la réclamation sera adressée à l'Etat successeur ayant le lien le plus direct avec le fait qui donne lieu à l'exercice de la protection diplomatique. S'il n'est pas possible d'identifier un Etat successeur unique ayant ce lien direct, la réclamation pourra être poursuivie contre tous les Etats successeurs. Les dispositions énoncées à l'article 7 s'appliquent *mutatis mutandis*.

4.   Lorsque l'Etat prédécesseur continue d'exister et la personne ou
la société possède la nationalité de l'Etat prédécesseur et celle de l'Etat
successeur, ou celle d'un Etat tiers, la question est régie par les règles
relatives à la protection diplomatique concernant la double ou multiple
nationalité.

CHAPITRE III:
DISPOSITIONS CONCERNANT DES CATÉGORIES
SPÉCIFIQUES DE SUCCESSION D'ETATS

ARTICLE 11:

Transfert d'une partie du territoire d'un Etat

1.   A l'exception des situations visées aux paragraphes suivants,
les droits et les obligations qui découlent d'un fait internationalement
illicite à l'égard duquel l'Etat prédécesseur a été soit l'auteur soit l'Etat
lésé, ne passent pas à l'Etat successeur, lorsqu'une partie du territoire
de l'Etat prédécesseur, ou tout territoire pour lequel celui-ci a la
responsabilité des relations internationales, devient partie du territoire
de l'Etat successeur.

2.   Les droits qui découlent d'un fait internationalement illicite
commis contre l'Etat prédécesseur passent à l'Etat successeur s'il
existe un lien direct entre les conséquences de ce fait et le territoire
transféré et/ou la population.

3.   Si des circonstances particulières l'exigent, les obligations
qui découlent d'un fait internationalement illicite passent à l'Etat
successeur, pourvu que l'auteur de ce fait ait été un organe de l'unité
territoriale qui plus tard est devenu un organe de l'Etat successeur.

ARTICLE 12:

Séparation de parties d'un Etat

1.   A l'exception des situations visées aux paragraphes 2 à 4, les
droits et les obligations qui découlent d'un fait internationalement
illicite à l'égard duquel l'Etat prédécesseur a été soit l'auteur soit l'Etat
lésé ne passent pas à l'Etat ou aux Etats successeurs lorsqu'une partie
ou plusieurs parties du territoire d'un Etat s'en séparent pour former un
ou plusieurs Etats et que l'Etat prédécesseur continue d'exister.

2.   Les droits qui découlent d'un fait internationalement illicite
commis contre l'Etat prédécesseur passent à l'Etat ou aux Etats
successeurs s'il existe un lien direct entre les conséquences de ce fait
et le territoire ou la population de l'Etat ou des Etats successeurs.

3.   Si des circonstances particulières l'exigent, les obligations qui découlent du fait internationalement illicite commis par l'Etat prédécesseur passent à l'Etat successeur pourvu que l'auteur de ce fait ait été un organe de l'unité territoriale de l'Etat prédécesseur qui plus tard est devenu organe de l'Etat successeur.

4.   Si les circonstances particulières indiquées aux paragraphes 2 et 3 du présent article l'exigent, les obligations qui découlent d'un fait internationalement illicite commis avant la date de la succession d'Etats sont assumées par l'Etat prédécesseur et l'Etat ou les Etats successeurs.

5.   Pour établir une répartition équitable des droits ou obligations des Etats prédécesseur et successeur, pourront être pris en considération des critères tels que l'existence de liens spéciaux avec l'acte qui engage la responsabilité internationale, l'étendue du territoire et la taille de la population, les participations respectives dans le produit national brut des Etats concernés à la date de la succession de l'Etat, la nécessité d'éviter l'enrichissement sans cause et toute autre circonstance pertinente. Les dispositions de l'article 7 s'appliquent *mutatis mutandis*.

6.   Le fait internationalement illicite d'un mouvement, insurrectionnel ou autre, qui parvient à créer un nouvel Etat sur une partie du territoire d'un Etat préexistant ou sur un territoire sous l'administration de ce dernier est considéré comme un fait de ce nouvel Etat d'après le droit international. En conséquence, l'Etat prédécesseur n'encourt pas de responsabilité pour des faits commis par le mouvement insurrectionnel ou autre.

ARTICLE 13:
Fusion d'Etats

Lorsque deux ou plusieurs Etats s'unissent pour former un nouvel Etat sans laisser subsister d'Etat prédécesseur, les droits ou obligations qui découlent d'un fait internationalement illicite à l'égard duquel l'Etat prédécesseur a été soit l'auteur soit l'Etat lésé passent à l'Etat successeur.

ARTICLE 14:
Incorporation d'un Etat dans un autre Etat préexistant

Lorsqu'un Etat est incorporé dans un autre Etat préexistant et cesse d'exister, les droits ou les obligations qui découlent d'un fait internationalement illicite à l'égard duquel l'Etat prédécesseur a été l'auteur ou l'Etat lésé passent à l'Etat successeur.

ARTICLE 15:

Dissolution d'un Etat

1.   Lorsqu'un Etat est dissout et cesse d'exister et que les parties de son territoire forment deux ou plusieurs Etats successeurs, les droits ou les obligations découlant d'un fait internationalement illicite à l'égard duquel l'Etat prédécesseur a été l'auteur ou l'Etat lésé passent, compte tenu du devoir de négocier et selon les circonstances mentionnées aux paragraphes 2 et 3 du présent article, à l'un, plusieurs ou à tous les Etats successeurs.

2.   Afin de déterminer lequel des Etats successeurs devient le titulaire des droits énoncés au paragraphe précédent, il sera notamment tenu compte de l'existence d'un lien direct entre les conséquences du fait internationalement illicite commis contre l'Etat prédécesseur et le territoire ou la population de l'Etat ou des Etats successeurs.

3.   Afin de déterminer lequel des Etats successeurs devient le titulaire des obligations énoncées au paragraphe premier, il sera notamment tenu compte, outre le facteur énoncé au paragraphe 2, du fait que l'auteur du fait internationalement illicite ait été un organe de l'Etat prédécesseur qui est devenu ensuite un organe de l'Etat successeur.

ARTICLE 16:

Etats nouvellement indépendants

1.   Quand l'Etat successeur est un Etat nouvellement indépendant, les obligations découlant d'un fait internationalement illicite commis par l'Etat prédécesseur ne passent pas à l'Etat successeur.

2.   Quand l'Etat successeur est un Etat nouvellement indépendant, les droits découlant d'un fait internationalement illicite commis contre l'Etat prédécesseur passent à l'Etat successeur si ce fait a un lien direct avec le territoire ou la population de l'Etat nouvellement indépendant.

3.   Le comportement, avant la date de succession d'Etats, d'un mouvement de libération nationale qui parvient à créer un Etat nouvellement indépendant, sera considéré comme le fait de ce nouvel Etat d'après le droit international.

4.   Les droits qui découlent d'un fait internationalement illicite commis avant la date de succession d'Etats par l'Etat prédécesseur ou un autre Etat contre un peuple bénéficiant du droit de disposer de lui-même passent après cette date à l'Etat nouvellement indépendant créé par ce peuple.

REFERENCES

1   Case Law

A   PCIJ CASES

Panevezys-Saldutiskis Railway Case, PCIJ, Series A/B No. 76, 35.

B   ICJ CASES

Application of the Convention on the Prevention and Punishment of the Crime of Genocide (Bosnia and Herzegovina v. Serbia and Montenegro), Judgment of 26 February 2007, ICJ Reports 2007.

Application of the Convention on the Prevention and Punishment of the Crime of Genocide (Croatia v. Serbia), Judgment of 3 February 2015, ICJ Reports 2015.

Case Concerning the Barcelona Traction, Light and Power Company, Limited (Second Phase) (Belgium v. Spain), Judgment of 5 February 1970, ICJ Reports 1970.

Case Concerning the Gabčíkovo-Nagymaros Project (Hungary v. Slovakia), Judgment of 25 September 1997, ICJ Reports 1997.

Certain Phosphate Lands in Nauru (Nauru v. Australia), Preliminary Objections, Judgment, ICJ Reports 1992.

East Timor (Portugal v. Australia), Judgment, ICJ Reports 1995.

C   OTHER COURTS AND TRIBUNALS

Bijelic v. Montenegro and Serbia, European Court of Human Rights, Judgment, 11 June 2009, Application no. 11890/05.

Sea-Land Service, Inc. v. The Islamic Republic of Iran, et al., Award No. 115–33–1, 22 June 1984, in: 6 *Iran-U.S. C.T.R.* 149.

D   ARBITRAL AWARDS

Administrative Decision No. 1, Tripartite Claims Commission, 25 May 1927, 6 UNRIAA 203.

Administrative Decision No. V, United States-German Mixed Claims Commission, 31 October 1924, in: 7 UNRIAA 119.

Claim of Finnish Shipowners against Great Britain in respect of the Use of Certain Finnish Vessels During the War (Finland v. United Kingdom), Award of Dr. Bagge, 9 May 1934, in: 3 UNRIAA 1481.

Emeric Koranyi & Mme. Ernest Dengcjel v. Romanian State, Hungary-Romania Mixed Arbitral Tribunal, Award of 27 February 1929, in: 8 *Recueil des decisions des tribunaux arbitraux mixtes* 980; in: (1929–1930) *Annual Digest* 64.

R.E. Brown (United States v. Great Britain), Award of 23 November 1923, 6 UNRIAA 120.

Hawaiian Claims case (Great Britain v. United States), Award of 10 November 1925, 6 UNRIAA 157.

In the Matter of the Chagos Marine Protected Area Arbitration (Mauritius v. United Kingdom), Award, 18 March 2015, PCA Case 2011-03.

Levy v. German State, French-German Mixed Arbitral Tribunal, Award of 10 July 1924, in: 4 *Recueil des décisions des tribunaux arbitraux mixtes* 726, in: (1923–1924) *Annual Digest*, case no. 27.

Mytilineos Holdings SA v. State Union of Serbia & Montenegro and Republic of Serbia, UNCITRAL, Partial Award on Jurisdiction, 8 Sept. 2006.

Pablo Nájera (France) v. United Mexican States, France-Mexico Claims Commission, Decision no. 30-A, 19 October 1928, in: 5 UNRIAA 466, (1927–1928) *Annual Digest* 52.

Sentence arbitrale en date des 24/27 juillet 1956 rendue par le Tribunal d'arbitrage constitué en vertu du Compromis signé à Paris le 15 juillet 1932 entre la France et la Grèce, Award of 24/27 July 1956, in: 12 UNRIAA 155; (1956) 23 ILR 91.

E DOMESTIC COURT DECISIONS

Alsace-Lorraine Railway v. Ducreux Es-qualité, France, Court of Cassation, Civil Chamber, 30 March 1927, in: (1928) 55 JDI 1034; (1928) I *Sirey* 300; (1927–1928) *Annual Digest* 85.

Baron A. v. Prussian-Treasury, Germany, Reichsgericht in Civil Matters, 19 December 1923, in: 107 ERZ. 382, in: (1923–1924) *Annual Digest* 60.

Crépet c. Etat belge et Société des forces hydro-électriques de la colonie, Belgium, Civil Tribunal of Brussels, 30 January 1962, (1962) *Journal des tribunaux* 242.

Dzierzbicki v. District Electric Association of Czestochowa, Poland, Supreme Court, First Division, 21 December 1933, in: (1934) OSP, no. 288, in: (1933–1934) *Annual Digest* 89.

Grillo, France, Conseil d'Etat, case no. 178498, 28 July 1999, in: *Tables du Recueil Lebon.*

Hespel, France, Conseil d'Etat, 2/6 SSR, case no. 11092, 5 December 1980, in: *Tables du Recueil Lebon.*

Kalmar v. Hungarian Treasury, Hungary, Supreme Court, 24 March 1929, case no. P.VI.5473/1928, in: *Maganjog Tara*, X, no. 75, in: (1929–1930) *Annual Digest* 61.

Kern v. Chemin de fer d'Alsace-Lorraine, France, Cour de Colmar (Première Ch, civile), 16 May 1927, in: (1929) 56 JDI 446.

Military Pensions (Austria) Case, Austria, Constitutional Court, 7 May 1919, case no. 126, in *Sammlung der Erkenntniss des österreichischen Verfassungsgerichtshofes*, vol. I (1919), no. 9, 17, in (1919–1922) *Annual Digest* 66.

Minister of Defence, Namibia v. Mwandinghi, Namibia, 25 October 1991, in: 1992 (2) SA 355 (NmS), in: 91 ILR 358.

Mordcovici v. P.T.T., Romania, Court of Cassation, 29 October, 1929, in: *Buletinul deciziunilor Inaltei Curti de Casatie*, LXVI (1929), Part 2, p.150, in: (1929–1930) *Annual Digest* 62.

Mutua et al. v. The Foreign and Commonwealth Office, United Kingdom, 21 July 2011, [2011] EWHC 1913 (QB) and of 5 October 2012, [2012] EWHC 2678 (QB).

Mwandinghi v. Minister of Defence, Namibia, Namibia, 14 December 1990, in: 1991 (1) SA 851 (Nm), in: 91 ILR 343.

Niedzielskie v. (Polish) Treasury, Poland, Supreme Court, 13 October 1926, in: *Rw.* III, 1485/26/I; 3 (1925–26) *Annual Digest* 74.

Niemiec and Niemiec v. Bialobrodziec and Polish State Treasury, Poland, Supreme Court, Third Division, 20 February 1923, in: 2 *Annual Digest*, case no. 33.

Olpinski v. Polish Treasury (Railway Division), Poland, Third Division, 16 April 1921, *O.S.P.*, I, no. 15, in: (1919–1922) *Annual Digest* 63.

Perriquet, Conseil d'Etat, France, case no. 119737, 15 March 1995, in: *Recueil Lebon.*

Personal Injuries (Upper Silesia) Case, Federal Republic of Germany, Court of Appeal of Cologne, 10 December 1951, in: NJW, 5 (1952), 1300, in: (1951) ILR 67.

Pittacos c. Etat belge, Belgium, Brussels Court of Appeal (2nd Chamber), 1 December 1964, *Journal des tribunaux*, 1965, 9; and Cour de cassation, 26 May 1966, *Pasicrisie belge*, (1966) Part I, 1221, also in: 48 ILR 22.

Poldermans v. State of the Netherlands, Netherlands, Court of Appeal of The Hague (First Chamber), 8 December 1955, in: (1959) NJ, no. 7 (with an analysis by Boltjes); (1957) ILR 69.

Samos (Liability for Torts) Case, Greece, Court of the Aegean Islands, 1924, N° 27, in: 35 *Thémis* 294; (1923–1924) *Annual Digest* 70.

Sechter v. Ministry of the Interior, Romania, Court of Cassation, 1929, in: (1930)17 (4) *Jurisprudenta Română a Inaltei Curti de Casatiesi Justitie*, 58; (1929–1930), *Annual Digest*, case no. 37.

Van der Have v. State of the Netherlands, Netherlands, District Court of The Hague, 12 January 1953, in: (1953) NJ, no. 133; (1953) ILR 80.

Vozneac v. Autonomous Administration of Posts and Telegraphs, Romania, Court of Cassation, 22 June 1931, in: (1932) *Jurisprudenta Română a Inaltei Curti de Casatiesi Justitie*, 36; (1931–1932) *Annual Digest*, case no. 30.

West Rand Central Gold Mining Company Ltd. v. The King, United Kingdom, Decision of 1 June 1905, in: (1905) LR; 2 KB, 391; *British International Law Cases*, vol. II (London: Stevens, 1965), 283.

Zilberszpic v. (Polish) Treasury, Supreme Court of Poland, First Division, 14 December 1928, in: Zb. OSN, 1928, no. 190; 4 (1927–1928) *Annual Digest* 82.

F   OTHER DECISIONS

International Conference on the Former Yugoslavia, Arbitration Commission, Opinion No 1, 29 November 1991, in: (1993) 92 ILR 166.

International Conference on the Former Yugoslavia, Arbitration Commission, Opinion No 13, Effects of War Damages on Division, 16 July 1993, in: 96 ILR 727.

2 Treaties

Abkommen zwischen der Regierung der Bundesrepublik Deutschland und der Regierung der Russischen Föderation über kulturelle Zusammenarbeit, 16 December 1992, in: BGBl., 1993, vol. II, 1256.

Accord du 27 mai 1997 entre le Gouvernement de la République française et le Gouvernement de la Fédération de Russie sur le règlement définitif des créances réciproques financières et réelles apparues antérieurement au 9 mai 1945, 19 December 1997 (Bill No. 97–1160, in: JORF, 15 May 1998).

Accord général entre le gouvernement de la République française et le gouvernement de la République arabe unie, in: La documentation française, 18 October 1958, no. 2473; (1958) *RGDIP* 738.

Additional Protocol to the Agreement on Reparation from Germany, on the Establishment of an Inter-Allied Reparation Agency, and on the Restitution of Monetary Gold of 14 January 1946, signed in Brussels on 15 March 1948, entered into force on 15 March 1948, in: 555 UNTS 104.

Agreement between the Government of the Federal Republic of Germany and the Government of the United States of America Concerning the Settlement of certain Property Claims, 13 May 1992, in: TIAS no. 11959.

Agreement between the Government of the United Kingdom of Great Britain and Northern Ireland and the Government of the Arab Republic of Egypt Regarding Compensation for British Property, Rights and Interests Affected by Arab Republic of Egypt Measures of Nationalisation and other Matters Concerning British Property in the Arab Republic of Egypt, entered into force on 28 March 1972, in: (1972) UKTS no. 62 (Cmd. 4995); 858 UNTS 3.

Agreement between the Government of the United Kingdom of Great Britain and Northern Ireland and the Government of Mauritius, 7 July 1982 (in force on 28 October 1982), in: (1983) UKTS no. 6 (Cmnd. 8785).

Agreement between the Government of the United Kingdom of Great Britain and Northern Ireland and the Government of the United Arab Republic Concerning Financial and Commercial Relations and British Property in Egypt, in: (1959) UKTS no. 35 (Cmd. 723); 343 UNTS 159; (1958) 14 *Rev. Égyptienne d.i.*, 364; (1960) 54 *AJIL* 511–519.

Agreement between the Government of the United States of America and the Government of the Socialist Republic of Vietnam concerning the settlement of certain property claims, signed in Hanoi, 28 January 1995, 2420 UNTS No. 43661.

Agreement between Italy and the United Arab Republic Relative to the Indemnisation of Italian Interests in Egypt with Protocol for the Application of the Exchange of Notes, 23 March 1965, entered into force on 5 September 1966, in: *Gaz. Off.*, No. 215, 1 April 1966; in: 7 *Diritto Internazionale*, 1966, Pt. II, at 231

Agreement between the State of Israel and the Federal Republic of Germany on Compensation, in: 162 UNTS 205.

Agreement for the Determination of the Amounts to be paid by Austria and by Hungary in satisfaction of their Obligations under the Treaties concluded by the United States with Austria on August 24, 1921, and with Hungary on August 29, *1921*, signed in Washington, 26 November 1924, 48 LNTS No. 1151, 69; 6 UNRIAA 199.

Agreement Establishing the Commonwealth of Independent States, UN Doc A/46/771, 13 December 1991, in (1992) 31 ILM 138.

Agreement on the Establishment of the Republic of Yemen and the Organisation of the Thirty-Month Interim Period, 22 April 1990, entered into force on 21 May 1990, in: (1990) 30 ILM 820.

Agreement on Reparation from Germany, on the Establishment of an Inter-Allied Reparation Agency and on the Restitution of Monetary Gold, signed in Paris on 14 January 1946, entered into force on 24 January 1946, in: 555 UNTS 69.

Agreement relating to the Separation of Singapore from Malaysia as an Independent and Sovereign State, signed at Kuala Lumpur, on 7 August 1965, 563 UNTS 89, No. 8206.

Agreement on Succession Issues of 29 June 2001 (Bosnia and Herzegovina, Croatia, Serbia, Slovenia, Macedonia) 2262 UNTS 251; (2002) 41 ILM 1–39.

Alma Ata Declaration, 21 December 1991, UN Doc A/46/60, 30 December 1991, (1992) 31 ILM 147.

Claims Convention between the United States and Panama, signed on 28 July 1926, ratified on 3 October 1931, in: 138 LNTS 120–126: 6 UNRIAA 301.

Comprehensive Peace Agreement between the Government of the Republic of the Sudan and the Sudan's People's Liberation Movement/Sudan People's Liberation Army, signed in May 2004.

Peace Treaty (U.K., Soviet Union, USA, France, Italy, Romania, Hungary, Bulgaria, Finland), signed on 10 February 1947 at Paris, entered into force on 15 September 1947, in: 49 UNTS 126; (1948) UKTS no. 50 (Cmd. 7481).

Protocol between the United States of America and Venezuela (1 May 1852, Caracas), in: Malloy W.M., *Treaties, Conventions, International Acts, Protocols and Agreements between the United States of America and other Powers, 1776–1909*, vol. II (Washington: US Govt., 1910).

Protocol I between the Federal Republic of Germany and the Conference on Jewish Material Claims against Germany, in; 162 UNTS 205; (1953) II BGBl. 85.

Protocol II between the Federal Republic of Germany and the Conference on Jewish Material Claims against Germany, in: 162 UNTS 205; (1953) II BGBl. 85.

Treaty Establishing Friendly Relations between the United States of America and Hungary, signed in Budapest on 29 August 1921, in 660 USTS; (1922) 16 *AJIL,* Suppl., 13–16.

Treaty on the Establishment of German Unity, 31 August 1990, in: (1991) 30 ILM 457; (1991) 51 *ZaöRV* 494.

Treaty of Peace between the Allied and Associated Powers and Austria; Protocol, Declaration and Special Declaration, St. Germain-en-Laye, 10 September 1919, entered into force on 16 July 1920, in (1919) UKTS No. 11 (Cmd. 400).

Treaty of Peace between Japan and Malaysia, signed on 11 September 1967, entered into force on 7 May 1968, in: (1969) 13 *Jap. Ann. Int'l L.* 209.

Treaty of Peace between Japan and the Republic of Indonesia, entered into force on 15 April 1958, in: 324 UNTS 227; (1959) 3 *Jap. Ann. Int'l L* 158.

Treaty of Peace between Japan and Singapore, signed on 21 September 1967, entered into force on 7 May 1968, in: (1969) 13 *Jap. Ann. Int'l L.* 244.

Vertrag zwischen der Bundesrepublik Deutschland und der Deutschen Demokratischen Republik über die Herstellung der Einheit Deutschlands [Treaty between the Federal

Republic of Germany and the German Democratic Republic on the Establishment of German Unity], 31 August 1990, (1990) II BGBl. 885; (1991) 30 ILM 463.

Vienna Convention on Succession of States in Respect of State Property, Archives and Debts, 8 April 1983, not yet in force, Official Records of the United Nations Conference on Succession of States in Respect of State Property, Archives and Debts, vol. II (United Nations publication, Sales No. E.94.V.6).

Vienna Convention on Succession of States in Respect of Treaties, 23 August 1978, entered into force on 6 November 1996, 1946 UNTS 3.

3   UN Documents

A   GENERAL ASSEMBLY RESOLUTIONS

Declaration of Principles of International Law Concerning Friendly Relations and Co-Operation Among States in Accordance with the Charter of the United Nations, GA Res 2625 (XXV), UNGAOR, 25th Sess, Supp No, UN Doc A/8082, (1970) 121.

Resolution 36/121 of 10 December 1981 (Question of Namibia).

Resolution 38/36 of 2 December 1983 (Question of Namibia).

Resolution 40/52 of 2 December 1985 (Activities of foreign economic and other interests which are impeding the implementation of the Declaration on the Granting of Independence to Colonial Countries and Peoples in Namibia and in all other Territories under colonial domination and efforts to eliminate colonialism, apartheid and racial discrimination in southern Africa).

Resolution 55/153 of 12 December 2000 (Nationality of Natural Persons in relation to the Succession of States).

Resolution 56/83 of 12 December 2001 (Responsibility of States for internationally wrongful acts).

Resolution A/60/264 of 12 July 2006 (Admission of the Republic of Montenegro to membership in the United Nations).

Resolution 65/308 of 25 August 2011 (Admission of the Republic of South Sudan to membership in the United Nations).

Resolution 67/19 of 29 November 2012 (Status of Palestine in the United Nations).

Resolution 71/292 of 22 June 2017 (Legal Consequences of the Separation of Chagos from Mauritius in 1965, Request for an Advisory Opinion).

B   INTERNATIONAL LAW COMMISSION

ILC, 'Addendum to First Report on Diplomatic Protection', by Mr. John R. Dugard, Special Rapporteur, 20 April 2000, UN Doc. A/CN.4/506/Add.1.

ILC, 'Commentaries to the Draft Articles on Responsibility of States for Internationally Wrongful Acts Adopted by the International Law Commission at Its Fifty-Third Session (2001)', Report of the International Law Commission on the Work of its Fifty-third Session, Official Records of the General Assembly, Fifty-sixth Session, Supplement No. 10(A/56/10), (2001) II(2) *Yearbook ILC*, 30.

ILC, 'Draft Articles on Diplomatic Protection with commentaries', (2006) II(2) *Yearbook ILC*, 23.

ILC, 'Draft Articles on Nationality of Natural Persons in Relation to the Succession of States', adopted by the ILC on second reading in 1999, ILC Report, U.N. Doc. A/54/10, 1999, ch. IV, paras. 44 and 45, in: (1997) II *Yearbook ILC*, 14.

ILC, 'Fifth Report on Succession in Respect of Treaties, prepared by the Special Rapporteur, Sir Humphrey Waldock', A/CN.4/256 and Adds.1–4, 10 April, 29 May and 8, 16 and 28 June 1972, A/8710/Rev.1, in: (1972) II *Yearbook ILC*, 292–298.

ILC, 'First Report on State Responsibility (addendum no. 4)', by Crawford J., Special Rapporteur, 26 May 1998, U.N. Doc. A/CN.4/490/Add.4.

ILC, 'First Report on Succession of States in Respect of Rights and Duties Resulting from Sources other than Treaties', by Mr Mohammed Bedjaoui, Special Rapporteur, 20th session of the ILC, 1968, UN Doc. A/CN.4/204, ILC Report, A/7209/Rev.1 (A/23/9), 1968, ch. III(C)(a), in: (1968) II *Yearbook ILC*, 94.

ILC, 'First Report on Succession of States in Respect of State Responsibility, by Special Rapporteur, Mr. Pavel Šturma', 69th session, 2017, A/CN.4/708, 31 May 2017.

ILC, 'Fourth Report on State Responsibility of the Special Rapporteur', Mr. Roberto Ago, 24th session of the ILC, 1972, U.N. Doc. A/CN.4/264 and Add.1, ILC Report, A/8710/Rev.1 (A/27/10), 1972, chp. IV(B), in: (1972) II *Yearbook ILC*, 71.

ILC, 'Guiding Principles Applicable to Unilateral Declarations of States Capable of Creating Legal Obligations', General Assembly Resolution 61/34 of 4 December 2006, in (2006) II(2) *Yearbook ILC*, 159.

ILC, 'Proposal by the Chairman of the ILC Sub-committee on Succession of States and Governments, Manfred Lachs', (1963) II *Yearbook ILC*, 260.

ILC, 'Report of the International Law Commission on the Work of its Twenty-Seventh Session', 5 May to 25 July 1975, Draft Articles on State Responsibility, U.N. Doc. A/10010/Rev.1, in: (1975) II *Yearbook ILC*, 47.

ILC, 'Report of the International Law Commission on the work of its Fifty-third session', Official Records of the General Assembly, Fifty-sixth session, Supplement No. 10 (A/56/10), chp. IV.E.2, 208, (2001) I *Yearbook ILC*, 202.

ILC, 'Report of the International Law Commission on the Work of its Fifty-Fourth Session', 29 April–7 June and 22 July–16 August 2002, ILC Report, A/57/10, 2002, chp. V, (2002) II(2), *Yearbook ILC*, 1.

ILC, 'Report of the International Law Commission', Official Records of the General Assembly, Seventy-first session, Supplement No. 10 (A/71/10), recommendation of the Working-Group on the long-term programme of work, Annex B: 'Succession of States in respect of State responsibility', Syllabus by Pavel Šturma, 409.

ILC, 'Second Report on Succession of States in Respect of State Responsibility, by Special Rapporteur, Mr. Pavel Šturma', 70th session, 2018, A/CN.4/719, 5 April 2018.

ILC, Titles and Texts of the Draft Articles on Responsibility of States for Internationally Wrongful Acts Adopted by the Drafting Committee on Second Reading, 26 July 2001, U.N. Doc. A/CN.4/L.602/Rev.1., (2001) II(2) *Yearbook ILC*, 30.

C OTHER UN DOCUMENTS

Decree on the Natural Resources of Namibia, Addendum to the Report of the United Nations Council for Namibia, 29 UN GAOR Supp. 24A, at 27–28, UN Doc. A/9624/add 1(1975).

Report of the Secretary-General on the Sudan, 12 April 2011, UN doc. D/2011/239.

UN Press Release, U.N. Doc PM/473, 12 August 1947 (Legal Department on the admission of Pakistan to the United Nations).

4   Domestic Law Instruments and Documents

Bundesgesetz über den Fonds für freiwillige Leistungen der Republik Österreich an ehemalige Sklaven und Zwangsarbeiter des nationalsozialistischen Regimes (Versöhnungsfonds Gesetz) (Federal Law Concerning the Fund for Voluntary Payments by the Republic of Austria to Former Slave Labourers and Forced Labourers of the National Socialist Regime), in: ÖBGBl., I No. 74/2000 of 8 August 2000, entered into force on 27 November 2000.

Constitution of Namibia, adopted by the Constituent Assembly of Namibia on 9 February 1990, entered into force on 21 March 1991, UN Doc. S/20967/Add.2.

Decision on Obligations of Public Authorities of the Republic of Serbia in Assuming Powers of the Republic of Serbia as Successor State to the State Union of Serbia and Montenegro, 12 June 2006.

Gesetz zur Errichtung einer Stiftung 'Erinnerung, Verantwortung und Zukunft', in: (2000) I BGBl., p. 1263.

Indian Independence Act (1947), 10 and 11 Geo. VI, c. 30; L.R. Statues 1947.

Indian Independence (International Arrangements) Order, Gazette of India (Extraordinary), 14 August 1947.

1947 Indian Independence (Rights, Property and Liabilities) Order, Gazette of India (Extraordinary), 14 August 1947, in: Whiteman M.M., *Digest of International Law*, vol. II (Washington: US Govt.,1973), 873.

5   Other Documents

Agreement between the United Arab Republic and Société Financière de Suez, 13 July 1958, UN Doc. A/3898, S/4089, 23 September 1958.

European Commission for Democracy through Law (Venice Commission), amicus brief, 20 Oct. 2008, opinion no. 495/2008, CDL-AD(2008)021.

Exchange of notes UK–UAR, in: (1960) 54 *AJIL* 511–519.

Letter from Russia to the UN Secretary-General, 24 December 1991, in UN Doc 1991/ RUSSIA, Appendix, 24 December 1991, 31 *ILM* 138.

Letter of US Secretary of State Mr. Marcy to French Minister Count Sartiges concerning the claims of French subjects as a result of the U.S. bombardment of Greytown in 1854, 26 February 1857, in: MS. Notes to French Leg. VI. 301; S. Ex. Doc. 9, 35 Cong. 1 sess. 3, in: Moore J.B., *History and Digest of the International Arbitrations to which the United States has been a Party*, vol. III (Washington: US Govt., 1898), 929–930.

6   Reports of the IDI and ILA

A   INSTITUT DE DROIT INTERNATIONAL

Institut de Droit international, 'Le caractère national d'une réclamation internationale présentée par un Etat en raison d'un dommage subi par un individu' (1965) 51-II *Annuaire de l'Institut de Droit international*, 157.

Institut de Droit international, 'Les effets des changements territoriaux sur les droits patrimoniaux', in: (1952) 44-II *Annuaire de l'Institut de Droit international*, 471.

Institut de Droit international, 'La protection diplomatique des individus en droit international. La nationalité des réclamations', in: (1965) 51-II *Annuaire de l'Institut de Droit international*, 157.

Institut de Droit international, 'Resolution on Responsibility and Liability under International Law for Environmental Damage', in: 67-II *Annuaire de l'Institut de Droit international*, 486–513.

Institut de Droit international, 'State Succession in Matters of Property and Debts', Deliberations, in: (2000–2001) 69 *Annuaire de l'Institut de Droit international*, 305.

Institut de Droit international, 'State Succession in Matters of Property and Debts', Rapport provisoire par le Rapporteur Georg Ress, 15 August 1999, in: (2000–2001) 69 *Annuaire de l'Institut de Droit international*, 140.

Institut de Droit international, 'State Succession in Matters of Property and Debts', Resolution, in: (2000–2001) 69 *Annuaire de l'Institut de Droit international*, 712.

Institut de Droit international, 'State Succession in Matters of State Responsibility', Deliberations, in: (2013) 75 *Annuaire de l'Institut de droit international*, 209.

Institut de Droit international, 'State Succession in Matters of State Responsibility', Deliberations, in: (2015) 76 *Annuaire de l'Institut de droit international*, 624.

Institut de Droit international, 'State Succession in Matters of State Responsibility', Final Report by Rapporteur Marcelo Kohen, in: (2015) 76 *Annuaire de l'Institut de droit international*, 511

Institut de Droit international, 'State Succession in Matters of State Responsibility', Provisional Report by Rapporteur Marcelo Kohen, in: (2013) 75 *Annuaire de l'Institut de droit international*, 123.

Institut de Droit international, 'State Succession in Matters of State Responsibility', Resolution, in: (2015) 76 *Annuaire de l'Institut de droit international*, 703.

B   INTERNATIONAL LAW ASSOCIATION

International Law Association, 'The Changing Law of Nationality of Claims, Interim Report', Interim Report, Francisco Orrego Vicuña, Committee on Diplomatic Protection of Persons and Property (2000), 28.

International Law Association, 'Final Report on Aspects of the Law of State Succession', Co-rapporteurs Władysław Czapliński and Marcelo G. Kohen, Report of the Seventy-Third Conference, Rio de Janeiro (2008), 250–263.

7   Books

Barde, J., *La notion de droit acquis en droit international public* (Paris: Publ. univ. de Paris, 1981).

Brownlie, I., *Principles of Public International Law*, 5th ed. (Oxford: Clarendon Press, 1998).

Crawford, J., *Brownlie's Principles of Public International Law*, 8th ed. (Oxford: OUP, 2013).

Crawford, J., *The Creation of States in International Law*, 2nd ed. (Oxford: OUP, 2006).

Crawford, J., *State Responsibility: The General Part* (Cambridge: CUP, 2013).

Distefano, G., Gaggioli, G. & Hêche A. (eds.), *La Convention de Vienne de 1978 sur la succession d'État en matière de traités: Commentaire article par article et études thématiques* (Brussels: Bruylant, 2015).

Donner, R., *The Regulation of Nationality in International Law*, 2nd ed. (Ardsley, NY: Transnational Publ., 1994).

Drinhausen, F., *Die Auswirkungen der Staatensukzession auf Verträge eines Staates mit privaten Partnern* (Frankfurt: Peter Lang, 1995).

Dugard, J., *International Law; a South African Perspective* 2nd ed. (Kenwyn: Juta, 2000).

Dumberry, P., *A Guide to State Succession in International Investment Law* (London: Elgar Publ., 2018).

Dumberry, P., *State Succession to International Responsibility* (Leiden: M. Nijhoff, 2007).

Dupuy, P.M., *Droit international public*, 4th ed. (Paris: Dalloz, 1998).

Gould, W.L., *An Introduction to International Law* (New York: Harpers & Brothers Publi., 1957).

Guggenheim, P., *Traité de droit international public*, vol. I (Geneva: Librairie de l'Université, 1953).

Hyde, C.C., *International Law Chiefly as Interpreted and Applied by the United States*, vol. I, 2nd ed. (Boston, MA: Little, Brown & Co., 1945).

Jakubowski, A., *State Succession in Cultural Property* (Oxford: OUP, 2015).

Jenning, R. & Watts, A., *Oppenheim's International Law, vol. I (Peace: Introduction and Part 1)* (London: Longman, 1996).

Juillard, P. & Stern, B. (eds.), *Les emprunts russes et le règlement du contentieux financier franco-russe* (Paris: Cedin Cahiers internationaux n°16, 2002).

Klappers, J. (ed.), *State Practice Regarding State Succession and Issues of Recognition* (The Hague: Kluwer Law International, 1999).

Kohen, M. (ed.), *Secession. International Law Perspectives* (Cambridge: CUP, 2006).

de Lapradelle, A. & Politis, N., *Recueil des arbitrages internationaux*, vol. III, 1872–1875 (Paris: Pedone, 1954).

Lauterpacht, H., *Oppenheim's International Law*, vol. I (London: Longmans Green & Co., 1955).

Mälksoo, L., *Illegal Annexation and State Continuity: The Case of the Incorporation of the Baltic States by the USSR (A Study of the Tension between Normativity and Power in International Law)* (Leiden: Martinus Nijhoff Publ., 2003).

Marek, K., *Identity and Continuity of States in Public International Law* (Geneva: Librairie Droz, 1968).

Moore, J.B., *Digest of International Law*, vol. VI (Washington, DC: G.P.O., 1906).

Moore, J.B., *History and Digest of the International Arbitrations to which the United States has been a Party*, vol. III (Washington, DC: US Govt., 1898).

O'Brien, J., *International Law* (London: Cavendish Publ. Ltd., 2001).

O'Connell, D.P., *The Law of State Succession* (Cambridge: CUP, 1956).

O'Connell, D.P., *State Succession in Municipal Law and International Law*, vol. I (Cambridge: CUP, 1967).

Ronzitti, N., *La successione internazionale tra stati* (Milan: Dott. A. Giuffrè, 1970).

Rousseau, C., *Droit international public*, vol. V (Paris: Sirey, 1983).

Sastry, T.S.N., *State Succession in Indian Context* (New Delhi: Dominant Publ. & Dist., 2004).

Schwarzenberger, G., *International Law as Applied by International Courts and Tribunals*, vol. I, 3rd ed. (London: Steven & Sons, 1957).

Verzijl, J.H.W., *International Law in Historical Perspective*, vols. V and VII (Leiden: A.W. Sijthoff, 1973).

Weston, B.H., Lillich, R.B. & Bederman, D.J., *International Claims: Their Settlement by Lump Sum Agreements, 1975–1995* (New York: N.Y.T.P., 1999).

Whiteman, M.M., *Digest of International Law*, vol. II (Washington: Dept. of State, 1973).

Wyler, E., *La règle dite de la continuité de la nationalité dans le contentieux international* (Paris: PUF, 1990).

8   Contributions to Collective Works

Abi-Saab, G., 'Que reste-t-il du «crime international»', in: *Droit du pouvoir, pouvoir du droit: Mélanges offerts à Jean Salmon* (Brussels: Bruylant, 2007), 69–91.

Atlam, H., 'National Liberation Movements and International Responsibility', in: M. Spinedi & B. Simma (eds.), *United Nations Codification of State Responsibility* (New York: Oceana, 1987), 35–56.

Cahin, G., 'Attribution of Conduct to a State: Insurrectional Movements', in: J. Crawford, A. Pellet & S. Olleson (eds.), *The Law of International Responsibility* (Cambridge: CUP, 2010), 247–256.

Cosnard, M., 'Les créances au titre de l'intervention occidentale de 1919–1922', in: P. Juillard & B. Stern (eds.), *Les emprunts russes et le règlement du contentieux financier franco-russe* (Paris: Cedin Cahiers internationaux, 2002), 121–149.

Czaplinski, W., 'Equity and Equitable Principles in the Law of State Succession', in: M. Mrak (ed.), *Succession of States* (The Hague: Martinus Nijhoff Publ., 1999), 61–73.

Degan, V.D., 'Equity in Matters of State Succession', in: R.S.J. Macdonald (ed.), *Essays in Honour of Wang Tieya* (Dordrecht: Martinus Nijhoff, 1993), 201–210.

Dugard, J., 'Continuous Nationality', in: *Max Planck Encyclopedia of Public International Law*, online ed. (OUP, 2006).

Dumberry, P., 'La succession d'Etats en matière de responsabilité internationale et ses liens avec la responsabilité des Etats en matière de traités', in: G. Distefano, G. Gaggioli & A. Hêche (eds.), *La Convention de Vienne de 1978 sur la succession d'État en matière de traités: Commentaire article par article et études thématiques* (Brussels: Bruylant, 2015), 1581–1608.

Eisemann, P.M., 'Emprunts russes et problèmes de succession d'États', in: P. Juillard & B. Stern (eds.), *Les emprunts russes et le règlement du contentieux financier franco-russe* (Paris: Cedin Cahiers internationaux, 2002), 53–78.

Garrido-Muñoz, A., 'Article 8', in: G. Distefano, G. Gaggioli & A. Hêche (eds.), *La Convention de Vienne de 1978 sur la succession d'État en matière de traités: Commentaire article par article et études thématiques* (Brussels: Bruylant, 2015), 261–294.

Gradoni, L., 'Article 2', in: G. Distefano, G. Gaggioli & A. Hêche (eds.), *La Convention de Vienne de 1978 sur la succession d'État en matière de traités: Commentaire article par article et études thématiques* (Brussels: Bruylant, 2015), 87–124.

Kohen, M.G., 'Le problème des frontières en cas de dissolution et de séparation d'États: quelles alternatives?', in O. Corten et al. (eds.), *Démembrement d'États et délimitations territoriales: L'utipossidetis en question(s)* (Brussels: Bruylant, 1999), 365–399.

Kohen, M.G., 'Succession of States in the Field of International Responsibility: The Case for Codification', in: M.G. Kohen, R. Kolb & D. Tehindrazanarivelo (eds.), *Perspectives of International Law in the 21st Century. Liber amicorum Professor Christian Dominicé in Honour of his 80th Birthday* (Leiden: M. Nijhoff, 2011), 161–174.

Kolliopoulos, A., 'Article 9', in: G. Distefano, G. Gaggioli & A. Hêche (eds.), *La Convention de Vienne de 1978 sur la succession d'État en matière de traités: Commentaire article par article et études thématiques* (Brussels: Bruylant, 2015), 295–335.

Mendelson, M., 'The Runaway Train: The Continuous Nationality Rule from the Panevezys-Saldutiskis Railway Case to Loewen', in: T. Weiler (ed.), *International Investment Law and Arbitration: Leading Cases from the ICSID, NAFTA, Bilateral Treaties and Customary International Law* (London: CMP, 2005), 97–149.

Mikulka, V., 'State Succession and Responsibility', in: J. Crawford, A. Pellet & S. Olleson (eds.), *The Law of International Responsibility* (Oxford: OUP, 2010), 291–296.

Mikulka, V., 'Succession of States in Respect of Rights of an Injured State', in: J. Crawford, A. Pellet & S. Olleson (eds.), *The Law of International Responsibility* (Oxford: OUP, 2010), 965–967.

Milanovic, M., 'The Spatial Dimension: Treaties and Territory', in: C.J. Tams, A. Tzanakopoulos & A. Zimmermann (eds.), *Research Handbook on the Law of Treaties* (Cheltenham: Edward Elgar, 2014), 186–221.

Pellet, A., 'Le crime international de l'Etat: un phœnix juridique', in: K. Koufa (ed.), *The New International Criminal Law: 2001 International Law Session* (Thessalonika: Sakkoulas, 2003), 281–351.

Stern, B., 'General Concluding Remarks', in: B. Stern (ed.), *Dissolution, Continuation and Succession in Eastern Europe* (The Hague: Martinus Nijhoff Publ., 1998), 197–210.

Stern, B., 'Responsabilité internationale et succession d'Etats', in: L. Boisson de Chazournes & V. Gowlland (eds.), *The International Legal system in Quest of Equity and Universality, Liber Amicorum Georges Abi-Saab* (Leiden: M. Nijhoff, 2001), 327–355.

Szabó, M., 'State Succession and the Jurisprudence of the European Court of Human Rights', in: C. Binder & K. Lachmayer (eds.), *The European Court of Human Rights and Public International Law Fragmentation or Unity?* (Baden-Baden: Nomos, 2014), 19–144.

Tanzi, A. & Iapichino, L., 'Article 15', in: G. Distefano, G. Gaggioli & A. Hêche (eds.), *La Convention de Vienne de 1978 sur la succession d'État en matière de traités: Commentaire article par article et études thématiques* (Brussels: Bruylant, 2015), 543–555.

Torres Bernárdez, S., 'Succession of States', in M. Bedjaoui (ed.), *International Law: Achievements and Prospects* (Dordrecht: M. Nijhoff/Unesco, 1995), 381–404.

Zimmermann, A. & Devaney, J.G., 'Succession to Treaties and the Inherent Limits of International Law', in: C.J. Tams, A. Tzanakopoulos & A. Zimmermann (eds.), *Research Handbook on the Law of Treaties* (London: Edward Elgar, 2014), 505–540.

9 Articles and Courses

Abi-Saab, G., 'The Uses of Article 19' (1999) 10 *EJIL* 339–351.

Binder, C., 'Sanum Investments Limited v. The Government of the Lao People's Democratic Republic' (2016) 17 *J. World Invest. & Trade* 280–294.

Booysen, H., 'Succession to Delictual Liability: A Namibian Precedent' (1991) 24 *Comp. & Int'l L.J. S. Afr.* 204–214.

Brockman-Hawe, B.-E., 'Succession, the Obligation to Repair and Human Rights; The European Court of Human Rights Judgment in the Case of Bijelic v. Montenegro and Serbia' (2010) 59(3) *ICLQ* 845–867.

Charpentier, J., 'Pratique française du droit international' (1970) *AFDI* 997–1099.

Cotran, E., 'Some Legal Aspects of the Formation of the United Arab Republic and the United Arab States' (1959) 8 *ICLQ* 346–390.

Czapliński, W., 'State Succession and State Responsibility' (1990) 28 *Canadian YIL* 339–359.

Drakidis, P., 'Succession d'Etats et enrichissements sans cause des biens publics du Dodécanèse' (1971) 24 *RHDI* 72–123.

Dumberry, P., 'The Controversial Issue of State Succession to International Responsibility in Light of Recent State Practice' (2006) 49 *German YIL* 413–448.

Dumberry, P., 'Is a New State Responsible for Obligations Arising from Internationally Wrongful Acts Committed before its Independence in the Context of Secession?' (2005) 43 *Canadian YIL* 419–453.

Dumberry, P., 'Is Turkey the "Continuing" State of the Ottoman Empire under International Law?' (2012) 59(2) *Netherlands ILR* 235–262.

Dumberry, P., 'New State Responsibility for Internationally Wrongful Acts by an Insurrectional Movement' (2006) 17(3) *EJIL* 605–621.

Dumberry, P., 'Obsolete and Unjust: the Rule of Continuous Nationality in the Context of State Succession' (2007) 76(2) *Nordic JIL* 153–183.

Dumberry, P., 'State Succession to State Contracts: A New Framework of Analysis for an Unexplored Question' (2018) 19 *J. World Invest. & Trade* 595–627.

Dumberry, P., 'Turkey's International Responsibility for Internationally Wrongful Acts Committed by the Ottoman Empire' (2012) 42 *Revue générale de droit* 562–589.

Dumberry, P., 'The Use of the Concept of Unjust Enrichment to Resolve Issues of State Succession to International Responsibility' (2006) 39(2) *RBDI* 506–528.

Fastenrath, U., 'Der deutsche Einigungsvertrag im Lichte des Rechts der Staatennachfolge' (1992) 44 *ÖZöRV* 1–54.

Focsaneanu, L., 'L'accord ayant pour objet l'indemnisation de la compagnie de Suez nationalisée par l'Egypte' (1959) *AFDI* 161–204.

Guggenheim, P., 'La pratique suisse 1965' (1966) 23 *ASDI* 65–118.

Hurst, C., 'State Succession in Matters of Torts' (1924) 5 *British YIL* 163–178.

Kelsen, H., 'Théorie générale du droit international public. Problèmes choisis' (1932) 42 *Rec. des Cours* 117–351.

Kohen, M.G., 'La création d'Etats en droit international contemporain' (2002) 6 *Bancaja Euromediterranean Courses of International Law* 543–636.

Lagrange, E., 'Les successions d'États: pratiques françaises' (2003) 63 *La. L.Rev* 1187–1240.

Lehner, O, 'The Identity of Austria 1918/19 as a Problem of State Succession' (1992) 44 *ÖZöRV* 63–84.

Monnier, J.-P., 'La succession d'Etats en matière de responsabilité internationale' (1962) 8 *AFDI* 65–90.

O'Connell, D.P., 'Recent Problems of State Succession in Relation to New States' (1970) 130 *Rec. des Cours* 95–206.

Oeter, S., 'German Unification and State Succession' (1991) 51(2) *ZaöRV* 349–383.

Piotrowicz R., 'Status of Yugoslavia: Agreement at Last' (2001) 77 *ALJ* 95–99.

Quint, P.E., 'The Constitutional Law of German Unification' (1991) 50 *Md. L.Rev.* 475–662.

Repousis, O.G., 'On Territoriality and International Investment Law: Applying China's Investment Treaties to Hong Kong and Macao' (2015) 37(1) *Michigan JIL* 113–190.

Shaw, M., 'State Succession Revisited' (1994) 5 *Finnish YIL* 34–98.

Stahn, C., 'The Agreement on Succession Issues of the Former Socialist Federal Republic of Yugoslavia' (2002) 96(2) *AJIL* 379–397.

Stavridi, J. & Kolliopoulos, A., 'L'Accord du 29 juin 2001 portant sur des questions de succession entre les Etats issus de la dissolution de l'ex-Yougoslavie' (2002) *AFDI* 163–184.

Stern, B., 'La succession d'Etats' (1996) 262 *Rec. des cours* 9–437.

Strydom, H.A., 'Namibian Independence and the Question of the Contractual and Delictual Liability of the Predecessor and Successor Governments' (1990) 15 *South African YIL* 111–121.

Šturma, P., 'State Succession in Respect of International Responsibility' (2016) 48 *George Washington ILR* 653–678.

Szurek, S., 'Epilogue d'un contentieux historique. L'accord sur le règlement des créances réciproque entre la France et la Russie' (1998) 44 *AFDI* 144–166.

Tams, C.J., 'State Succession to Investment Treaties: Mapping the Issues' (2016) 31(2) *ICSID Rev.* 314–343.

Udina, M., 'La succession des Etats quant aux obligations internationales autres que les dettes publiques' (1933) 44 *Rec. des Cours* 665–773.

Volkovitsch, M., 'Righting Wrongs: Toward a New Theory of State Succession to Responsibility of International Delicts' (1992) 92 *Columbia LR* 2162–2214.

Zemanek, K., 'State Succession after Decolonization' (1965) 116 *Rec. des cours* 181–300.

10   Theses

Atlam, H.M., Succession d'Etats et continuité en matière de responsabilité internationale, Thesis, Université de droit, d'économie et des sciences d'Aix-Marseille (France), 1986.

Peterschmitt M., La succession d'États et la responsabilité internationale pour fait illicite, Mémoire de DES, Université de Genève/Institut Universitaire de hautes études internationales (Switzerland), 2001.

INDEX

Algeria
  independence, 39, 132, 134, 139
  National Liberation Front (FLN), 39, 139
Allied and Associated Powers
  and Austria-Hungary break-up, 95
  Inter-Allied Reparation Agency, 100
Alsace-Lorraine, transfer of, 67, 81
annexation of States, *see* incorporation
     of States
armed struggle, *see* insurrectional movements
Australia
  Certain Phosphate Lands in Nauru
     case, 140
  East Timor dispute with Portugal, 137
Austria
  and Austria-Hungary break-up, 95
  Reconciliation Fund Law, 74
Austria-Hungary, break-up of, 95
autonomous entities
  devolution agreements, 36, 39, 144
  internationally wrongful acts, 103

Baltic States, and USSR break-up, 92
Belgium
  and Congo independence, 133
  independence, 101
Boer Republics, *see* South Africa
break-up of States, continuing States after, 92
Brown case, *see R.E. Brown* case
Burma, British annexation of, 117

Catalonia referendum 2017, 2
cession of territory, *see* transfer of territory
Chagos Islands, 73
changes of government, 28
codification, 1, 7, 9, 16, 29
Colombia, dissolution of Union of, 31, 121
colonies, *see also* newly independent States
  cession of, 73
  colonisers' responsibility for acts of, 118
  decolonisation, 1, 77, 129, 138
Congo (DRC), independence, 133

continuing States
  after break-up of States, 92
  nationality, 67
  non-succession principle, 93
  responsibility for pre-succession acts, 43,
     99, 133
  States considered to be, 94
  successor States and, 119
  treaty entry by, 94
  war reparations to, 100
continuous nationality
  application of, 10, 66
  diplomatic protection and, 66, 69
  jurisprudence, 71
  non-application of, 69
  successor State reparation claims, 68
Crete, lighthouses arbitration (*France v.
     Greece*), 81
Croatia Genocide Convention case, 5, 11, 20,
     22, 107, 109, 120, 127
Czech Republic
  and Austria Reconciliation Fund Law, 74
  as successor State, 48, 124
Czechoslovakia
  and Austria-Hungary break-up, 95
  break-up of, 1, 50, 72, 119
  Gabčíkovo-Nagymaros Project case, 48, 84,
     124, 128
  successor States, 48, 124

date of the succession of States, definition of, 17
DDR (German Democratic Republic), *see*
     Germany
decolonization, *see* colonies
Democratic Republic of the Congo,
     independence, 133
devolution, *see also* separation
  of obligations, 50
  separation of part of State, 77, 91
devolution agreements
  autonomous entities, 36, 39, 144
  characteristics of, 30